Collins
English for Exams

Practice Tests for
IELTS

D1508714

Collins

HarperCollins Publishers
The News Building
1 London Bridge Street
London
SE1 9GF

First edition 2013

© HarperCollins Publishers 2013

ISBN 978-0-00-749969-4

Collins is a registered trademark of HarperCollins
Publishers Limited

www.collinselt.com

A catalogue record for this book is available from the
British Library

Typeset in India by Aptara

Printed in China by RR Donnelley APS

Written by: Peter Travis
             Louis Harrison

Sample answer sheets reproduced by permission of
Cambridge ESOL.

Contents

Title	Topic	Page number
Introduction		4
Overview of IELTS examination		6
Strategies for success		8
Test 1	Listening	31
	Reading	38
	Writing	50
	Speaking	51
Test 2	Listening	52
	Reading	60
	Writing	71
	Speaking	73
Test 3	Listening	74
	Reading	81
	Writing	92
	Speaking	94
Test 4	Listening	95
	Reading	102
	Writing	112
	Speaking	114
General Training Test A	Reading	115
	Writing	127
General Training Test B	Reading	128
	Writing	140
Mini-dictionary		141
Audio script		156
Sample answer sheets		172
Listening and Reading answer key		175
Writing: model answers		178
Speaking: model answers		183
Acknowledgements		190

Introduction

Who is this book for?

Practice Tests for IELTS will prepare you for the IELTS test whether you are taking the test for the first time or re-sitting the test. It has been written for learners with band score 5–5.5 who are trying to achieve band score 6 or higher. The book, with its answer key and model answers, has been designed so that you can use the materials to study on your own. However, the book can also be used as part of IELTS preparation classes.

Content

Practice Tests for IELTS is divided into three sections. The first section contains an introduction, an overview of the IELTS examination, and strategies for success in the exam. The second section contains four complete Academic tests and two General Training tests for Reading and Writing. The third section contains a mini-dictionary, a full audio script, sample answer sheets, answer keys for the Listening and Reading papers, and model answers for the Writing and Speaking questions.

Specifically the book contains:

- **Tips for success** – essential advice for success in your exam
- an **Overview of the IELTS examination** – a quick reference to IELTS whenever you need to remind yourself of what to expect on exam day
- **Quick guides** – brief summaries of the question types for each part of the exam
- **Challenges and solutions** – strategy and skill reviews to help you learn how to overcome the most common challenges in each part of the test
- **Practice tests** – four complete Academic tests and two General Training tests for Reading and Writing
- **Mini-dictionary** – definitions and examples of the most important high-level vocabulary from *Practice Tests for IELTS* (definitions are from Collins COBUILD dictionaries)
- **Audio script** – the full texts of what you will hear in the Listening and Speaking sections
- **Sample answer sheets** – familiarize yourself with the answer sheets used in the Listening, Reading and Writing sections of the IELTS exam
- **Answer keys** – the answers for all the questions in the Listening and Reading sections
- **Model answers** – example answers for the Writing and Speaking sections, all of which would achieve the highest marks in the IELTS test
- **CD** – MP3 files with all of the Listening passages, questions from the Speaking tests and the model answers for the Speaking tests.

Tips for success

Make a plan to succeed and start by following these tips.

- **Register for the test early.** If you are applying for university check the application deadlines. Make sure that you register to take the test well before the deadline to ensure that your scores arrive on time.
- **Find out the score requirements for the universities you want to apply to.** Degree programmes that have minimum-score requirements typically post them on their admissions websites.
- **Start to study early.** The more you practise, the more you will improve your skills. Give yourself at least one month to complete all of the practice tests in this book. Spend at least one hour a day studying and don't give up. Remember, by using this book, you are on your way to high scores in the IELTS test!
- **Time yourself** when you complete the practice tests.
- Don't be afraid to make your own notes on the page. For example, writing down the definitions to words you don't know will help you remember them later on.
- Read or listen to the model answers as many times as you need to.
- In the Writing test, return to the questions and try to come up with new responses. Keep practising until creating responses within the time limits becomes easy for you.

Using the book for self-study

Having access to someone who can provide informed feedback on your answers to the Writing and Speaking questions is an advantage. However, you can still learn a lot working on your own or with a study partner, who is willing to give and receive feedback.

Ideally, you should begin by working through the *Challenges and solutions* for each part of the exam. Try to carry out the suggested activities as these will help you to develop the skills you will need to do well in each section.

When you are ready to try the practice tests make sure you attempt the Writing and Speaking tasks. These are skills that can only be improved through extensive practice. At the same time, you should aim to become well informed about a wide variety of subjects, not just those covered in the book. The IELTS Writing and Speaking tests can cover almost any topic considered to be within the grasp of a well-educated person.

Practise writing to a time limit. If you find this difficult at first, you could focus first on writing a high-quality response of the correct length. Then you could start to reduce the time allowed gradually until you are able to write an acceptable answer within the time limit. You should become familiar enough with your own handwriting that you can accurately estimate the number of words you have written at a glance.

Model answers should be studied to identify the underlying approach and effect on the reader. Do not memorize essays or letters or attempt to fit a pre-existing response around another exam question. By working through the practice tests in the book, you should develop the skills and language to effectively express your own responses to unseen exam questions on the day.

Overview of the IELTS examination

The International English Language Testing System (IELTS) is jointly managed by the British Council, Cambridge ESOL Examinations and IDP Education, Australia.

There are two versions of the test:

- Academic
- General Training.

The Academic test is for students wishing to study at undergraduate or postgraduate level in an English-medium environment.

The General Training test is for people who wish to migrate to an English-speaking country.

There are separate Reading and Writing modules for the Academic and General Training IELTS tests.

The test
There are four parts to the test.

Listening	30 minutes, plus 10 minutes for transferring answers to the answer sheet. There are 4 sections in this part of the test.
Reading	60 minutes. There are 3 texts in this section, with 40 questions to answer.
Writing	60 minutes. There are 2 writing tasks. Your answer for Task 1 should have a minimum of 150 words. Your answer for Task 2 should have a minimum of 250 words.
Speaking	11–14 minutes. There are 3 parts in this section. This part of the test will be recorded.

Timetabling – Listening, Reading and Writing must be taken on the same day, and in the order listed above. Speaking can be taken up to seven days before or after the other modules.

Scoring – Each part of the test is given a band score. The average of the four scores produces the Overall Band Score. You do not pass or fail IELTS; you receive a score.

IELTS and the Common European Framework of Reference
The CEFR shows the level of the learner and is used for many English as a Foreign Language examinations. The table below shows the approximate CEFR level and the equivalent IELTS Overall Band Score.

CEFR description	CEFR code	IELTS Band Score
Proficient user	C2	9
(Advanced)	C1	7–8
Independent user	B2	5–6.5
(Intermediate – Upper Intermediate)	B1	4–5

This table contains the general descriptors for the band scores 1–9.

IELTS Band Scores		
9	Expert user	Has fully operational command of the language: appropriate, accurate and fluent with complete understanding
8	Very good user	Has fully operational command of the language, with only occasional unsystematic inaccuracies and inappropriacies. Misunderstandings may occur in unfamiliar situations. Handles complex detailed argumentation well
7	Good user	Has operational command of the language, though with occasional inaccuracies, inappropriacies and misunderstandings in some situations. Generally handles complex language well and understands detailed reasoning
6	Competent user	Has generally effective command of the language despite some inaccuracies, inappropriacies and misunderstandings. Can use and understand fairly complex language, particularly in familiar situations
5	Modest user	Has partial command of the language, coping with overall meaning in most situations, though is likely to make many mistakes. Should be able to handle basic communication in own field
4	Limited user	Basic competence is limited to familiar situations. Has frequent problems in understanding and expression. Is not able to use complex language
3	Extremely limited user	Conveys and understands only general meaning in very familiar situations. Frequent breakdowns in communication occur
2	Intermittent user	No real communication is possible except for the most basic information using isolated words or short formulae in familiar situations and to meet immediate needs. Has great difficulty understanding spoken and written English
1	Non user	Essentially has no ability to use the language beyond possibly a few isolated words
0	Did not attempt the test	No assessable information provided

Marking

The Listening and Reading papers have 40 items, each worth one mark if correctly answered. Here are some examples of how marks are translated into band scores.

Listening   16 out of 40 correct answers: band score 5
23 out of 40 correct answers: band score 6
30 out of 40 correct answers: band score 7
Reading   15 out of 40 correct answers: band score 5
23 out of 40 correct answers: band score 6
30 out of 40 correct answers: band score 7

Writing and Speaking are marked according to performance descriptors.

Writing – Examiners award a band score for each of four areas with equal weighting:

• Task achievement (Task 1)
• Task response (Task 2)
• Coherence and cohesion
• Lexical resource and grammatical range and accuracy

Speaking – Examiners award a band score for each of four areas with equal weighting:

• Fluency and coherence
• Lexical resource
• Grammatical range
• Accuracy and pronunciation

For full details of how the examination is scored and marked, go to: **www.ielts.org**.

Strategies for success

Quick guide

Definition
The Listening test, which is the same in both the Academic and the General Training IELTS exams, tests your comprehension of English lectures, monologues and conversations. The test includes different types of listening passages spoken by a range of native speakers. Some passages are about academic topics, while others focus on experiences that a student may encounter on and off campus. The Listening test is the same for both the IELTS Academic and IELTS General Training test.

Targeted skills
In order to do well in the Listening test, you must be able to:
- understand main ideas
- identify specific details
- identify a speaker's opinion and attitude
- answer questions within the given time.

The Listening passages
The Listening paper contains four sections with a total of 40 questions. There are four different types of passage in each Listening test.

The first two sections deal with social needs. The first passage will be a conversation, for example between a customer and a shop assistant or two friends making plans. The second passage will be a monologue, for example a guest on a radio show or someone explaining a service at university.

The last two sections focus on an academic context. The third passage will be a conversation with up to four people who might be discussing an assignment or talking to a tutor about their studies. The forth passage will be a monologue and feature a lecture or academic talk.

Questions
A variety of question types accompany each Listening passage. These can include any of the following:
- multiple choice
- matching
- plan / map / diagram labelling
- sentence / chart / form completion
- summary completion
- classification.

Timing
You will have **30 minutes** to answer the questions and 10 minutes to transfer your answers to the answer sheet. A sample answer sheet is provided at the end of this book. The recording is played once only.

Challenges and solutions

» **CHALLENGE 1: 'I don't know a lot of the words that I hear in the audio recordings or see in the questions.'**

SOLUTION: Expand your vocabulary. Sections 3 and 4 of the Listening test focus mainly on academic contexts. There are several word lists available that present the most common words found in academic settings. The Academic Word List (AWL), developed by Averil Coxhead, is a list of 570 words that are commonly included in introductory college texts. Getting to know these words will likely help you perform better in the test and prepare for entering English-language courses. Read as widely as possible before the exam in order to expand your general vocabulary.

SOLUTION: Use the context – words or phrases around unknown words – in recordings, questions, or answer options to help you work out meaning. In the Listening test, speakers will often provide a number of clues for the meaning of key terms. See the table below for common ways that speakers give context clues for key terms. To practise, try listening to English-language news programmes. Announcers often make the meaning of new terms clear by using these types of clues.

Ways of giving context clues			
Repetition	**Rewording**	**Definition signposts**	**Giving examples**
The speaker will repeat a key term several times in the same paragraph.	The speaker will often reword a phrase so that the meaning of a term is clearer. A rewording often includes the following phrases: • *By that, I mean ...* • *What I'm talking about here is ...* • *In other words, ...*	Speakers use certain terms to introduce a definition, including: • *This refers to ...* • *This means ...* • *That's a ...* • *I think a definition is in order here.*	In order to clarify a definition, speakers will give examples. Listen for the following phrases for examples: • *like* • *such as* • *you know*
Example	**Example**	**Example**	**Example**
*Animals use **camouflage** to protect themselves from predators. An animal might blend in with the background to **camouflage** itself.*	*Why do companies **vet** new hires? I mean, why do they **perform background checks and check out the potential employee's history**?*	*It's a matter of agency. **I think a definition is in order here.** Agency is people's ability to make choices that will influence their futures.*	*Engaging in recreational activities, **such as** jogging or playing an instrument, has been shown to reduce stress levels.*

» **CHALLENGE 2: 'I get lost as I listen to lectures in the Listening test.'**

SOLUTION: Sometimes it's difficult to stay focused throughout the academic lectures in the IELTS test. One way to avoid problems with this is to practise identifying the organizational structure of IELTS Listening passages. If you understand how each passage is generally structured, you will be better able to predict what type of information will be included in the lecture and where this information will appear in the lecture. If you lose concentration while listening, you just have to think about how the passage is structured in order to get back on track. Note that nearly all of the academic lectures in the IELTS Listening test follow one of the following common organizational structures:

- definition
- compare and contrast
- process
- classification
- theory / support
- pros and cons (advantages and disadvantages)
- cause and effect.

To practise, try listening to some of the lectures on the CD for this book. See if you can identify what types of structures they follow.

SOLUTION: Listen for signposts. A signpost is a word or phrase that is used to signal a specific type of information in a Listening passage. For example, some signposts signal the introduction of a new topic (e.g. *On a different note ...*), while others signal the definition of a key term (e.g. *By that, I mean ...*). By listening for signposts, you can get a better sense of what is happening in the lecture, which will help you become focused again. To practise, listen to a recording of a lecture from this book and write down all the signpost words you hear. Then check your notes against the script. How many did you notice?

SOLUTION: Recognize what information is important and what is not. During a Listening passage, speakers often digress, or talk about information that is not directly related to the main topic of the lecture or conversation. If you get lost while you are listening, recognizing digressions will help you refocus on the important information. See the table below for words and expressions that are often used to introduce digressions.

Expressions that signal digressions
Now, this won't be in the test, but it's interesting to think about.
You don't have to write this down, but consider that ....
Just as an aside, I want you all to know that ...
This is only somewhat related, but ...
It doesn't really make a difference to what we're discussing today, but don't you think that ... ?
Don't let this confuse you, because it doesn't really apply to what we're talking about today.
This may be oversimplified, but for the purposes of today's lecture, it's really all you need to know about X.

» **CHALLENGE 3: 'I don't always understand the conversations in the audio recordings – there's so much back and forth and corrections and other stuff.'**

SOLUTION: Unlike written language, spoken language is more informal and includes interruptions, mispronunciations, repetitions, clarifications, pauses, intonation changes to make a point, and so on. The Listening passages in the IELTS test are authentic-sounding lectures and conversations and include many common features of spoken language.

Try listening to the audio passages in this book and notice features like interruptions, mistakes, and repetitions. These features are included in order to make the Listening passages sound more natural. By noting and understanding how speakers use these features, you will become more accustomed to the flow of the Listening passages in the IELTS test.

Common features of spoken English			
	Interruptions	**Mistakes / Corrections**	**Repetition**
Examples	*Sorry ...* *Wait; what about ... ?* *A: So you're a fresher and—* *B: A second year, actually.*	*Now, their meaning is entirely explicit – or rather, entirely implicit. Another difference between the two animals is that salamanders – sorry, I mean lizards – can live in a much drier environment.*	*OK, this is important.* *Let me say that again.* *Did you get that?*
Notes	Typically, if someone interrupts another person, the information is important. For example, a person might interrupt the other speaker to give correct or updated information.	When a speaker misspeaks, be sure to write down the correction, since answer options for detail questions are often based on these.	Repeated information is often tested in the IELTS test. If you hear repeated information, write it down in your notes.

SOLUTION: Get used to the flow of native English by exposing yourself to as much natural English as possible. The more exposure you have to native-English speech, the more you'll understand the English used in the IELTS test. Ways of increasing your exposure to spoken English include:

- watching TV programmes or films. The TV programmes don't have to be educational – comedies and dramas include great examples of natural spoken English. While you watch, note how people often interrupt each other, correct themselves after making a mistake, or quickly change topics. If you find this difficult, try watching films with subtitles. Listening can be easier when you can read to check understanding.
- joining an English-language speaking club. You might find that your university, local library, or community centre has one. By joining, you will not only be able to practise speaking English, you will also have the opportunity to hear native speakers and take part in natural conversations.

» **CHALLENGE 4: 'I don't always understand the speakers. Sometimes they talk too fast.'**

SOLUTION: The speakers in the Listening passages in the IELTS test are native speakers of English. Differences in pronunciation and speed reflect the way that native speakers of English actually talk. There are many common English reductions that you may hear in the IELTS test. Reductions are shortened forms of certain word combinations that omit sounds or blend two or more words. Reductions are very common in the Listening passages of the IELTS test, so make sure you know how they are formed. Study the table below for common reductions. You can practise by listening to audio passages from this book and noticing the reductions. Are some harder to understand than others? Focus on them, and listen as many times as it takes for the meanings to become clear.

Common reductions

Who did you go to the cinema with?	→	Whodja go to the cinema with?
What did you do that for?	→	Whatdja do that for?
When did you finish?	→	Whendja finish?
Where did you get those shoes?	→	Wheredja get those shoes?
How did you do in the test?	→	Howdja do in the test?
How have you been doing?	→	Howvya been doing?
Don't you like him?	→	Doncha like 'im?
Did you talk to her?	→	Didja talk to 'er?
What are you going to do?	→	Whataya gonna do?
How about this one?	→	How 'bout this one?
I'm trying to finish my homework.	→	I'm tryna finish my homework.
A lot of people were there.	→	Alotta people were there.
I don't know.	→	I dunno.
I've got to go now.	→	I've gotta go now.
Could you help me with this?	→	Couldja help me with this?

SOLUTION: Listen to some English-language podcasts or radio programmes. At first, practise listening to only a minute or two of the programme at a time. As your comprehension improves, increase the listening time. When you listen, focus on understanding the speakers' pronunciation throughout the entire programme. Listen to the programmes as many times as you need to until you understand the main ideas.

SOLUTION: If possible, purchase a digital recording device with variable-speed playback capabilities. Using a variable-speed digital recorder, you can record English-language radio broadcasts, television programmes, and podcasts. At first, you can play back the media at a slow speed. As your comprehension level improves, you can increase the playback speed until you are listening to the broadcasts at their original speed.

» **CHALLENGE 5: 'None of the answer options "feels" right. It's as if what the speakers say and the answer options are not related.'**

SOLUTION: The writers of the IELTS test are looking to see if you can understand and interpret what is said, how it is said, and what it may or may not mean. Therefore, it's important to understand how correct answer options are created so you will be able to identify the correct option more easily.

One extremely common feature of correct answer options in the IELTS test is the rewording of key information. Basically, a correct answer option will always contain key words that you've heard in the lecture or conversation. However, the correct answer typically mixes up the information and doesn't contain the exact wording from the Listening passage. In other words, the correct answer will often include paraphrased information from the Listening passage. Information in answer options may be paraphrased by:

- changing key content words (using synonyms)
- including general information about a concept that is described in detail in the listening
- changing the voice of the information from passive to active (or vice versa) in the answer option (e.g. *The boy hit the ball* versus *The ball was hit by the boy*). The passive voice is formed by using a form of the verb *be* + past participle.

Study the examples below of how paraphrasing may be used in the IELTS test. If you want to practise, after you complete a test in this book, try to identify the paraphrase types used in some of the answer options. This may help you improve your ability to recognize correct and incorrect answers.

Paraphrase type	You'll hear this	You'll see a question like this	You'll see answer options like this
Changes to content words	*The bengal scampered swiftly.*	How did the tiger run?	Fast ✓ Slowly ✗
Specific to general	*OK, you'll just need to tell me your address, date of birth, and student ID number.*	What does the secretary ask for?	Some personal information ✓ A change-of-address form ✗

✓ correct answer option
✗ incorrect answer option

SOLUTION: Use a process of elimination. Read each answer option carefully and draw a line through those that contain:

- information that states the opposite of the facts and details presented in the passage
- information that does not answer the question
- the exact wording from the passage. Remember, the correct answer typically paraphrases information from the passage, so an answer option that includes the same wording is probably incorrect.

SOLUTION: Don't spend too much time answering any one question. Remember, you have only 30 minutes to answer all of the questions in the Listening test. Therefore, if you aren't certain of an answer, select whatever answer you feel is the most appealing and move on to the next question. You will not be penalized for choosing an incorrect answer.

Reading test

Quick guide

Definition
The Reading test tests your ability to understand written English. The test includes different types of reading passages that are based on a variety of subjects.

Targeted skills
In order to do well in the Reading test, you must be able to:

- understand basic vocabulary in context
- quickly scan a written passage and understand its main ideas and supporting details
- understand more detailed information
- understand how information is organized
- understand inferences, opinions, relationships, paraphrases, and the purpose of a passage
- answer questions within the given time.

The Reading passages (Academic test)

The Reading test includes three reading passages with a total of between 2,000 and 2,750 words. The texts and the questions get progressively more difficult. The texts are similar to those found in magazines, newspapers or textbooks. The subjects are of general academic interest and of a type that would be accessible to someone about to enter university. At least one text will contain detailed logical argument.

The Reading passages (General Training test)

The Reading test has three sections. The first section includes texts that are aimed at social survival and contains commonplace texts such as letters, advertisements and leaflets. The second section contains texts with a work-based context, whilst the third section involves reading a more extended piece of text that will be descriptive or instructive but not argumentative.

Questions

There are usually 40 questions in total. The questions will be in a variety of formats including:

- multiple choice
- matching
- diagram labelling
- sentence / chart completion
- true / false
- matching headings / summaries
- classification.

Timing

You will have **60 minutes** to read and answer the questions. Your answers must be written onto the answer sheet within the 60 minutes as, unlike in the Listening test, there is no extra time allowed for this. A sample answer sheet is provided at the end of this book.

Challenges and solutions

» **CHALLENGE 1: 'I don't know a lot of the words that I see in the passages or in the questions.'**

SOLUTION: Expand your vocabulary. There are several ways to increase your vocabulary. For one, there are several word lists available that present the most common words found in academic settings. The Academic Word List, developed by Averil Coxhead, is a list of 570 words that are commonly included in introductory college texts. Getting to know these words will likely help you perform better in the test and prepare you for entering English-language courses.

SOLUTION: Use a learner's dictionary when you study. Dictionaries such as the *Collins COBUILD Advanced Dictionary* and *Collins COBUILD Key Words for IELTS* offer clear definitions, example sentences and grammar information to help you expand your knowledge and use of everyday and academic vocabulary. In this book, you will find definitions for challenging or unfamiliar words, much like you would in the IELTS Reading passages. These definitions come from the *Collins COBUILD Advanced Dictionary*.

SOLUTION: Use context clues. Context clues are the words and phrases that surround key words. Using these clues will help you determine the meanings of unfamiliar words. The author may use a number of strategies to provide context clues for key words, including giving examples of the key word, contrasting the meaning of the key word with an opposite idea, or giving an indirect definition of a key word. To practise finding and using context clues, try reading a 300-word excerpt from a newspaper or a university textbook. Pay attention to the strategies that the authors use to help you work out the definitions of difficult words.

Strategies for using context clues		
Strategy	**Key words**	**Example**
Pay attention to **examples** that appear near the highlighted word. If you are familiar with the examples, you can use them to determine the meaning of the highlighted word.	such as including consists of this includes like	*The graphic shows expenditure on household items, **like** going to the supermarket or buying gifts.*
Look for key words that signal a **contrast** from a previous idea. If you know the meanings of the words from surrounding sentences, you'll know that the highlighted word has an opposite meaning.	Unlike X ... On the other hand, X ... While ... But ... However, ...	***Unlike** most mammals, few of which are venomous, the platypus produces a noxious substance that can cause extreme pain in humans.*
Look for **indirect definitions** of terms in the sentences that surround the highlighted word. These definitions may include an easier synonym of the highlighted word or information that helps clarify its meaning.	and meaning that	*In the southwestern United States, the sunflower is ubiquitous, **and** it is difficult to find a garden that doesn't include the plant.*

SOLUTION: Learn how to look at word parts, like prefixes and suffixes, to determine the meanings of unknown words. Many English words are formed through the use of prefixes, which go at the beginnings of words, and suffixes, which go on the ends of words. By learning the meanings of common English prefixes and suffixes, you will be able to guess the meaning of unknown words.

» **CHALLENGE 2: 'I often run out of time before completing all of the questions.'**

SOLUTION: Use skimming and scanning skills to find the answers to the questions.

Skimming is when you quickly read a passage, paying attention only to the most important ideas. By skimming, you can often identify the key ideas that many questions are based on in a short amount of time. This way, you can avoid running out of time during the test.

In order to skim effectively, make sure you know where to find the most important ideas. Regardless of the different organizational styles for passages, important ideas often appear in the same places. See the table below for information on where to find the most important ideas in a passage.

Part of the passage	Skimming strategy
Introduction	• Read **the last two–three lines** in the introductory paragraph. These lines will typically describe the main idea of the passage.
Body paragraphs	• Read **the first two–three lines** in the body paragraphs. These sentences will describe the main ideas of the paragraphs. • Read **the last two–three lines** in the body paragraphs. These lines will often explain how each paragraph relates to the main idea of the passage. These lines will also help you understand how the body paragraphs are related to one another.

Scanning is when you read the passage quickly in order to find specific key words or ideas. After you've read a question and its answer options, you should make a note of any key words or ideas, like names, terms or numbers, that will help you answer the question. Then scan the passage, looking specifically for those key words.

Remember, you don't need to understand every word perfectly while you skim or scan a passage. The most important part is to find the information you need in order to answer the questions quickly and correctly.

To practise skimming and scanning, find an article with 600–700 words in a university textbook. First, skim the article and write down the most important ideas on a piece of scrap paper. Then, try scanning the article for key words and dates. The more you practise skimming and scanning, the faster and more accurate you will get, so try to practise every day.

SOLUTION: Time yourself whilst doing the test. You should not spend more than 20 minutes on each Reading passage and you should try to allow more time for the later passages as the texts and questions get progressively more difficult. While you work on the questions, be sure to glance at your watch. Avoid spending too long on one particular question; skip it and return to it later. This will help you avoid getting stuck on one question and wasting your time.

» **CHALLENGE 3: 'The passages are often complicated and confusing – sometimes I get lost as I'm reading them.'**

SOLUTION: Understand the basic organizational styles found in the IELTS Reading test. If you lose concentration or become confused while you are reading, you just have to think about how the passage is structured in order to get back on track. See the table below for the most common organizational structures of the longer Reading passages and how the information in these passages is often arranged.

	Classification	Compare and contrast	Cause / Effect	Problem / Solution	Theory / Support
Introduction	Introduces what will be classified in the passage	Introduces two ideas, things or events	Introduces an event or process	Introduces a problem	Introduces a theory
Body paragraphs	Present 2–3 **different types or features** of the subject being classified	The first body paragraph describes several **features of the first subject**. In the following paragraphs, the author presents **corresponding features of the second subject**, pointing out how these are **similar to or different from** those of the first subject.	The first body paragraph describes 1–2 **causes** for an event or process. Then, the author describes the **effects**, or consequences, of the causes.	Provide 2–3 **solutions** to the problem	Provide 2–3 **pieces of evidence** to support the theory

To practise, read each of the passages in this book. See if you can identify the organizational structure of each passage. Make a note of how the body paragraphs are organized and whether they fit these patterns.

SOLUTION: Look for linking words and phrases or signposts as you read. Linking words and phrases are used to connect the ideas in different sentences. For example, some linking words and phrases signal the introduction of a new topic (e.g. 'Another example of X is …'), while others signal a process or sequence of events (e.g. 'First, …'). Linking words and phrases often appear at the beginning of a new paragraph, though they can appear in the middle part of a paragraph as well. By paying attention to these words and how they are used, you can get a better sense of what is happening in the passage. In turn, this will help you avoid becoming confused by the information in the passage.

SOLUTION: Answers to questions will usually appear in order. For example the answer to Question 2 will usually be found after the answer to Question 1. In longer texts you will often find that each question relates to a particular paragraph. As you work through the practice tests in this book pay attention to how the answers appear in the text and whether they do always follow each other in order.

SOLUTION: Write down key words and ideas as you read the questions and answer options. Then you can refer to your list of key words and quickly scan for them in the reading passage. Whilst doing this remember to also look out for synonyms of the words that appeared in the questions.

» **CHALLENGE 4: 'I have a hard time telling the difference between major supporting details and minor facts.'**

SOLUTION: Try to understand the role of the details in the passage. By understanding how the details that you are confused about relate to the ideas in the passage, you will be able to sort the major details from the minor ideas. Use the steps below to start understanding the roles of details in a passage.

	Steps for differentiating between major supporting details and minor facts
Step 1	Skim the first paragraph to find the topic sentence. Topic sentences are sentences that express the main topic of a passage or paragraph. Regardless of the passage type or organizational style of a passage, it will have a major point that it is trying to make. The introduction will usually provide a brief background of the main topic and then present a topic sentence that summarizes the main point of the passage.
Step 2	Skim the body paragraphs to find the topic sentence for each paragraph. The topic sentences are usually located within the first two or three lines of the body paragraphs. By locating the topic sentences, you can start to understand what the main argument of the passage is and how the author has organized the flow of ideas.
Step 3	Once you've located the topic sentences and the main point of the passage is clear to you, quickly review the details that you are unsure about. Again, when you review details, make sure you scan the passage for the key words associated with those details in order to save time.
Step 4	When you read a sentence containing a detail you are unsure about, ask yourself the following question: If you were to leave out that particular detail, would the main point of the passage be weakened? If the answer is 'Yes', the detail in question is probably a major detail. On the other hand, if leaving out the detail would not majorly change or weaken the main point of the passage, then the detail is a minor fact.

» **CHALLENGE 5: 'None of the answer options "feels" right.'**

SOLUTION: Familiarize yourself with the question types and the skills required to answer each one. In the Reading test, there are several possible question types. By learning which skills each question type tests, you will better understand what to look for in a correct answer, which should help improve your intuition about the correct answers. Look at the *Quick guides* for details about the question types.

SOLUTION: Understand how correct answer options are created. While the correct answers in the Reading test will vary in many ways, remember that one common feature of correct answers is the rewording of key information. A correct answer will always contain key information that you've read in the passage. However, the information is typically mixed up so that the correct answer doesn't use the exact wording from the passage. In other words, the correct answer will include paraphrased information from the Reading passage. Information in an answer may be paraphrased by:

- changing key words (i.e. using synonyms)
- including general information about a concept that is described in detail in the passage
- changing the voice of the information from active to passive (or vice versa). The passive voice is formed by using the verb *be* + past participle.

To practise recognizing paraphrased information, complete a Reading test from this book, then try to identify the paraphrase types used in some of the answer options. This may help you improve your ability to recognize correct and incorrect answers.

SOLUTION: Use a process of elimination. A process of elimination involves reading each answer option carefully and eliminating options that are incorrect. Typically, you can eliminate answer options that contain:

- information that contradicts the facts and details presented in the passage
- information that does not answer the question
- the exact wording from the passage. Remember, the correct answer typically paraphrases information from the passage, so an answer option that includes the same wording is probably incorrect.

SOLUTION: Skip questions you are unsure about. You can always return to previous questions. However, you have only 60 minutes to answer all of the questions in this test. For some people, it's easier to answer difficult questions once they've had some time to think about them. So if you find that you're spending too much time on one question and you aren't certain of the answer, move on to the next question or the next passage. You may find that it's easier to answer a difficult question when you return to it later.

Writing test

Quick guide

Definition
The Writing test tests your ability to write an appropriate response to a question coherently and with a range of vocabulary and grammatical structures. For each question, you will be required to understand the task, know how to write a well-organized essay, and incorporate main ideas and details to answer the question.

Targeted skills
In order to do well in the Writing test you must be able to:
- understand instructions that introduce the Writing task and identify the key points to address in your answer
- write in the appropriate register and format
- create a well-organized essay that is easy for the reader to follow
- use a range of vocabulary and grammatical structures accurately
- answer questions within the given time.

The questions (Academic test)
In the Academic test there are two Writing tasks. In the first task you are required to write about an information graphic such as a table or chart. You could be asked to describe, summarize, compare or evaluate the information. The minimum word length is 150 words. In the second task you write an essay on a given topic. The minimum word length is 250 words.

The questions (General Training test)
In the General Training test there are two Writing tasks. In the first task you are required to respond to a problem or situation by writing an informal / semi-formal / formal letter asking for information or explaining a situation. The minimum word length is 150 words. In the second task you write an essay on a given topic. The minimum word length is 250 words.

Timing

The entire Writing test takes approximately **60 minutes** to complete. You are advised to spend 20 minutes on the first task and 40 minutes on the second task.

Challenges and solutions

» **CHALLENGE 1: 'I don't have time to write complete answers.'**

SOLUTION: Be aware of how much time you have. On the day of the test wear a watch. While you work, keep an eye on the time. Use the following timing guide while you write.

Timing for Task 1: Total time: 20 minutes		Timing for Task 2 Total time: 40 minutes	
Time on the clock	What you should be doing	Time on the clock	What you should be doing
20–18 minutes	Review notes and write a quick outline. Underline key words. Just write a few words to help you remember what you will write down.	40–35 minutes	Read the question carefully, underline key words and brainstorm the topic. Try to come up with as many points as you can.
18–4 minutes	Write your answer. Be sure that you use paragraphs and that you deal with the specific details in the question.	35–4 minutes	Write your essay. Be sure that your essay has clear paragraphs. Try to include personal details to support your key points.
4–0 minutes	Review and edit your work. Be sure to look for misspelled words and ungrammatical sentences.	4–0 minutes	Review and edit your essay. Be sure to look for misspelled words and ungrammatical sentences.

SOLUTION: Practise doing timed tasks before the test. Start by allowing yourself an extra 15 minutes over the suggested time limit and slowly reduce this until you can complete the tasks with a few minutes to spare. You will need this time to read through your work to check for mistakes.

» **CHALLENGE 2: 'I'm afraid that the examiner will not understand the ideas in my essay.'**

SOLUTION: Use linking words and phrases. They connect two sentences together by indicating a shift in focus, continuing in the same line of thinking, drawing a conclusion, clarifying a point, indicating sequence, and so on. If you use linking words and phrases throughout your essay, you will be able to improve the flow of your response and make it easier to understand. Use the following table as a reference for linking words and phrases and their uses.

Function	Linking words and phrases	
Shift in focus	but	nonetheless
	conversely	on the contrary
	despite	on the other hand
	however	still
	in contrast	though
	nevertheless	yet
Continuing in the same line of thinking	additionally	furthermore
	also	in addition
	and	likewise
	besides	that moreover
Drawing a conclusion	accordingly	hence
	as a result	indeed
	consequently	therefore
	for that reason	thus
Clarifying a point	in other words	that is to say
	specifically	namely
Indicating sequence	after	later
	as soon as	meanwhile
	before	next
	finally	soon
	in the first place	then
Giving examples	For example, ...	
	Take X, for instance, ...	
	One example of X is ...	

SOLUTION: Work on improving your spelling. While a few misspelled words won't affect your score, if you spell a lot of words incorrectly, it may keep the examiner from understanding your meaning. One way to improve your spelling is to read a lot. This is because the more you see words in English, the more you will understand how common words are spelled. Another way to help your spelling is to practise writing. When you check your writing, circle all the misspelled words and make sure you learn how to spell them correctly.

SOLUTION: Don't use an idiomatic expression unless you are sure you know what it means. When the examiners score your essay, they will look at how well you can use idiomatic expressions. However, if you use an idiomatic expression incorrectly, it will only harm your score.

» **CHALLENGE 3: 'I have trouble talking about opinions.'**

SOLUTION: Know when you will be required to express opinions. For example, Question 1 in the General Writing paper may ask you to write a letter of complaint, which will involve giving your opinion. Question 2 in both the Academic and the General Training test involves writing an essay in which you will describe your opinion on a particular topic. Use the table below to help you know when and how to use opinion language.

Question	What opinion you might have to give	Expressions you can use in your response
Question 1 **Academic Writing**	A summary of what is presented in the graph / table / chart	It seems to me that ... The data shows ...
Question 1 **General Training Writing**	In a letter of complaint, your opinion of a service you received	As far as I am concerned, ... In my opinion, ...
Question 2 **Academic and** **General Training Writing**	Express agreement or disagreement with the main topic and provide reasons to support this position.	• I feel that ... • I think X is a good / bad idea. • I support / oppose ... • In my opinion, X is good / bad ... • My view is that X is positive / negative ... • I agree / disagree with the claim that ... • While some people think that ..., I personally believe that ... • I know that some people feel differently, but it's my opinion that ... • It's my opinion that ... • I agree / disagree with the idea that ... • Other people might disagree, but my view is that ...

» **CHALLENGE 4: 'I have difficulty knowing how to write formal letters.'**

SOLUTION: You are required to write a letter in the General Training IELTS test and this is often formal or semi-formal in register. Keep a record of useful set expressions often found in formal letters such as letters of complaint, letters requesting information or letters of application. Here are some examples of phrases that are often used to start and end a letter as well as some used in the body. Add any more as you come across them.

Section of letter	Set expression
Beginning	I am writing with reference to ... I am writing with regards to ... With reference to (your letter / advertisement), ...
Body	Please find enclosed ... I would be grateful if you could ... Unless ... I will be forced to ...
End	I look forward to hearing from you soon. I hope this information will help you. Do not hesitate to contact me should you require any further information.

SOLUTION: One of the areas you will be assessed on is your ability to identify and use the correct register for a piece of writing. During your preparation, try to keep a record of examples of formal and informal language. This includes the use of contractions and idiomatic English as well as the practice of using understatement when making a complaint. Here are some examples. Add more as you come across them.

Category	Informal	Formal
Use of contractions	I'm / You're / It's	I am / You are / It is
Vocabulary	Idiomatic language: Up to my ears in work Put up with	Very busy Tolerate
Tone	I was really angry when I discovered ...	I was rather disappointed to discover ...
Grammar	Active	Passive Use of inversion: 'Should you ...' 'Had I ...'
Punctuation	Exclamation marks Ellipses (...) indicating a pause	No exclamation marks Use of colon and semi-colon

» **CHALLENGE 5: 'I find it difficult expressing what I can see in the graphs and charts.'**

SOLUTION: Task 1 in the Academic Writing test often contains a graph, table or diagram, which you are asked to describe. Make sure you are familiar with the different types of graphic you are likely to be presented with. Knowing the correct words will immediately help you with your opening sentence, such as: 'The graph shows the increase in ...' Typical graphics include:

Bar charts
Line graphs
Pie charts
Tables
Flow charts
Diagrams

SOLUTION: It can sometimes be useful to give a very brief summary of the structure of the graphic. For example, should you have to describe a bar chart or line graph you could begin by explaining what the vertical and horizontal axes shows. This will help you both understand the information in the graphic and enable you to give a clearer explanation of what you can see.

SOLUTION: To describe graphics accurately it is vital you learn some of the common phrases and set expressions used to describe movement or trends. These include set phrases like 'a slight increase', 'a gradual improvement', and 'a steady fall'. Remember also that many of these expressions can be used in different forms. You will find many examples in newspaper articles describing economic or business issues. Add any new ones you find to these examples.

Adjective + noun	Verb + adverb
a sharp fall a drastic increase a gradual decline	fell sharply increased drastically declined gradually

» **CHALLENGE 6: 'I often find myself using the same words again and again in my writing.'**

SOLUTION: Learn synonyms for common words that appear in the test. *Collins COBUILD Key Words for IELTS* contains lots of synonyms for important IELTS words. To practise, reread one of the Reading passages in this book. Choose 10 to 15 key words that appear in the passage. Then look in a thesaurus for synonyms of these words and make a list to study and learn. You can then use these synonyms in your paraphrased sentence. See below for examples of how to use synonyms in your paraphrases.

Original wording	Paraphrased version using synonyms
A Lazarus taxon is a **species** that was once **believed** to have been extinct, but is later found to be **alive**.	Types of **organisms** that were **thought** to be extinct and are later found to **still exist** are called a Lazarus taxon.
One advantage of **using** surveys for **data collection** is that it **allows researchers** to **ask consumers questions** about their attitudes and shopping behaviour.	**Conducting** surveys in order to **collect data** is **advantageous** because it **gives scientists** the opportunity to **question customers** about their attitudes and shopping behaviour.

SOLUTION: Don't copy the words and ideas exactly as they appear in the question. Paraphrasing is putting the ideas from a source into your own words. If you simply copy words and sentences, you will receive fewer marks than if you use your own words. To avoid copying, check the original question after you create a paraphrase. Is the sentence structure and vocabulary different? If your paraphrase is too similar to the original, be sure to change it by using different types of sentence structures and synonyms of key words.

SOLUTION: Practise paraphrasing. The best way to improve your paraphrasing skills is to practise. Find a text, such as a newspaper article, and then choose a paragraph to paraphrase. Put the passage away and try paraphrasing. When you are done, compare your paraphrase with the source. Did you change key words by using synonyms? Also, did you change the sentence structures? Practise paraphrasing one paragraph a day until you feel confident about your paraphrasing skills.

» **CHALLENGE 7: 'I have a hard time choosing what to write about in Task 2.'**

SOLUTION: Practise brainstorming techniques. Brainstorming involves thinking about the topic and trying to come up with major supporting details quickly. For example, one technique you might find useful when discussing a problem is to spend a minute or two writing down all of the points you can think of for both sides of the argument. Don't worry about whether the points you're writing down are good or not – sometimes, writing down a weak point will help you think of a better one. Try this technique for the topics in this book.

When you are done, review your notes from the brainstorming. Can you think of a way to adjust the technique so it works better for you?

SOLUTION: Don't waste time considering which point to support. When you are writing the essay, you should choose the position that is easiest for you to support. You can determine this by looking at the notes you've created when you brainstormed. Which side has more points? Also, remember that there are no right or wrong opinions in the IELTS test. In other words, you are not being graded based on your opinions themselves. What's really important is how well you support your opinion in your essay.

SOLUTION: Don't be afraid of making up personal examples to include in your essay. In Task 2 you are often invited to use your own experience to support your answer. However, nobody is going to check whether your personal examples are true or not. If you have to change the details of one of your examples so that it supports your key point better, go ahead and do it. It will make your essay even stronger.

SOLUTION: Make a list of familiar topics and practise coming up with key points for them. Give yourself about two to three minutes to think of key points for each topic. That way, you'll get used to thinking of supporting points in timed conditions like you'll have to on the day of the test. Use the topics from the list below or try to come up with your own topics.

- Some people think it is important to get a degree from a top university in order to get a good job. Others feel that real-world experience is more helpful for getting a good job. Which do you think is more important and why? Use reasons and specific examples to support your answer.
- Teachers are the most influential people in a child's life. Do you agree or disagree? Use specific reasons and examples to support your answer.
- Some people think that having a good diet is the most important factor for physical health. Others think that exercise plays a larger role in health. Which do you think is true and why? Use reasons and specific examples to support your answer.
- It is best to travel before starting a career. Do you agree or disagree? Use specific reasons and examples to support your answer.

Speaking test

Quick guide

Definition
The Speaking test, which is the same in both the Academic and the General Training IELTS exams, tests your ability to use spoken English in as realistic a setting as possible. The test is recorded.

Targeted skills
In order to do well in the Speaking test, you must be able to:
- understand and respond to questions
- express your opinion, discuss and speculate on common subjects
- speak at length coherently
- speak accurately and fluently using a good range of vocabulary and grammatical structures
- speak with clear pronunciation.

The questions
The Speaking test has three parts. Part 1 is an interview during which the examiner asks you very general questions to give you the chance to talk about yourself. In Part 2 you are required to talk on a subject for between one and two minutes. You will be given a card, which will tell you what to include in your talk. You are given one minute to prepare. When you have finished your long turn the examiner will ask you a question or two to bring Part 2 to an end. In Part 3 the examiner will invite you to discuss the topic from Part 2 further by asking you several questions.

Timing

The entire test lasts between 11 and 14 minutes.

Part 1: 4–5 minutes
Part 2: 3–4 minutes
Part 3: 4–5 minutes

Challenges and solutions

» **CHALLENGE 1: 'I'm not sure how much I have to say in answer to the examiner's questions in Part 1.'**

SOLUTION: Try to see Part 1 as a chance for the examiner to get to know more about you and treat the exercise like a simple conversation. On the one hand you don't want to give overly long answers but equally you should avoid giving short, uncommunicative responses. This is particularly the case with questions such as 'Do you …?' or 'Have you …?' where you should *not* answer simply 'Yes' or 'No'.

SOLUTION: Practise answering Part 1 questions by giving a reason or example to extend your answer. For example, if the examiner asks 'Is your hometown a nice place to live?' think of a reason why it is or it isn't. If you are asked 'What kind of food do you like to eat?' don't just reply 'Indian food' or 'Pizza'. Think of a particular meal you have eaten recently and why you enjoyed it.

» **CHALLENGE 2: 'I'm not confident I'll have anything to say during the interview section.'**

SOLUTION: The questions in Part 1 are about you and your experiences. You might be asked about your hobbies and interests, where you live, your family or your studies. Think of more questions you might be asked on the following subjects and how you would answer them.

Subject	Possible questions
Where you live	Do you get many tourists where you live? …
Your hobbies or interests	Can you think of any hobbies or interests you enjoyed as a child that you no longer have? …
Your friends and family	Who do you most take after in your family? …
Your daily routine	What time do you like to get up? …
Your studies	What was your favourite subject at school? …
Your favourite TV programmes / films / books / music	Have you read a book lately that you really enjoyed? …
The food you like / don't like	What kind of food do people in your country like to eat? …

SOLUTION: Try to use a variety of functional language when responding to questions rather than repeating the same phrases again and again. For example, the following expressions can all be used as an alternative to 'I like ...' or 'I don't like ...'

- I quite fancy ...
- I'm quite fond of ...
- I've always been keen on ...
- I've got a soft spot for ...
- I'm not a big fan of ...
- I'm not that bothered about ...
- I can't bear ...
- ... doesn't really appeal to me.
- I've never really fancied ...

» **CHALLENGE 3: 'I'm not sure how to spend the one-minute preparation time in Part 2.'**

SOLUTION: There are various ways to prepare for Part 2. Some people like to make bullet-pointed notes based on the prompts in the question. Others will use a mind map or spidergram to brainstorm ideas for their talk. The important point is you should not attempt to write full sentences but simply note key words to remind you of what to say. Remember that people tend to lose focus when they feel nervous. By preparing an outline, you will feel more confident when you give your response, which will keep you from rambling.

SOLUTION: Some people prefer not to make notes but to spend the one minute visualizing what they are going to say. This approach is useful if the task is asking you to describe a past event and you can give your talk in the form of a story or anecdote. In this case think in terms of:

- the setting (where and when the event took place)
- the people involved in the story
- what happened / the key events
- how you felt about the experience.

Remember not to stray from the question when using this approach.

» **CHALLENGE 4: 'In Part 2 I worry that I'll either run out of time before finishing or I won't have enough to say.'**

SOLUTION: Time yourself when you practise for Part 2 so you get a feel for how long one to two minutes is. By timing yourself, you will learn how to pace yourself when giving your responses. That way, you won't speak too fast (or too slowly) and you will be able to give a complete response during the allotted time.

SOLUTION: Focus on quality and not quantity. The examiners are not concerned with how much information you can provide in the given time. Rather, they want to know if you can give a response that adequately answers the question.

» **CHALLENGE 5: 'I'm worried that my talk will be disorganized and I'll go from one subject to the next.'**

SOLUTION: Try using the question as a guide to structure your talk. The question always comes in four parts with the final part often asking you to describe how you feel about the topic, the significance of the event or why you like or dislike something you've been describing. Spend the first half of your long turn talking about the first three questions and then the final half responding in more detail to the forth question.

SOLUTION: Use signposting words and expressions to help you structure your thoughts and to help the examiner follow your talk. Some common signposting vocabulary appears below.' Add any new items as you learn them.

Signposting	Set expression
Comparing and contrasting	In contrast to ... In spite of this, ... Having said that, ... At the same time, ... On the one hand, ... On the other hand, ... Compared to ...
Cause and effect	To have a huge effect / impact on ... To result in ... To lead to ... To be the cause of ... On account of ... With the aim of ... In order to .... As a consequence, ... Owing to ...
Giving examples	For example, ... For instance, ... Take ... for example ... To give you an example, ... By way of example, ... To illustrate this, ...
Addition	The first / second reason ... Furthermore, ... In addition, ... What's more, ...
Drawing conclusions	Weighing up the pros and cons, ... So, all in all, ... To sum up, ... So, in general, ...

» **CHALLENGE 6: 'I'm scared to speak. It's not common to give opinions in my country.'**

SOLUTION: Be aware that there are no right or wrong opinions in the IELTS test. In other words, you are not being graded based on your opinions. What's really important is how well you support your views in your response. For questions that require you to say what you think about a subject, try to determine which opinion would be easiest to support. If you think of it this way, you will feel more confident about giving your opinions because you will know that you can support them. Also, remember that giving an opinion in the IELTS test is just part of a task – it's not an activity that exposes you or your personal feelings.

SOLUTION: You will often be asked to give your opinion in Part 3 of the exam. During your preparation, think about what your opinion is on the questions in this book and others that you find. If you really have no opinion on a subject, say so but attempt to speculate on what your opinion might be. For example: 'I've never really given that much thought actually ... I suppose it's possible that ...'

SOLUTION: When giving your opinion, try to avoid repeating 'I think' and use a variety of alternative expressions. Here are some examples:

- It seems to me that ...
- As far as I'm concerned, ...
- I've always been of the opinion that ...
- As I see it, ...
- Speaking for myself, ...
- If you ask me, ...
- To my mind, ...
- In my view, ...
- For my part, ...
- I don't really have an opinion one way or the other. I suppose ...
- It's not something I've given much thought to. Perhaps ...

» **CHALLENGE 7: 'I'm worried that the examiners won't understand me. My pronunciation is bad.'**

SOLUTION: Record yourself speaking English. Start by recording yourself while you speak the model answers found in this book. When you are done, compare your recording with that of the speaker. How is your pronunciation different from the speaker? Keep recording your voice until you sound more like the speaker. For extra practice, download an English-language news programme or podcast. Write down a section of the programme. Then record yourself while you read the transcription. Compare the recording of your voice with the original newsreader. Can you match the pronunciation and intonation of the native speaker? Keep practising until you do.

SOLUTION: Ask your friends to listen to a recording of you speaking English. Sometimes it is hard to judge whether or not your language is easy to understand. By listening to your speech, your friends might be able to point out pronunciation problems that you hadn't noticed. In particular, ask your friends if it is easy to understand what you are saying. What parts do they have difficulty understanding? Using the feedback from your friends, practise speaking the words that you had the most trouble with until it is easy for others to understand your speech.

SOLUTION: Listen to as much English as possible. When you listen to native English speakers talk, make sure to notice important pronunciation and intonation patterns. You might want to try listening to English-language radio programmes while you work or watching English-language television in your free time. Then, start using the pronunciation and intonation patterns you hear to sound more like a native speaker. This will greatly improve the clearness of your English.

SOLUTION: Find opportunities to practise speaking English with native English speakers. To find native English speakers in your area, try going to tourist attractions in your city, like museums or landmarks. You may also want to join an English-language speaking club at your school. If your school doesn't have an English-language speaking club, check for one at the local library.

SOLUTION: Don't forget that the stress of many words may depend on whether you use the word as a noun or a verb. For the words listed below, the first syllable is stressed if you use the word as a noun. The second syllable is stressed if you use the word as a verb. If you choose to use these words in your responses in the Speaking test, make sure you use the correct pronunciation.

combat	conduct	confine
conflict	construct	contest
contract	contrast	convert
decrease	discount	frequent
impact	incline	increase
insert	invite	object
perfect	permit	present
proceed	produce	protest
record	refuse	reject
research	rewrite	survey
transfer	update	upgrade

Test 1

SECTION 1   *Questions 1–10*

01

Questions 1–5

Complete the details in the form below.

*Write **NO MORE THAN ONE WORD AND/OR A NUMBER** for each answer.*

z-Mobile Services	
Incident Report Sheet	
Example	*Answer*
Postcode	CN2 1EB
Mobile phone number	07890 **1** _____ 570
Name	**2** _____ Green
Crime Reference Number	CZ- **3** _____ -5
4 _____ Mobile Equipment Identity (IMEI) number	Not known
Time, date of theft	1–2pm, 16 **5** _____

Questions 6–10

Choose the correct letter, A, B or C.

6   The caller's phone was stolen
    A   when he went to the toilet.
    B   from the table.
    C   from his pocket.

7   The caller will have to pay a charge
    A   for a new phone.
    B   if his phone is stolen again.
    C   in 12 months' time.

8   The delivery address is
    A   34 Solent Gardens.
    B   34 Solent House.
    C   34 Solent Grove.

9   The caller's IMEI number
    A   can be found on the side of the phone battery.
    B   is made up of 15 digits.
    C   cannot be found.

10   The operator
    A   transfers the caller to a colleague.
    B   will ring the caller back the next day.
    C   asks the caller to ring back.

SECTION 2   *Questions 11–20*

02

Questions 11–13

Choose THREE letters, A–G.

Which **THREE** things did the presenter say he enjoyed about his holiday?

    A the food

    B the weather

    C the nightlife

    D the journey

    E the people he met

    F His children had a good time.

Questions 14–16

Write NO MORE THAN THREE WORDS for each answer.

Which **THREE** radio shows does the presenter recommend Sally listen to?

14 _____

15 _____

16 _____

Questions 17–18

Choose the correct letter, A, B or C.

17 What does John object to?

    A the time of day the programmes are on

    B the lack of time guests have to answer questions

    C the interviewers' questions

18 How does John think the problem could be solved?

    A have further live radio shows

    B put the radio shows on at different times

    C extend the show on the Internet

Questions 19–20

Choose TWO letters, A–E.

Which **TWO** things does Clive want to hear more of on the radio station?

    A younger guests

    B music for older people

    C consumer issues for older people

    D older presenters

    E health problems faced by older people

SECTION 3   *Questions 21–30*

03

Questions 21–25

Complete the notes below.

Write **NO MORE THAN THREE WORDS** *for each answer.*

PRESENTATION INFORMATION	
Day	**21** _____
Subject	**22** _____
Length	**23** _____
Technical equipment needed	**24** _____
Location	**25** _____

Questions 26–30

Which person is responsible for the following tasks?

Write the correct letter, **A**, **B** *or* **C**, *next to questions 26–30.*

NB   You may use any letter more than once.

> **A** Simon
> **B** Kelly
> **C** Fiona

26 introduce and end the talk
27 talk about the historical perspective
28 talk about the contemporary situation
29 book the technical equipment
30 build the presentation

Questions 31–37

*Choose the correct letter, **A**, **B** or **C**.*

31 The speaker thinks

    A university is a similar experience to school or college.

    B students need more tutor support at university.

    C a lot of students have difficulties at university.

32 Which chart, **A**, **B** or **C**, shows the degree of poor time management skills amongst male and female students?

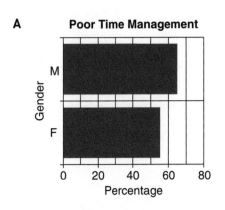

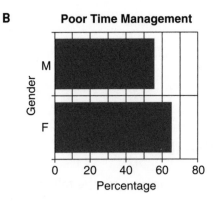

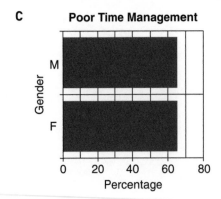

33 The speaker thinks it's important that

    A the academic planner is kept safe somewhere.

    B the academic planner is put somewhere it can be seen easily.

    C students remember to collect their academic planner.

34 When filling in the academic planner students should

    A ignore non-academic occasions.

    B try to keep visits home to a minimum.

    C add all important academic and non-academic dates.

35 Initially, the academic planner will

    A give the wrong impression about the amount of work there is.

    B show some days are busier than others.

    C give a clear idea of busy periods.

36 According to the tutor, students should organise their studies

    A so that they have time for coffee breaks.

    B so that they don't miss any seminars or lectures.

    C as if it were a normal working day.

37 The tutor makes the point that

    A cookery students do well when writing essays.

    B cooking and essay writing share certain characteristics.

    C cooking is a complicated process.

Questions 38–40

*Choose **THREE** letters, **A–G**.*

Which **THREE** things does the tutor recommend?

    A When planning self-study, note the time you should spend studying.

    B Break tasks down into individual stages.

    C Avoid working in the evenings.

    D Put time aside for favourite TV programmes.

    E Do household tasks at regular times.

    F Avoid the library if your friends are there.

READING PASSAGE 1

*You should spend about 20 minutes on **Questions 1–12**, which are based on Reading Passage 1 below.*

Invasive species

Britain's rivers and estuaries are being invaded at an alarming rate by a small furry-clawed crab all the way from China. So how did a crab travel so far and why are naturalists so concerned? The mitten crab first arrived in Europe on ships sailing from Asia. It then spread rapidly from Portugal to Sweden and was first reported to be in the River Thames in 1935. From the Thames, it spread across the United Kingdom at a very rapid rate: by 1999 mitten crabs had spread across 448 km of British coastline, sometimes walking miles overland to reach the next river. A team from the University of Newcastle found that UK rivers are being invaded three times faster today than in 1935. And there's little wonder – a single female crab can carry between 250,000 and 1,000,000 eggs so mitten crab colonies expand very rapidly. Furthermore, cleaning up pollution from Britain's rivers is simply helping the invaders.

The mitten crab is one example of many invasive species that have found their way from their original habitat into foreign lands. There are several ways invasive species move from country to country: they may expand their territory naturally as their colony grows; but far more frequently an invasion is associated with human activity. The main causes include shipping, deliberate introduction for hunting or work, and the escape of pets into the wild. The introduction of the mitten crab to Europe was probably accidental: ships taking on water to use as ballast to keep the vessel steady on its journey from Asia to Europe also took on the unwanted guests and carried them to new areas to colonise. Elsewhere, invasive species have been purposefully introduced by man. In 1859, 24 rabbits were introduced into Australia by Thomas Austin so that he could hunt them for recreation. Unfortunately, like the mitten crab, rabbits are prolific breeders: a single pair of rabbits are able to increase to 184 individual rabbits in just one and a half years and they spread at a rate of 130 km per year. Soon the population in Australia was out of control and had spread throughout the continent. Another domestic creature introduced from India into Australia in the 1800s was the dromedary camel. Camels were initially brought to work as pack animals to carry heavy loads across the hot desert interior of Australia. By 1920 it was estimated that around 20,000 camels were being used to transport goods. However, with the arrival of trains and cars, camels were released into the wild where their numbers had increased to around one million by 2008. Finally, the trade in animals as pets can enable a species to colonise areas far away from their native land.

Between 2000 and 2006 the U.S. Fish and Wildlife Service recorded 1.5 billion animal shipments made into America. 92% of these imported animals were then sold as pets, with the rest imported for research, education and zoos. While most of these animals were fish, the imports also included reptiles and mammals. When these pets escape and begin to breed, it can create serious problems. An example of this is in Florida, where in the 1990s a number of pet Burmese pythons – a snake native to south east Asia – escaped their outdoor enclosures when a major hurricane hit the state. Today, it is estimated that up 30,000 snakes inhabit the wetlands of the Florida Everglades. Burmese pythons, which can grow up to 20 feet long, are thriving on their new diet of native species, including endangered creatures, and are more than capable of competing with the American alligator for food.

The impact of invasive species is not to be underestimated. Katherine Smith, a conservation biologist at Brown University in Providence, Rhode Island states that 'A huge amount of money goes into the myriad effects that invasive species have.' Smith continues, 'They destroy infrastructure. They cause public health threats. They harm livestock and native animals. They disrupt ecosystems. The dollar values really do increase quickly.'

When a non-native species finds its way into a new and vulnerable environment the damage can be more or less serious as the invader out-competes the local wildlife, brings in new disease or destroys the environment.

The Australian dromedary camel, forming the largest herd of wild camels in the world, competes for food with native species and may have aided the local extinction of preferred species such as the quandong tree. The Australian government estimate that the camel is responsible for AUS$10 million in damage to infrastructure and competition for livestock food every year. Even more damaging is the effect rabbits are having in Australia. Apart from the economic loss to the wool industry, estimated at AUS$95 million annually, rabbits compete with sheep for food. The animals have a devastating environmental impact. Close grazing of grass leads to soil erosion and has significantly altered the composition of extensive areas of land. While the real impact of the mitten crab in the UK is not known at present, scientists have noted that the crab is causing riverbank erosion as it burrows into the mud, forming a network of tunnels that make the riverbanks unstable.

Invasive species are very difficult to manage once they have become established. Various methods have been tried to keep the populations under control. In Australia, 85,000 were culled and various methods have been tried to keep rabbit populations under control including poison and destruction of their warrens or homes. The latest idea in the UK to control the mitten crab is even simpler: catch them and give them to restaurants to sell as a tasty meal.

Questions 1–3

Do the following statements agree with the information given in Reading Passage 1? *Write*

TRUE	*if the statement agrees with the information*
FALSE	*if the statement contradicts the information*
NOT GIVEN	*if there is no information on this*

1   Mitten crabs originated in Vietnam.

2   Crabs need water to spread.

3   Making rivers less dirty has aided the invasion of the mitten crab.

Questions 4–7

Look at the following items (Questions 4–7) and the list of reasons.

Match each item with the reason for their introduction.

*Write the correct letter, **A–E**, next to Questions 4–7.*

NB *There are three more reasons than you will need.*

Animal	Reason
4 mitten crab	**A** was introduced as a predator species to protect plants from pests
5 rabbit	**B** escaped while being used as a pet
6 dromedary camel	**C** escaped from laboratories conducting experiments on animals
7 Burmese python	**D** introduced by someone who enjoyed shooting
	E came with water used to balance ships at sea
	F were carried over by trains
	G used to carry large loads across inhospitable areas

Questions 8–11

Complete the summary below.

*Choose **NO MORE THAN TWO WORDS** from the passage for each answer.*

Write your answers in spaces 36–40.

The effects of the introduction of non-native species can bring them into **8** _____ with native animals. Dromedary camels may have helped the **9** _____ a native plant. Rabbits have led to the degradation of **10** _____ across large areas of Australia. At the moment, the impact of the mitten crab is **11** _____.

Question 12

Which of the following statements reflects the claims of the writer in the reading passage?

*Choose the correct letter, **A**, **B** or **C**.*

The writer of the article views invasive species as

    A a natural development.

    B a hard problem to manage.

    C a good business opportunity.

READING PASSAGE 2

*You should spend about 20 minutes on **Questions 13–29**, which are based on Reading Passage 2 below.*

Private space

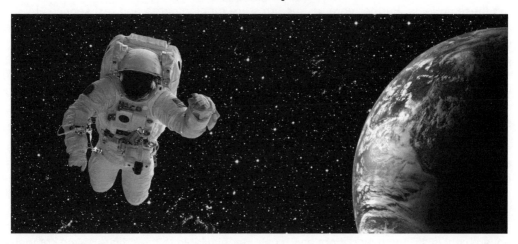

A It's a remarkable achievement: the question is no longer 'How can we send humans into space?' but 'How can we keep them there?' Spaceflight is reaching a turning point where new technologies in engine development, better understanding of aerodynamics and materials for body construction are making spaceflight possible for private industry.

B The history of space exploration, until relatively recently, has been one of big government-backed projects like the Space Shuttle, Mars Landers and Long March rockets. But the most recent launches to the International Space Station (ISS) have been very special for at least three reasons. Firstly, along with 450 kg of scientific equipment, food and clothes, the rocket was carrying ice cream for the three space station astronauts. Secondly, the rocket was unmanned, being guided into docking position and back to earth again by remote control and automated systems. Finally, the rocket was commissioned from a private company by NASA.

C When the privately owned rocket delivered its goods to the ISS, it marked a milestone in the evolution of space flight and vindicated NASA's decision to delegate routine supply flights to the space station. The flight has been a long time in development. It started with President George W Bush announcing his Vision for Space Exploration, calling for the ISS to be completed. Under the next President, America's Space Shuttles were retired leaving NASA with no other choice but to look for alternative methods of supplying the ISS. The initiative was part of an effort to commercialise the space industry in order to decrease costs and spread the investment in the industry across a wider group than governments.

D The initiative had many attractions for NASA. By outsourcing to the private sector the routine business of taking food and equipment to and from low-earth orbit, NASA can theoretically free up money to do things that it really wants to prioritise: missions such as sending astronauts to Mars and landing on asteroids by the 2030s. Now that the Space Exploration

Technologies Corporation (SpaceX) has proved that private enterprise can be players in space exploration, firms are pouring money into developing new spacecraft built to transport cargo, to mine asteroids and to carry passengers into space.

E In the last half of the twentieth century only government-backed agencies like NASA and Russia's ROSCOSMOS were capable of running space programmes due to the gigantic investment costs and uncertain payoffs. However, SpaceX and similar companies are proving that the former conditions are no longer relevant as new solutions are coming to light. Commercial companies like Boeing are able to raise large sums of money to run these projects. Furthermore, as the firms are running cargo and taxi services to lower orbits, the break-even point is lower, the technology is cheaper and they have the benefit of years of experience in commercial aviation and space flight. Opening space programmes to the commercial sector has the additional advantage of generating more solutions to old problems. An analogy is the invention of the Internet: when the technology went into the commercial sector, no one could have envisioned the development of social network sites. Likewise, no one can predict where commercial enterprise will take the space industry.

F The uncertainty surrounding where the space industry will end up is a problem as well as an asset and it is unsettling private investors who like to invest in relatively certain prospects. At the moment the industry is dominated by big-spending billionaires like the owner of SpaceX. In addition, the relatively small number of companies in the area could pose a problem in the future. The commercial space industry is still very new and there is no guarantee that progress will be smoother. For one thing, no one is sure that the business model is sound: government is still the major, if not only, customer available to the private space companies. The other problem is that space travel is high risk: the loss of space shuttles Challenger in 1986 and Columbia in 2003 illustrates that even the most carefully planned launches have unavoidable risks associated with them. The question is what would happen to the industry if another accident occurred. Finally, many space experts are doubtful that, even if private industry takes over the 'taxi' role for low-orbit missions, NASA will be able to achieve its ambitions, given its squeezed budgets and history of being used for political purposes. Furthermore, NASA may have created another space race, this time between government and private industry. If NASA doesn't go to Mars or the asteroid belt, its private competitors certainly have plans to do so.

G In spite of all of these risks, many argue that it is critical for the private sector and federal government to work together to push further into space.

Questions 13–18

Reading Passage 2 has seven paragraphs, A–G.

Which paragraphs, **A–F**, contain the following information?

*Write the correct letter, **A–F**, next to Questions 13–18.*

13 NASA being able to spend money on important projects
14 events leading to the commercialisation of spaceflight
15 new developments that have made spaceflight more accessible
16 an automated rocket that successfully completed a mission
17 the great dangers of space travel
18 new answers being found to previous questions

Questions 19–25

Choose the correct letter, A, B, C or D.

19 Which is NOT mentioned as making private space flight possible?

A new methods of constructing the rockets

B modern substances from which to build the rockets

C understanding better how air moves round objects

D new methods of making space suits

20 Why are the recent launches special?

A Their destination was the International Space Station.

B They carried clothes.

C They were not managed by a private company.

D The rocket is not owned by a government.

21 In order to make NASA look for other spaceflight providers, the US government

A invested in private space companies.

B started to build the international space station.

C stopped using the Space Shuttle.

D allowed private companies to fly into space.

22 Private companies

A need to reduce the cost of space projects.

B have social network sites.

C are able to fly rockets at high orbits.

D act as ferries to and from the space station.

23 At present, the private space industry is characterised by

A uncertainty about how to make profits.

B companies controlled by individuals.

C companies too small to raise the amount of money needed.

D government interference.

Questions 24–29

Complete the summary below.

*Choose **NO MORE THAN TWO WORDS** from the passage for each answer.*

Write your answers in spaces 24–29.

There are a number of problems with commercial space projects. To start with, the
24 _____ might not be sound. There is also great **25** _____ attached to
space flight – what would happen if there was another **26** _____ ? Experts doubt
whether NASA can fulfil its **27** _____ as it has often been under **28** _____
pressure. Moreover, the development may lead to a **29** _____ between NASA and the
private space industry.

READING PASSAGE 3

You should spend about 20 minutes on **Questions 30–40**, which are based on Reading Passage 3 on the following pages.

Questions 30–34

Reading Passage 3 has six paragraphs, A–F.

Choose the correct heading for paragraphs **B–F** from the list below.

Write the correct number, **i–ix**, next to Questions 30–34.

List of Headings
i Shielding the earth from the atmosphere
ii Bouncing back the sun's rays from earth
iii The effect of volcanoes on the atmosphere
iv Criticisms of geoengineering
v Trapping greenhouse gases
vi The root of the problem
vii Why attempt geoengineering?
viii Protecting glaciers
ix The need for action

Example	Answer
Paragraph **A**	**ix**

30 Paragraph **B**

31 Paragraph **C**

32 Paragraph **D**

33 Paragraph **E**

34 Paragraph **F**

Engineering a solution to climate change

A   Looking at the rate of climate change and the disastrous effects it is having on the world, scientists are concerned that we are acting too slowly. Many are now looking to geoengineering – large-scale human interventions to change the world's climate – to counteract global warming. The schemes range from the mundane to science fiction but all come from the same impulse: if we don't do something now, it may be too late to do anything.

B   Climate change is now so rapid that, in the very near future, the Arctic will be ice-free during winter as less ice forms during winters and more melts in summer. Scientists say that tackling climate change isn't a problem we need to deal with in 10 or 20 years' time; we need to look at radical solutions now. A study has shown that the technologies to produce these geoengineering projects already exists and could be in place for around $5 billion a year. This is a bargain when compared with the cost of reducing carbon dioxide emissions, a major greenhouse gas: that figure stands at somewhere between $200 and $2,000 billion.

C   So what exactly are scientists planning to do to deal with global warming in the short term? Among the main schemes are shielding the earth from the sun's rays either at ground or atmospheric level, or capturing the carbon produced by industry and sinking it back into the ground or the sea. Shielding the world has produced ideas that range from simple science to science fiction. One suggestion has been to make the roofs of buildings and roads whiter to reflect the sun's rays back into space. While this has the advantage of simplicity, it simply won't make much difference, reflecting only 0.15 watts per square metre, averaged across the planet. To put this into perspective, to stop earth warming we need to increase heat loss by about 3.7 watts per square metre averaged over the world. Another idea is to protect the Greenland ice field by covering it in giant sheets of reflective material. If this works, it could help in the Antarctic where the giant Filchner-Ronne ice shelf is melting rapidly. If this glacier disappears completely, it would raise sea levels, causing catastrophic flood damage around the planet.

D   If reflecting heat back from the ground has little effect, there are two alternatives: seeding clouds and replicating volcanic activity. The first idea is to make clouds whiter by increasing the amount of rain in them. Sending salt particles into clouds should 'seed' the clouds with more raindrops. Clouds carrying more raindrops would be whiter and better reflectors of sunlight. This could be good news for the earth and in addition could be stopped when necessary with the salt completely clear from the skies within ten years. Unfortunately, other research indicates that creating whiter clouds may have unwanted side effects, producing adverse weather conditions in the region and changing ocean currents. A much older idea is to replicate the effect volcanoes have had on the atmosphere. A volcanic eruption sends large amounts of ash and sulphur into the air, which block the sun and create cooler conditions. For example, when Mount Pinatubo erupted in 1991, it produced a sulphur dioxide cloud, which reduced average global temperatures by one degree centigrade. Geoengineers have long put forward the idea of circulating particles of sulphur in the atmosphere to counteract global warming. The particles would be delivered by aircraft or balloons spraying them into the atmosphere. However, this also has unpredictable effects on the amount and pattern of rainfall. Furthermore, this method would delay the recovery of the ozone layer over the Antartic by 30 to 70 years. More ambitious geoengineering projects have included placing billions of reflective balloons between the sun and the earth and putting giant mirrors into orbit. Scientists have criticised these approaches as 'science fiction' and say they are unlikely to happen due to the huge costs involved.

E   Whatever actions we take to block or reflect the heat from the sun, we will still need to reduce the amount of carbon dioxide in the atmosphere. Various geoengineering projects have been proposed to do this. Carbon capture technologies range from planting trees, which naturally use carbon dioxide as they grow, to pumping carbon back into the earth and trapping it there. This is a good idea but would only account for about 0.5 watts per square metre. Carbon capture technologies are already in use at power stations where the greenhouse gas is taken at point of production and pumped underground into depleted gas and oil reserves. However, the technology to do this is not very efficient. Other ideas for taking carbon out of the atmosphere include seeding the oceans with iron. This would increase the growth of plankton which, like trees, use carbon naturally. Unfortunately, this would only account for 0.2 watts per square metre.

F   Proponents of geoengineering have never regarded the earth-changing engineering projects as a complete solution. Nevertheless, the concept as a whole attracts many criticisms. One is that the problem of climate change is of such huge scale and complexity that there will not be one single solution. All proposals so far have advantages and disadvantages. The biggest problem of all is that many of the projects are untested and any of the proposals may have unforeseen consequences. For example, we could not suddenly stop a geoengineering scheme: keeping temperatures artificially low for a period then taking away the cause of this would cause the temperature to rise again rapidly. Furthermore, global engineering solutions to the problem of climate change would need the agreement of all the world's leaders: having an American solution, a Chinese solution, a Brazilian solution, and so on simply wouldn't be politically acceptable. But the biggest downfall is that geoengineering projects could reduce the political and popular pressure for reducing carbon emissions, as politicians point to geoengineering for an answer rather than tackling the real cause of climate change: human activity.

Questions 35–40

Classify the following as typical of

    A *land-based reflection*

    B *atmospheric reflection*

    C *carbon capture*

*Write the correct letter, **A**, **B** or **C**, next to Questions 35–40.*

35 removes carbon dioxide as soon as it is produced

36 increases the reflectivity of white clouds

37 cleans carbon dioxide from the air naturally

38 would increase the number of small plants and animals in the sea

39 may help prevent rising water levels

40 is similar to the effect volcanoes have on the atmosphere

WRITING TASK 1

You should spend about 20 minutes on this task.

> *The table below shows the change in some household types in Great Britain from 1971 to 2007.*
>
> *Summarise the information by selecting and reporting the main features, and make comparisons where relevant.*

Write at least 150 words.

PEOPLE IN HOUSEHOLDS BY TYPE OF HOUSEHOLD AND FAMILY					
Great Britain: household types	**Percentages**				
	1971	1981	1991	2001	2007
One person	6	8	11	12	12
One-family households					
Couple					
No children	19	20	23	25	25
Dependent children	52	47	41	39	36
Non-dependent children	10	10	11	9	9
Lone parent	4	6	10	12	12

WRITING TASK 2

You should spend about 40 minutes on this task.

Write about the following topic:

> *Tourism is one of the fastest growing industries and contributes a great deal to economies around the world. However, the damage tourism can cause to local cultures and the environment is often ignored.*
>
> *To what extent do you agree or disagree?*

Give reasons for your answer and include any relevant examples from your knowledge or experience.

Write at least 250 words.

SPEAKING

PART 1: Introduction and interview

Listen to Track 05, pressing pause after each question to answer.

PART 2: Individual long turn

Before you read the task card, listen to Track 06.

> Describe a well-known person you admire.
>
> You should say:
>> who this person is
>>
>> what this person does
>>
>> why this person is well known
>
> and explain what it is about this person you admire.

PART 3: Two-way discussion

Listen to Track 07, pressing pause after each question to answer.

Test 2

LISTENING

SECTION 1   *Questions 1–10*

08

Questions 1–3

Choose the correct letter, A, B or C.

> *Example*
>
> Seb's course looks like it will be
>
>   **A**   too difficult.
>
>   **B**   too easy.
>
>   **C**   enjoyable.

1   Some of Lydia's classmates

    A   are going into town later.

    B   have already been into town.

    C   haven't got time to go out.

2   Seb says he

    A   is cooking a meal for his host family.

    B   doesn't think he'll want to eat in town.

    C   has already eaten.

3   Lydia's teacher

    A   has asked her to do some shopping.

    B   advised her not to stay out late.

    C   told her the shops stay open longer that evening.

Questions 4–7

Complete the notes below.

*Write **NO MORE THAN THREE WORDS AND/OR A NUMBER** for each answer.*

YOUR HOST FAMILY DETAILS

Your host family are Mr and Mrs Andrews.

Address   **4** _____ Mayweather Road, Coldfield

Bus service   Number **5** _____

Local landmarks   The house is opposite the **6** _____ .

Telephone number   01764 **7** _____

Question 8

*Choose the correct letter, **A**, **B** or **C**.*

8 Lydia needs to find

   A a stationer's.

   B a grocer's.

   C a chemist's.

Questions 9–10

Complete the sentences below.

*Write **NO MORE THAN THREE WORDS** for each answer.*

9 Seb is looking for a _____ .

10 They both have a voucher for the _____ in the city library.

Questions 11–16

Choose the correct letter, A, B or C.

11 The self-access centre

    A is always available.

    B is generally quiet.

    C gets busy during exams.

12 The Internet PCs

    A should be used for no more than half an hour.

    B must not be used to access Facebook.

    C are generally used to study English.

13 Usernames and passwords

    A are created by the teachers.

    B are issued during induction.

    C are created by students.

14 The help desk

    A is staffed by technicians.

    B offers language support.

    C is only open when two members of staff are available.

15 Photocopying of reference books

    A is not allowed.

    B is done by teachers.

    C has a small cost.

16 The high–spec PCs

    A can be used to browse the Internet.

    B are available for word processing.

    C may need a CD-ROM.

Questions 17–20

Complete the sentences below.

*Write **NO MORE THAN THREE WORDS AND/OR A NUMBER** for each answer.*

17 Students can purchase a _____ from the help desk.

18 The graded readers can be borrowed for a maximum of _____.

19 The centre opens at 8.30 and closes at _____, Monday to Friday.

20 On occasion the room is _____ by a teacher and might not be available.

Questions 21–24

Choose the correct letter, A, B or C.

21 Jacob says that

    A he needs to do more research.

    B he read widely before writing the draft.

    C he isn't confident about his main points.

22 The tutor thinks Jacob

    A has presented both sides of the argument well.

    B needs to do more work on the content.

    C has organised the essay very well.

23 The ideas Jacob expresses in the essay

    A should be re-ordered.

    B are poorly presented.

    C don't make sense.

24 The tutor suggests that Jacob

    A look at the use of paragraphs in other pieces of writing.

    B read one or two textbooks on writing skills.

    C read widely to develop his vocabulary.

Questions 25–27

Complete the tutor's notes below.

*Write **NO MORE THAN THREE WORDS** for each answer.*

Very natural use of **25** _____. Well done!
Try using higher level **26** _____ in your essays.
The sentences are sometimes too **27** _____.

Questions 28–30

Choose THREE letters, A–F.

What does the tutor suggest?

    A Try some worksheets to practise formal writing.

    B Check spelling carefully.

    C Use more advanced vocabulary.

    D Buy a thesaurus.

    E Use some of the synonyms the tutor has suggested.

    F Find alternative words to those that are underlined.

Questions 31–34

Choose the correct letter, A, B or C.

31 Work experience is required

    A to get a professional job.

    B to do a postgraduate degree.

    C to join an undergraduate course.

32 Graduates on placements

    A develop skills employers require.

    B are transferred to various posts.

    C should avoid making too many demands on employers.

33 Placements can offer the opportunity

    A to make an impact on the working environment.

    B to get to know important people in the area of work.

    C to meet new and interesting people.

34 Placements can lead to

    A future employment with the same organisation.

    B a better class of postgraduate degree.

    C greater influence with large organisations.

Questions 35–37

Choose THREE letters, A–E.

Students on placements could

     A help improve the quality of research within the organisation.

     B support people receiving long-term treatment following serious injury.

     C run counselling sessions.

     D have the chance to offer feedback on counselling sessions they attend.

     E contribute to teacher-development programmes.

Questions 38–40

Complete the notes below.

*Write **NO MORE THAN THREE WORDS** for each answer.*

It is the responsibility of the student **38** _____ an interview.

It is **39** _____ to have a CRB check when working with certain clients.

Forms for the CRB check can be obtained from **40** _____.

READING

READING PASSAGE 1

*You should spend about 20 minutes on **Questions 1–12**, which are based on Reading Passage 1 on the following pages.*

Questions 1–5

Passage 1 has six paragraphs, **A–F**.

Choose the correct heading for paragraphs A–D and F from the list of headings below.

*Write the correct number, **i–ix**, next to Questions 1–5.*

List of Headings
i Improvements to faba bean farming
ii Increasing productivity to secure the future of legume farming
iii The importance of legumes
iv The nutritional value of legumes
v The effect of farming on the environment
vi Legumes in the diet of ancient peoples
vii The importance of reducing meat consumption
viii Archaeological discoveries
ix Legumes as a provider of protein

1 Paragraph **A**
2 Paragraph **B**
3 Paragraph **C**
4 Paragraph **D**

Example	*Answer*
Paragraph **E**	**i**

5 Paragraph **F**

A   The health benefit of legumes has been widely known for centuries. Also known as pulses or, more commonly, beans, they belong to an extremely large category of vegetables containing over 13,000 species. Only grains supply more calories and protein to the world's population. Today, agricultural researchers and scientists are experimenting with varieties of legumes that are easier to harvest, more resistant to disease and yield better crops.

B   Beans are often referred to as 'the poor person's meat' but this label is unfair – considering the health benefits of legumes, they should really be called 'the healthy alternative to meat'. Beans contain a rich and varied supply of nutritional substances, which are vital for keeping in good health. Diets rich in beans are used to help with a variety of health issues including lowering cholesterol levels, improving blood sugar control in diabetics, reducing the risk of many cancers, lowering the risk of heart disease and lowering blood pressure. Beans are a good source of protein but are often considered to be an 'incomplete' protein as they lack the essential amino acids that we need to complete our diet. Foods from animals (meat, fish, eggs, dairy products), on the other hand, contain protein and amino acids. However, many cultures combine beans with grains to form a complete protein that is a high-quality substitute for meat – rice and soy in Japan, corn and beans in Mexico, rice and lentils in the Middle East. Beans are also a good source of fibre, giving the consumer between 5 and 8.6 grams of fibre per 100 grams eaten. Fibre is an important ingredient in a healthy diet with great benefits to our digestive system and in reducing cholesterol levels, which in turn reduces our risk of heart disease. Fibre also helps us to feel full and control our appetite.

C   Why is it important to substitute meat as much as possible? First of all because of the health implications – red meat in particular has a high fat content. Secondly, antibiotics and other chemicals are used in the raising of poultry and cattle. Thirdly, the cost to the environment is much greater in raising cattle than it is in growing crops. To produce a kilogram of beef, farmers need to feed the cow 15 kilograms of grain and a further 30 kilograms of forage.

D   Little wonder then that legumes have been used from ancient times. According to Trevor Brice in *Life and Society in the Hittite World*, the Hittites, an ancient people living in Anatolia from the eighteenth century BC, ate a wide variety of legumes including peas, beans, faba beans, chickpeas and lentils. And in ancient Egypt, Ramses II is known to have offered 11,998 jars of beans to the god of the Nile. Archaeologists have found the remains of legumes on land beneath Lake Assad in Syria dating back to 8,000 BC and, astonishingly, a 4,000-year-old lentil seed found during an excavation in Turkey has been germinated, allowing scientists to compare the ancient variety with the organic and genetically engineered varieties of today. Professor Nejat Bilgen from Dumlupinar University, who led the archaeological team, said that the lentils were found in a container dating from the Bronze age. The plant grown from the ancient lentil was found to be 'pretty weak' in comparison with modern varieties.

E   Modern agricultural research has tended to focus on grain production, breeding new varieties of wheat and other crops rather than improving the varieties of legumes, which can suffer from low yields and unstable harvests. For this reason, farmers started to abandon them in favour of more dependable crops, which had had the benefits of scientific improvement. Recently, scientists have returned to legumes to identify desirable characteristics such as height, good crop production and resistance to pests in order to cross different plants with each other and produce a new, improved variety. Using traditional breeding methods agricultural scientists are transforming the faba bean into a variety that is easier to grow. Traditional varieties are undependable as they rely on insects to pollinate them. But faba bean types that can self-fertilise naturally were discovered and this gene is being bred into new varieties. Other faba bean varieties have been found that produce higher yields or shorter crops. Faba bean plants tend to grow tall and fall over in the field making them difficult to harvest mechanically so breeding plants that are 50% shorter means they are more stable. Unlike the traditional plants, the new faba bean plants end in a flower – this means that more of the plant's energy is transformed into producing beans instead of unusable foliage.

F   With the new varieties, farmers in some regions are achieving a marked rise in production – between 10 to 20% improvement. Scientists have also managed to develop a commercial faba bean able to resist the parasitic weed Orobanche, which has been known to destroy whole fields of the crop. The future of legumes and the farmers who grow them is becoming brighter. Legumes are an important source of nourishment for humans and also for the soil: the beans take nitrogen directly from the atmosphere and fix it into the soil to provide nutrients for other crops and save the farmer the cost of artificial fertiliser. Making legumes a profitable crop for the future may prove an essential factor in feeding growing populations.

Questions 6–11

Do the following statements agree with the information given in Reading Passage 1? *Write*

TRUE	*if the statement agrees with the information*
FALSE	*if the statement contradicts the information*
NOT GIVEN	*if there is no information on this*

6 Legumes are second to grain in providing people with calories and protein.

7 Beans can help to cure heart disease.

8 Antibiotics are used when farming animals for food.

9 Scientists have the opportunity to see how similar modern and ancient lentil plants are.

10 Agricultural scientists are making the faba bean easier to grow in dry areas.

11 New varieties of faba bean can destroy parasitic weeds.

Question 12

What is the best title for Reading Passage 1?

Choose the correct letter A, B or C.

A   The health benefits of beans and pulses

B   Diet in ancient times

C   Agricultural scientists give legumes a new lease of life

*You should spend about 20 minutes on **Questions 13–29**, which are based on Reading Passage 2 below.*

What is dyscalculia?

When you look at the morning newspaper or check a news webpage, numbers are everywhere: the date is 12th September; it's 16°C in London; England lose 2–1 at football; the time is 12.30. But for people with dyscalculia, dealing with numbers presents a particular everyday difficulty. Dyscalculia is a learning difficulty in mathematics. It was originally uncovered by Kosc – a Czech researcher – after research into damage to parts of the brain involved in mathematical cognition. Dyscalculia can have two causes: brain damage or 'acquired dyscalculia' and developmental dyscalculia – or dyscalculia from birth. Whichever the cause, dyscalculia has three features: problems with mathematics; problems with mathematics only, not other areas of learning; and the assumption that these problems are rooted in brain activity.

Unlike dyslexia – difficulties with words – dyscalculia has been relatively little studied until recently. Very little is known about its causes, prevalence or how to treat it. Estimates indicate that between 3% and 6% of the population could be affected. The figures refer to children who only have difficulties with maths but have good or excellent performance in other areas of learning. People with dyscalculia have difficulty with the most basic aspects of numbers and mathematics, but this does not mean that the person affected has difficulty with higher mathematical reasoning or arithmetic. In fact, the evidence from brain-damaged dyscalculic people shows that an individual might suffer dyscalculia but can even show great ability in abstract mathematical reasoning.

Dyscalculia appears to be related to an ability shared between humans and many other animals. This is called 'subitizing' and is the capacity to count the number of objects by briefly looking at them. Subitizing seems to be an innate skill present in humans from birth and is a useful survival skill for humans and animals: there is a big advantage in being able to count how many predators or prey there are. Experiments with babies show that we are able to count at a very early age: if a baby sees a doll put behind a screen then another doll is also put behind the screen, the baby expects to see two dolls when the screen is removed. Babies will look longer at things they didn't expect to see, so if the screen is removed and the baby sees only one doll or three dolls, they stare at this unexpected sight longer, proving our ability to count from infancy. Dyscalculia could be explained by the lack of this innate capability. Genetic causes could include known genetic disorders such as Fragile X syndrome. However, as well as genetic factors, there could also be environmental causes such as drinking alcohol during pregnancy, which can result in underdevelopment of the brain.

There are many signs of dyscalculia including some well established and some less well researched. There are a number of symptoms that we are relatively certain of. Firstly, counting: whilst discalculic children can learn the sequence of numbers – 1, 2, 3, 4, 5, etc – they have difficulty counting backwards or forwards, particularly in twos or threes. Secondly, they find learning and remembering number facts difficult and often lack confidence even when they have the right answer. They can't use rules correctly either; for instance they may know that 4 + 2 = 6 but not be able to see that $2 + 4 = 6$ or understand the concept of addition. Thirdly, they have problems with numbers with zeros and don't understand that the numerals 10, 100 and 1,000 are the same as the words ten, one hundred and one thousand. Fourthly, dyscalculic children may not be good at using money or telling the time. Concepts of speed or temperature may be difficult for them to fully understand. Finally, they may have problems in understanding directions or in following a map.

Diagnosing and treating dyscalculia is not straightforward as there are many reasons for being bad at maths including poor teaching, lack of motivation and inability to concentrate for long periods of time. An important result of present research will be to improve our methods for identifying children with dyscalculia. The treatment of the problem, however, is a different matter. Many people think that, because the cause of dyscalculia is in the brain, it can't be treated. But this is a misunderstanding. Every time we learn a new fact or skill, our brain changes. Furthermore, if we practise a new skill extensively the brain changes considerably. This is related to a property of the brain called 'plasticity', which simply means the ability of the brain to develop and change, particularly during childhood. Dyscalculia could be treated by experiences at home, providing an environment that encourages children to count. Schools could pay more attention to making sure children understand basic mathematical concepts before dealing with more advanced ideas; they should, for example, avoid teaching the division of fractions before ensuring children have understood to concept of division. Teaching maths through a multi-sensory approach using speech, sound, writing and reading simultaneously has been shown to be a good approach. Finally, maths should be taught in short blocks of time and lessons should build on what was taught previously.

Questions 13–16

Complete the sentences below.

*Write **NO MORE THAN TWO WORDS** from the passage for each answer.*

13 A person with dyscalculia cannot solve basic _____ problems.

14 The condition was first discovered by a researcher investigating _____ to the brain.

15 Dyscalculia can be caused by injury to the brain or it can be present

_____ .

16 Other aspects of _____ are not affected by dyscalculia.

Questions 17–22

Do the following statements agree with the information given in Reading Passage 2?
Write

TRUE	*if the statement agrees with the information*
FALSE	*if the statement contradicts the information*
NOT GIVEN	*if there is no information on this*

17 There is not much information on how many people have dyscalculia.

18 People with dyscalculia are not able to do advanced maths.

19 *Subsitizing* means knowing how many things there are by counting them.

20 Experiments show that babies are able to count to four.

21 One explanation is that people with dyscalculia have not inherited a common ability.

22 Drinking alcohol may be linked to the development of dyscalculia.

Questions 23–29

Classify the following as typical of

A *reasons for being bad at maths*

B *plasticity*

C *dyscalculia*

D *the treatment of dyscalculia*

*Write the correct letter, **A, B, C** or **D**, next to Questions 23–29.*

23 limiting maths teaching to short periods

24 being unmotivated to learn

25 the brain developing, especially when young

26 not associating words about figures with numbers

27 needing practice at telling the time

28 using all the senses when doing maths

29 poor concentration for longer lengths of time

READING PASSAGE 3

You should spend about 20 minutes on Questions 30–40, which are based on Reading Passage 3 below.

Crowdmapping

One of the most exciting mass movements today is crowdmapping: sharing data collectively to produce a visualisation on a map giving almost-instant information on current events. Crowdmapping produces a picture of events on the ground as they happen by taking text messages and social media feeds together with geographic data to distribute real-time, interactive information on events such as revolutions, wars, humanitarian crises and natural disasters. This new application of social networking can bring fresh insights into events, which can be nearly impossible to cover through traditional methods of journalism where individuals report into a central newsroom. It has the additional advantage of mapping longer-term trends that fall in and out of the news.

Technologies like mobile phones and the world wide web have made it possible for those people caught up in a war or natural disaster to broadcast information from the affected area and for this information to be collected in a way that emergency aid services can use and act on. In a disaster situation the most current information is essential because the needs of, for example, flood victims change minute by minute. It enables response organisations to get an understanding of a crisis situation quickly (thus it is sometimes called *crisis mapping*), give targeted aid to people most in need and form a network of reliable reporters on the ground to check information going to the live updated map. When an emergency situation arises, a small army of volunteers comes together to collect incoming information and put it on the map. Some of the information comes from official sources such as the United Nations, but the most powerful aspect of data collection is the ability to pull information from Twitter posts, emails and text messages. Once this information is available, volunteers collaborate via the Internet to put data on to a map, which is updated every second to build a comprehensive picture of the scale and severity of the disaster. Volunteers from all over the world translate the messages coming in from the disaster zone into English and plot the information on the live interactive map.

One of the originators of crowdmapping is Ushahidi. The developers of crowdmapping software began the project in Kenya to map reports of violence after a controversial election result in 2008. Later, in 2010 in Haiti, a similar approach of collectively sharing information to help emergency services deal with the situation was adopted. A small team released a free phone number – 4636 – to allow victims of the 7.0-magnitude earthquake to text their requests for medical aid, water and shelter. Over 1,000 workers and volunteers around the globe, contacted via Facebook, translated the messages, mostly in Haitian Creole. They then prioritised and geolocated the requests for help via crowdmapping software. Through this service, emergency response teams were able to save the lives of hundreds of people and send food, water and medicine to tens of thousands. The success of Project 4636 led to the development of crowdmapping when dealing with critical and even non-critical situations.

Most recently, crowdmapping has been used to track violent activity in warzones and areas with uprisings. In one country, when the people rose up against their leader, the United Nations monitored the escalating violence via a crowdmap to provide them with information on what was happening in the country. In another country, rebel fighters reported people who were missing, killed or arrested according to eyewitnesses. Other uses for the software have included the Danish people's attempt to map the extent of CCTV surveillance in their country. Since the project began, 2,220 CCTV cameras have been photographed and verified by journalists. However, not all attempts at crowdmapping have been successful. The attempt to map an uprising in one country was cut short when the authorities took the country offline and, when the Internet was brought back, the crowdmap had been forgotten.

There are other downsides to crowdmapping. According to George Chamales, there are security challenges: it must be ensured that the system stays operational and that the information collated is not misused. Firstly, the lead crowdmap tends to be the one that is set up first and has the most users. Unfortunately, the organisation behind the first crowdmap may not be the best one to manage the complex process of collecting and managing the data. Secondly, there are several platforms for producing crowdmaps including commercial products and open-source projects like Ushahidi. Some have even been developed for a particular crisis such as the nuclear meltdown in Fukushima – all of these have their own disadvantages: commercial software may need to patch bugs in the programme; open source software may overlook security in favour of functionality. The information collected needs to come from trustworthy sources, which are then relied on for more reports; this may make the person sending the report a potential target in war situations. Finally, there is the human element in processing the information, relying on thousands of volunteers to translate, categorise and prioritise the information. There is an obvious risk in giving strangers access to messages generated in dangerous circumstances: messages may be deleted and the sender's identity may be compromised.

While the introduction of any new technology has flaws, George Chamales believes that crowdmapping cannot afford to go through the same maturation as other technologies: the risks to people using it in hostile political situations are too great and could lead to them being arrested or killed. Furthermore, over time the technology may be labelled as dangerous, leading organisations to shun an extremely useful instrument. The answer, Chamales believes, can be found in developing standards through collaboration between IT security experts and the crowdmapping movement. New challenges and issues will arise with each crisis mapped by the people affected, but George Chamales thinks that establishing security standards would be a good starting point to allow this valuable new form of networking to evolve.

Questions 30–34

Label the diagram below using words from the box.

*Write the correct letter, **A–E**, in spaces 30–34.*

> **Crowdmapping actions**
>
> **A**   interactive map
>
> **B**   social media feeds
>
> **C**   emergency services
>
> **D**   volunteers collect and translate
>
> **E**   official sources

Crowdmapping

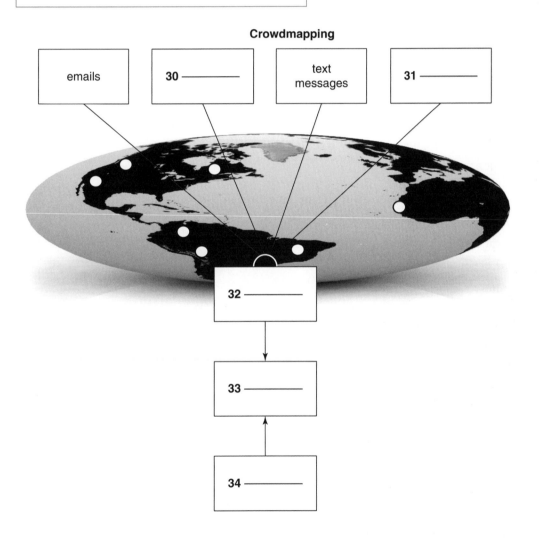

emails	30 ———

text messages	31 ———

32 ———

33 ———

34 ———

Questions 35–40

Choose the correct letter, A, B, C or D.

35 Crowdmapping aims to produce data on

    A historical and future patterns of behaviour.

    B political events.

    C interactive maps.

    D events after earthquakes only.

36 Crowdmapping allows emergency services to

    A contact journalists.

    B help everyone who needs it.

    C check information online.

    D act quickly in specific areas.

37 The operation relies heavily on

    A a project in Kenya.

    B a small team.

    C people translating messages.

    D emergency response teams.

38 The fourth paragraph contains examples of crowdmapping in

    A countries with no internet access.

    B natural disasters.

    C areas of conflict.

    D a country with a lot of traffic cameras.

39 Which is NOT a disadvantage of crowdmapping?

    A the inability of some organisations to handle the data effectively

    B unreliable information

    C security being compromised

    D computer crashes

40 What is the best way to deal with the problems associated with this new technology?

    A wait for problems to be resolved

    B arrest people using it incorrectly

    C agree common practices to make crowdmapping secure

    D change the process when new problems arise

WRITING

WRITING TASK 1

You should spend about 20 minutes on this task.

> *The graphs below show the percentage of people holding full driving licences in Great Britain by age and sex.*
>
> *Summarise the information by selecting and reporting the main features, and make comparisons where relevant.*

Write at least 150 words.

Full car driving licence holders: by sex and age

Great Britain

Percentages

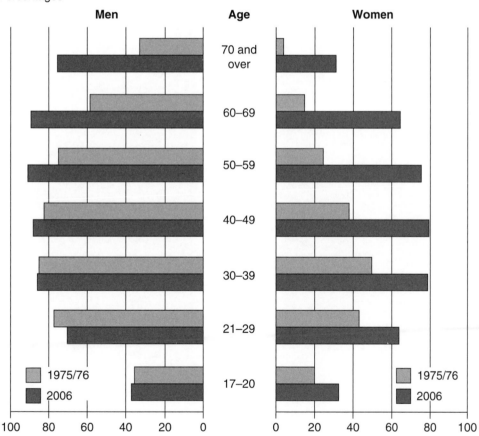

WRITING TASK 2

You should spend about 40 minutes on this task.

Write about the following topic:

> A huge number of students choose to study English independently on a self-study basis rather than attend a formal course. However, without the assistance of a teacher, students often find it difficult to manage their studies.
>
> To what extent do you agree or disagree?

Give reasons for your answer and include any relevant examples from your knowledge or experience.

Write at least 250 words.

SPEAKING

PART 1: Introduction and interview

Listen to Track 12, pressing pause after each question to answer.

PART 2: Individual long turn

Before you read the task card, listen to Track 13.

Describe a hobby you had as a child.

You should say:

> what the hobby was
>
> how old you were when you had the hobby
>
> how you spent your time on the hobby

and explain what it was about the hobby that interested you.

PART 3: Two-way discussion

Listen to Track 14, pressing pause after each question to answer.

Test 3

SECTION 1   *Questions 1–10*

15

Questions 1–4

Complete the form below.

*Write **NO MORE THAN THREE WORDS AND / OR A NUMBER** for each answer.*

Example	Answer
Modal	Ford Fiesta
Registration	3R1 **1** _____
Current mileage	**2** _____ miles
Estimated yearly mileage	6,000 a year
Overnight parking	**3** _____
Cover	Third party **4** _____
No claims bonus	6 years

Questions 5–7

*Choose **THREE** letters, **A–G**.*

Which additional cover does Liam want?

    A   Legal

    B   14-day cover courtesy car

    C   Driver Injury

    D   Protected no claims bonus

    E   Breakdown

    F   Lost car key

    G   Windscreen

Questions 8–10

Complete the form below.

Write **NO MORE THAN THREE WORDS AND/OR A NUMBER** *for each answer.*

Name	Liam Byrd
Address	35 Bottiville Crescent, Birmingham
Postcode	**8** _____
Date of birth	11/11/1969
Telephone	0121 677 9887
Payment by	**9** _____
Card number	**** **** **** 1551
Security number	***
How did the customer hear about Hartline?	**10** _____

Questions 11–20

Questions 11–14

Complete the sentences below.

*Write **NO MORE THAN THREE WORDS AND/OR A NUMBER** for each answer.*

11 Every year more than _____ people try to climb Mont Blanc.

12 Approximately _____ reach the top every day in the summer months.

13 In July 2007 there were 30 fatalities, chiefly due to _____.

14 One danger is _____ caused by other climbers.

Questions 15–17

*Choose the correct letter, **A**, **B** or **C**.*

15 How did Katherine do her most recent climb?

    A in a group

    B with a guide

    C on her own

16 Why did Katherine find her first climb of Mont Blanc difficult?

    A because of poor weather conditions

    B because of the time she was climbing

    C because the route was crowded

17 What did Katherine do on her second climb that made it easier?

    A She spent a few days in Chamonix beforehand.

    B She did the climb over two days.

    C She climbed smaller peaks for training.

Questions 18–20

*Choose **THREE** letters, **A–F**.*

What has experience taught Katherine about climbing Mont Blanc?

    A Be in good physical condition.

    B Have the right climbing equipment.

    C Wear several layers of clothing.

    D Protect yourself from the sun.

    E Climb with others.

    F Acclimatise yourself to the altitude first.

17

SECTION 3   *Questions 21–30*

Questions 21–23

*Write **NO MORE THAN THREE WORDS** for each answer.*

21 When do Elaine and Adam decide to meet for revision?

_____

22 What item does Adam think will help them work independently on revision?

_____

23 How does Elaine suggest they spend their revision time between meetings?

_____

Questions 24–28

Complete the sentences below.

*Write **NO MORE THAN THREE WORDS** for each answer.*

24 It's best to avoid taking notes _____.

25 Relate _____ to key theories and arguments.

26 Using diagrams can help keep a lot of information _____.

27 Bullet points can enable you to highlight _____.

28 Keep a record of your sources, such as the _____.

Questions 29–30

*Choose the correct letter, **A**, **B** or **C**.*

29 In future revision sessions Adam suggests using past papers

    A to try to predict future exam questions.

    B to test each other.

    C to discuss the questions.

30 Elaine suggests

    A adding essay practice to the timetable.

    B doing essays under exam conditions.

    C asking a tutor to mark their essays.

SECTION 4 *Questions 31–40*

18

Questions 31–33

Choose the correct letter, A, B or C.

31 According to the text, shared space
  A is very popular in the Netherlands.
  B reduces the number of cars in an area.
  C improves the dynamic between drivers and pedestrians.

32 Shared space design results in
  A fewer road signs.
  B stronger boundaries between pedestrians and motorists.
  C increased local employment.

33 Supporters of shared space argue that it
  A leads to new businesses opening.
  B makes people happier to shop in the area.
  C encourages wildlife.

Questions 34–37

Match the groups A–D with their concerns about shared space 34–37.

  A *Motorists*
  B *Blind people*
  C *Cyclists*
  D *Supporters of shared space*

34 Insufficient experience amongst planners
35 A lack of important signage
36 Intimidation by motorists
37 The loss of familiar street furniture

Questions 38–39

Choose TWO letters, A–D.

People will be able to answer the questions

    A on the Internet.

    B at the local library.

    C at the proposed site.

    D at home.

Question 40

Choose the correct letter, A, B or C.

Questions must be designed so that they

    A do not reflect the views of the campaign group.

    B do not require an understanding of shared space.

    C are easy to answer.

READING

READING PASSAGE 1

*You should spend about 20 minutes on **Questions 1–12**, which are based on Reading Passage 1 below.*

Seas beneath the sands

A   Look at a map of North Africa from Egypt to Algeria. Almost everything outside the Nile Valley and south of the coastal plain appears to be lifeless sand and gravel deserts. But peer deeper, under the sand, and you will find water. Under the Sahara lie three major aquifers, strata of saturated sandstones and limestones that hold water in their pores like a wet sponge. The easternmost of these, extending over two million square kilometres, contains 375,000 cubic kilometres of water—the equivalent of 3,750 years of Nile river flow. It is called the Nubian Sandstone Aquifer System, and lately it has come to the attention of practitioners of a subspeciality of nuclear science known as isotope hydrology.

B   Isotope hydrology, which studies the atoms of the two elements making up groundwater— oxygen and hydrogen—and the trace elements in it, like carbon and nitrogen, is able to determine when, give or take a couple of thousand years, today's groundwater fell to earth as rain. In the case of the Nubian Aquifer, some water in the system is thought to be one million years old, but most of it fell between 50,000 and 20,000 years ago. Since then, as the region has slowly turned to desert, there has been little addition of water to the aquifer. What lies beneath the ground is called fossil water, and it will likely never be recharged.

C   Because the Nubian Aquifer is shared among four nations, and because Libya and Egypt are now going forward with big water-pumping projects that tap the Nubian Aquifer, the International Atomic Energy Agency (IAEA), co-recipient of the 2005 Nobel Peace Prize, is trying to bring the countries together in a joint effort to plan for a rational shared use of the water.

D   The stakes are certainly high. Egypt eventually hopes to use almost half a billion cubic metres of groundwater annually—more than the volume of Lake Erie. Libya is already pumping water from the Kufra Oasis, in its southeast corner, through a four-metre-diameter pipeline to its thirsty coastal cities. When fully operational, that project will pump some 3.6 million cubic metres per day. Still, at current extraction rates, the aquifer is not likely to be depleted for a thousand years.

E   Dr Taher Muhammad Hassan of the EAEA (Egyptian Atomic Energy Authority) says "One thing that isotope studies have shown us is that there is surprisingly little aquifer recharge from the Nile. Nile water has a younger isotopic profile, and samples from wells dug as close as five kilometres from the river show no sign of the Nile fingerprint. In fact, some of that well water is dated at 26,000 years old." Hassan is confident there is little likelihood of international conflict over aquifer sharing. "We know that the velocity of underground flow in most places is just two metres a day," he says. "It's like sucking a thick milkshake through a straw—it doesn't happen fast, and eventually it stops completely." Even Libya's big extraction plans for Kufra will probably have only a minor effect on Egypt's East Uweinat farming area, given the distance between the two. If Kufra's water table drops 200 metres, the Egyptian side might see a drop of only 10 centimetres.

F   At al-Agouza West in Egypt, a 10-story drilling rig, the same kind used to drill oil wells, has reached 800 metres and is now evacuating the drilling mud and widening the bore. It has taken 20 days to penetrate layers of shale and clay to reach the saturated sandstone—the basement of the Nubian formation is some 1,800 metres deep here—at a cost of about $400,000. Once the well is ready for testing, the ministry engineers check its static and dynamic levels with a sounder, a kind of fisherman's bob at the end of a tape measure that rises and falls with the water table.

G   Dr Khaled Abu Zeid, of the Egyptian non-profit Center for Environment and Development of the Arab Region and Europe (CEDARE), stresses the social context of water-resource development, and the need to keep in mind traditional water users as well as new users. Small farmers and Bedouin who rely on shallow wells should not be ignored in favour of the big development schemes. "They need water today," he says, "and will still need it tomorrow. We must not let it run dry because deeper wells are more cost-effective. But neither should we have an absolutist conservationist approach, in which we try to keep fossil water in some kind of 'museum' for their benefit."

H   The director of the Groundwater Research Institute at the Nile Barrage, Dr Ahmed Khater, finds it ironic that in a desert region like the Middle East, petroleum geology is much better understood than subsurface hydrology. "But water is what makes our life possible here, and we must use it wisely," he says. He cites the experience of President Nasser's "New Valley" project in the 1960s, which proposed a massive resettlement of Nile Valley farmers to the western oases. It was a failure. "These isotope studies hold the promise of learning more about what is really our most precious asset—water, not oil," he says. Nasser, he notes, got the New Valley project's motto wrong. "He said, 'When settlers come, then we will find water.' He should have said, 'When we find water, then settlers can come.'"

Questions 1–4

Complete the table below.

*Choose **NO MORE THAN THREE WORDS** from the passage for each answer.*

Nubian Sandstone Aquifer system	
Extent	**1** _____ 375,000 km³ of water
Formation	The majority of the **2** _____ between 50,000 and 20,000 years ago.
Flow	water moves only **3** _____ a day in most places
Depth	The **4** _____ of the formation is 1,800 metres deep.

Questions 5–12

Reading Passage 1 has eight paragraphs, *A–H*.

Which paragraph contains the following information?

*Write the correct letter, **A–H**, next to Questions 5–12.*

  5 dating the age of the water

  6 understanding underground water through studying isotopes

  7 the process of water collection

  8 review of the likelihood of conflict

  9 the importance of water for North-Saharan countries

10 layers of porous rock holding water under the desert

11 attention to the needs of local people

12 cross-country project for the use of water

READING PASSAGE 2

*You should spend about 20 minutes on **Questions 13–27**, which are based on Reading Passage 2 below.*

High intensity training

Endurance vs intensity

The traditional view of exercise is that more is better. But now a new form of exercise is challenging the old view and causing debate between traditionalists and proponents of a new form of exercise, High Intensity Training (HIT). Current recommendations from the US Department of Health and Human Services say adults aged between 16 and 64 should take two kinds of exercise every week: aerobic and muscle-strengthening. Aerobic exercise covers activities that make you breathe harder and your heart beat faster – activities such as walking quickly, swimming or playing a relaxed game of tennis. Muscle-strengthening exercises work all the major muscle groups in a person's body – legs, hips, back, chest, abdomen, shoulders and arms. The US Department of Health and Human Services recommends that adults do two hours and thirty minutes of moderate-intensity aerobic activity per week and muscle-strengthening activities on at least two days per week. A lot of people, perhaps understandably, never meet these targets, usually citing lack of time as the main reason.

However, a recent study has removed the old excuse. Professor Martin Gibala, from Canada's McMaster University, has published research in the Journal of Physiology that shows doing less exercise can be more effective than time-consuming periods of aerobic and muscle-strengthening activities. High Intensity Training is very simple: it involves a warm-up period followed by a short burst of intense activity, usually 30 seconds to one minute, then a recovery period where you exercise at a gentler pace for a couple of minutes, then another short period of high-energy activity. After a second recovery phase, there is more energy-intensive exercise before slowing down for a while, then stopping. That's all your exercise for the day. This cycle of warm up / intense activity / recovery / intense activity, etc can be applied to a variety of sports such as cycling, jogging and swimming.

How does it work?

There are a number of different explanations as to why HIT seems to be more effective than endurance exercise. Firstly, exercising at low intensity only burns calories while you are active so that the minute you stop, you also stop burning calories. In contrast, high-intensity exercise continues to work on your metabolism a long time after you have finished – and this can be up to 24 hours later – so that you continue burning calories for longer. Secondly, HIT builds your muscles, replacing fat with muscle mass. The third theory is that the sprint-and-recover cycle doesn't give the body the chance to store energy in the same way as training over a long period: the body needs to use all the energy in one go rather than maintain the same energy level over a longer period and still being able to reserve some as fat. The final theory is HIT combines both aerobic and muscle-strengthening activities and uses many more muscles than regular exercise – up to 80% of the muscles in the body, compared with up to 40% for moderate jogging or cycling.

There have been numerous experiments into HIT. In one conducted by a team from the University of Colorado led by Kyle Sevits, five male volunteers were tested to measure the number of calories a typical HIT workout burns. The volunteers, aged between 25 and 31, were tested to make sure their hearts were healthy, and their body composition and resting metabolic rates were measured. The participants ate a specific diet, then taken to a hospital room where researchers were able to control the air intake and determine the oxygen, carbon dioxide and water content of the air. Through these indices researchers were able to measure how many calories the volunteers burned. While each person lived in the room, they were kept on their strict diet and could only watch TV or use a computer. However, on one day they were asked to participate in HIT on a gym bike, pedalling as fast as they could for five 30-second periods with four-minute recovery periods between. The results were startling: the volunteers burned an average of an extra 200 calories on the workout day in spite of doing high-intensity activity for just 2.5 minutes. Other experiments have revealed similar results. In Japan, a team from the National Institute of Fitness and Sport separated individuals into two groups. The first group trained five days a week over six weeks, taking an hour of moderate-intensity exercise per day, totally five hours per week. The oxygen intake of this group improved by an average of 9%. The second group's training sessions were eight 20-second intense workouts followed by ten seconds of rest. Their oxygen intake improved by 15%.

Benefits to health

Good oxygen intake is a sign of a healthy adult but the workout routine has shown other health benefits in diabetes. Scientists at Herriot Watt University in Edinburgh found that short bursts of high-intensity activity every few days reduced the risk of contracting diabetes due to the beneficial effects on blood sugar. Similarly, a study in 2011 by Professor Gibala found that insulin sensitivity improved by 35% after just two weeks, which is important in enabling glucose digested from food to get to our cells and provide energy. Endurance is also increased: one study in 2006 found that eight weeks of doing high-intensity workouts meant subjects could exercise twice as long as they could before the study, while maintaining the same pace. Additionally, HIT increases the fat burnt and sustains more muscle. Finally, HIT stimulates production of human growth hormone (HGH) by up to 450% during the 24 hours after the workout has finished. HGH is not only responsible for increased calorie burning but also slows down the ageing process. It seems that HIT could keep us fitter and younger for longer.

Questions 13–17

Do the following statements agree with the information given in Reading Passage 2?
Write

TRUE	*if the statement agrees with the information*
FALSE	*if the statement contradicts the information*
NOT GIVEN	*if there is no information on this*

13 The traditional view of exercise questions the effectiveness of long periods of activity.

14 Aerobic exercise includes tennis, walking and football.

15 Many people fail to do the recommended amount of exercise.

16 Some now believe that being active for shorter periods is better for our health.

17 HIT involves a 10-minute cool-down period.

Questions 18–22

Choose the correct letter, A, B, C or D.

18 Low-intensity activity

    A burns calories after you stop.

    B lets the body store fat.

    C doesn't take much time.

    D uses all the body's energy reserves.

19 High-intensity training

    A retains both muscle and fat tissue.

    B is only good for muscle-building.

    C makes use of under half of our muscles.

    D is done in cycles of rest and activity.

20 In one experiment, participants

    A were all middle aged.

    B were slightly unhealthy.

    C ate a high-fibre diet.

    D were kept in a controlled environment.

21 Researchers measured

    A the air intake.

    B how much TV they watched.

    C how fast they pedalled.

    D how much energy they used.

22 In the Japanese experiment

    A there were two groups of men.

    B the groups trained simultaneously.

    C scientists measured the amount of oxygen used in training.

    D both groups had intensive training sessions.

Questions 23–27

Complete the text below.

*Choose **NO MORE THAN TWO WORDS** from the passage for each answer.*

A study has found that HIT **23** _____ the chance of getting diabetes. Another study
found that HIT improves **24** _____, enabling individuals to exercise for longer
periods while **25** _____ a similar pace. More fat is **26** _____ and the
27 _____ of human growth hormone increases enormously.

READING PASSAGE 3

You should spend about 20 minutes on **Questions 28–40**, which are based on Reading Passage 3 on the following pages.

Questions 28–32

Passage 3 has six paragraphs, A–F.

*Choose the correct heading for paragraphs **B–F** from the list below.*

*Write the correct number, **i–ix**, next to Questions 28–32.*

List of Headings
i The collapse of the Neanderthal population
ii The origin of modern humans
iii Humanity's prehistoric mother
iv Routes out of Africa
v Attributes of humans and Neanderthals
vi The human migration
vii What did Neanderthals look like?
viii The diversity of African populations
ix Tracing back our DNA

Example	Answer
Paragraph **A**	**ii**

28 Paragraph **B**

29 Paragraph **C**

30 Paragraph **D**

31 Paragraph **E**

32 Paragraph **F**

A   Among prehistoric archeologists, Ksar Aqil has an almost mythical status, but the site is little known outside professional circles. The migration of modern humans out of Africa and the Near East's position as a bridge between continents and cultures, as well as nearly a century of scientific research, are all woven into the story of Ksar Aqil. Current perspectives on human evolution and mankind's colonization of the globe are based upon fossil evidence, as well as excavated artifacts and biogenetic data. These lines of inquiry indicate a relatively recent evolution of modern humans, *Homo sapiens sapiens*, in Africa about 200,000 years ago.

B   The latest, and arguably most powerful, analytical tool available to those investigating human origins comes from molecular biology. Geneticists have found that examination of the DNA from tiny structures inside the cell, called mitochondria, provided a means to measure human biogenetic relationships on a time scale spanning hundreds of thousands of years. Mitochondria, also known as the powerhouse of the cell because they generate chemical energy, possess their own genome, and mitochondrial DNA (mtDNA) is inherited exclusively from the mother. Dramatic results released in 1987 by researchers at the University of California at Berkley indicated that all mtDNA present in people today stems from a single female who lived about 200,000 years ago in Africa. This woman was called "Mitochondrial Eve," the genetic mother of all of earth's present-day population.

C   Tens of thousands of years before Beirut became a meeting place of East and West, the Levantine coastal strip and the Arabian Peninsula to the south were corridors through which our common ancestors moved out of Africa and into Asia, Europe, Australia and, lastly, the Americas. The region also has the distinction of being a place where Neanderthals (*Homo sapiens neanderthalensis*) and our immediate ancestors co-existed and indeed interbred. Although the evolutionary split between Neanderthals and the ancestors of modern humans occurred sometime between 440,000 and 270,000 years ago, according to research, a little Neanderthal DNA, between one and four per cent, exists in all peoples alive today, except for those in Africa. It is probable that our Neanderthal heritage resulted from interbreeding that happened in the Near East sometime between 80,000 and 45,000 years ago.

D   According to proponents of the "out of Africa" theory, the exodus of anatomically modern humans probably occurred in waves. One early migration into the Near East occurred prior to 130,000 years ago, and an examination of a modern map of the Horn of Africa and adjacent parts of Arabia shows there are two obvious routes this migration could have taken. One involves crossing from northern Egypt into the Sinai Peninsula, the other crosses the Bab el-Mandab strait to reach modern-day Yemen, perhaps by watercraft. It is likely that both these routes were taken at different times, as they were navigable, presented no significant hazards and were frequented by the animals our early ancestors tracked and hunted. Given the geographic position of the Near East as a bridge between Europe and Asia, this region formed the trunk through which our family tree branched out from its African roots, both geographically and genetically. When modern humans entered the area over 130,000 years ago, the Neanderthals were in residence, and it seems they curtailed the extent of the newcomers' settlement for a while. When another wave of modern humans began migrating from Africa about 50,000 years ago, perhaps due to population pressure on resources and territory, our ancestors ultimately became the sole inhabitants of places like Ksar Aqil.

E   If this contest had been based on physical strength alone, the Neanderthals would have won hands down. Modern humans, however, had developed cognitive, physical and cultural abilities that provided an advantage, ultimately leading to the Neanderthals being relegated to geographically marginalized refugees. Neanderthals differed from modern humans in a number of ways, perhaps most noticeably in their skull anatomy, which featured a sloped forehead, a large projection at the back of the skull called an occipital bun, pronounced eyebrow ridges, and no chin. Physically robust and more powerfully built than our ancestors, their massive but relatively short stature was more efficient in cold climates like Europe's. In common with modern humans, they possessed a gene essential for language development, and some paleoanthropologists believe they were capable of complex speech patterns. The Neanderthals apparently were not suited to activities like long-distance running. The energy cost of locomotion was apparently 32 per cent higher in Neanderthals, resulting in a daily dietary requirement between 100 and 350 calories greater than that of modern humans living in similar environmental settings. Our ancestors may, therefore, have had a competitive edge simply by being more fuel-efficient.

F   What exactly happened to the Neanderthals no one knows. Modern peoples migrating into Southwest Asia and on to Europe may have displaced them. Undoubtedly, contact led to a variety of interactions, some clearly resulting in opportunities for interbreeding, others involving physical conflict and competition for resources. The Neanderthals' demise may also have been linked to rapid climatic swings between 50,000 and 30,000 years ago, which created further pressure on their already divided and isolated populations.

Questions 33–39

Classify the following as typical of

    A *Neanderthals*

    B *humans*

    C *both*

*Write the correct letter, **A**, **B** or **C**, next to Questions 33–39.*

33 the ability to develop language

34 the absence of one particular facial feature

35 the ability to run long distances

36 needing to consume lots of calories

37 greater physical strength

38 being small in height

39 making up at least 96% of our genes

Question 40

What is the best title for Reading Passage 3?

*Choose the correct letter, **A**, **B** or **C**.*

    A The decline of Neanderthal man

    B The site where humans and Neanderthals met and mixed

    C The migration of humans into Europe

WRITING TASK 1

You should spend about 20 minutes on this task.

> *The graph below shows the perceived danger and actual likelihood of being a victim of crime.*
>
> *Summarise the information by selecting and reporting the main features, and make comparisons where relevant.*

Write at least 150 words.

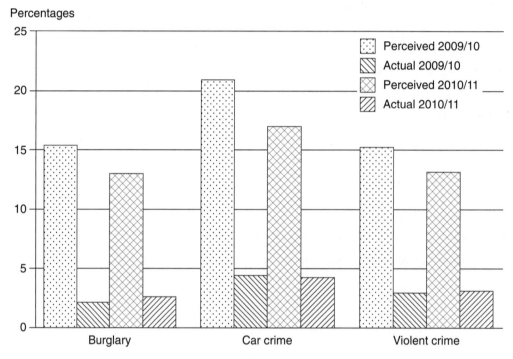

Perceived and actual likelihood of being a victim of crime: by crime type

WRITING TASK 2

You should spend about 40 minutes on this task.

Write about the following topic:

> *The position of women has changed a great deal in many societies over the past 50 years. But these societies cannot claim to have achieved gender equality.*
>
> *To what extent do you agree or disagree?*

Give reasons for your answer and include any relevant examples from your knowledge or experience.

Write at least 250 words.

SPEAKING

PART 1: Introduction and interview

Listen to Track 19, pressing pause after each question to answer.

19

PART 2: Individual long turn

Before you read the task card, listen to Track 20.

20

> Describe a possession that is very important to you.
>
> You should say:
>
> what the possession is
>
> how long you have had it
>
> how often you use it
>
> and explain what it is about this possession that makes it so important.

PART 3: Two-way discussion

Listen to Track 21, pressing pause after each question to answer.

21

Test 4

SECTION 1   *Questions 1–10*

22

Questions 1–3

Complete the notes below.

*Write **NO MORE THAN THREE WORDS AND/OR A NUMBER** for each answer.*

Example	Answer
The customer is going to France for	1 week

Traveller's cheques can be replaced within **1** _____.

Having a little cash is useful for things like **2** _____.

The bank charges for ATM withdrawals with a **3** _____.

Questions 4–7

Complete the table below.

*Write **NO MORE THAN TWO WORDS AND/OR A NUMBER** for each answer.*

Order	Collect in branch	Home delivery
Monday–Thursday	Next day	Next day
4 Before _____ p.m.	10 a.m.	**5** _____ p.m.
Friday–Saturday	Tuesday	Tuesday
6 _____	10 a.m.	**7** _____ p.m.

Questions 8–10

Choose the correct letter, A, B or C.

8 The bank will buy back unused traveller's cheques

  A free of charge.

  B for a small fee.

  C if they are returned in good condition.

9 Sandra does not want Euros because she

  A already has some.

  B will be given some.

  C will be buying some at the airport.

10 On Tuesday Sandra will

  A collect the cheques from the branch.

  B be at work.

  C sign for the cheques at home.

SECTION 2 *Questions 11–20*

Question 11

Choose the correct letter, A, B or C.

11 NUS extra cards

    A are offered free to all students.

    B are recognised internationally.

    C give you a year's-worth of discounts.

Questions 12–15

Complete the notes below.

*Write **NO MORE THAN THREE WORDS AND/OR A NUMBER** for each answer.*

> ### *Student Railcards*
>
> For young people between 16 and 25
>
> Mature students 25+ studying **12** _____
>
> Get **13** _____ train fares in the UK
>
> Discounts for theatre tickets and **14** _____
>
> 1 year £28
>
> 3 years **15** _____

Questions 16–17

Choose TWO letters, A–E.

Local bus operators offer bus passes

A especially for students.

B for various lengths of time.

C that are cheaper the longer the period.

D for use only for commuting.

E that can be used by your friends.

Questions 18–20

Write the correct letter, A, B or C, next to questions 18–20.

Which places are useful for the following?

A Household items

B Vintage clothes

C Second-hand textbooks

18 The university campus

19 Charity shops

20 Car boot sales

SECTION 3   *Questions 21–30*

24

Questions 21–25

Complete the notes below.

*Write **NO MORE THAN THREE WORDS AND/OR A NUMBER** for your answer.*

Autumn term: Key dates	
Term starts	15th September
Release timetables	15th September
Release **21** _____	14th October
All assignments online	by **22** _____
Release grades for first assignment	**23** _____
Release **24** _____ for Belgium trip	29th October
Belgium trip	**25** _____

Questions 26–30

Choose the correct letter, A, B or C.

26 The college is trying to

    A significantly reduce the amount of paper it uses.

    B be careful about the amount of documents it produces.

    C discover why students keep losing their work.

27 According to the text, students at the college

    A are not allowed to print documents.

    B have restrictions on how many pages they can print.

    C have to pay to do any printing.

28 The college

    A has permission to reproduce the quizzes.

    B wants the students to give them feedback about the quizzes.

    C thinks the online quizzes are more effective than the paper ones.

29 The tutor explains that

    A the quizzes are easy to find on the intranet.

    B the quizzes will be online for a few weeks only.

    C the majority of the quizzes are online.

30 The online quiz system

    A occasionally doesn't work.

    B keeps the quiz results confidential.

    C allows tutors to identify areas where the students may be having difficulties.

SECTION 4   *Questions 31–40*

25

Questions 31–34

Complete the sentences below.

*Write **NO MORE THAN THREE WORDS** for each answer.*

31 _____ times are less common within the family.

32 We may eat more than we need due to our _____.

33 Eating habits can be affected by both _____ emotions.

34 People who are _____ are more likely to eat more due to negative emotions.

Questions 35–39

Answer the questions below.

Which type of hunger relates to the points below?

*Write **E** for emotional hunger. Write **P** for physical hunger.*

35 Experiences a sudden urge to eat

36 Hungers for any type of food

37 Needs to satisfy the hunger as soon as possible

38 Will stop eating once full

39 Will feel no sense of guilt after eating

Question 40

*Choose the correct letter, **A**, **B** or **C**.*

40 People suffering from obesity can be helped by

    A taking the pressure off them about feeling guilty.

    B understanding why they have negative feelings.

    C pinpointing stressful moments that can cause emotional hunger.

READING PASSAGE 1

*You should spend about 20 minutes on **Questions 1–16**, which are based on Reading Passage 1 below.*

Raining Ice

In May 2012, disaster struck a mountainous region of China's Gansu province. 40 people were killed and 29,300 people evacuated when a brief but extremely violent hailstone storm swept across Min County. Houses collapsed, roads were blocked and crops were destroyed. The extreme weather also affected the power supply and communications in the region. When you consider that hailstones can reach sizeable proportions, the damage they can cause is understandable. The world's largest hailstone was found after a storm in South Dakota and measured 20.5 cm in diameter with a 47 cm circumference – this was after melting caused it to lose 5 cm from its original size. Apart from China and the US, other parts of the world that frequently suffer from hailstorm damage include Russia, India and northern Italy.

Hail is a form of solid precipitation created within cumulonimbus clouds. Cumulonimbus clouds are caused by heating from below and cooling from above. As the earth is heated during the day by the sun, air close to the ground becomes warmer. Hot air is less dense than cold air and therefore lighter so it rises and, as it does so, it becomes cooler. The warm air reaches a cold point called the condensation level where the water vapor condenses and turns back to a liquid form. As the warm air rises to the condensation level, it becomes less able to keep its moisture and condenses into large clouds, which are often called thunderheads. The process of condensation releases heat into the surrounding air making the air rise even faster and release more moisture. These huge clouds are complex systems in their own right, containing large amounts of energy resulting in updrafts and downdrafts – vertical winds that can reach speeds over 176 km per hour and help in the formation of hail.

Hail grows in the thunderhead's main updraft where most of the cloud is 'supercooled' water: water that is still liquid even though its temperature is below 0°C. This water will stay in liquid form until it encounters something on which to freeze. There are other particles within the cloud – small frozen raindrops or soft ice particles – called graupel. When the supercooled water hits the graupel, it freezes around it, creating a hailstone. However, this is just the start of the hailstone's journey. A hailstone's eventual size depends upon the intensity of the storm in which it is born. To form a golf ball-sized hailstone requires over ten billion supercooled drops of water and a time span of between five and 10 minutes. This accumulation of additional ice is a process called *accretion* and takes place in areas of the cloud rich in supercooled water. Accretion takes place in two ways, resulting in two distinguishable kinds of hailstone. In the first process, strong updrafts, which lift the top of the cloud into part of the atmosphere known as the troposphere, take the hailstone through the supercooled layer where it accretes ice, making it heavy enough to fall back through the cloud. On falling, it encounters other strong updrafts, which take it back though the supercooled layer where it grows and falls again. An updraft of 35–55 km per hour will form small hailstones; hailstones that are 5 cm in diameter require updrafts of 88 kph and hailstones that are 12 cm in diameter need updrafts of 160 kph to grow. The other process involves the hailstone falling slowly through a layer of the cloud rich in supercooled water.

The first process results in hailstones with concentric layers usually alternating between clear and cloudy ice, indicating how it was produced. The opaque layer forms when supercooled water drops freeze quickly onto the growing hailstone and trap tiny air bubbles inside the ice giving it a milky appearance. The next layer – the transparent layer – forms when larger drops of supercooled liquid water hit the hailstone. Here the freezing process is slower, allowing air bubbles to escape and clear ice to form. Hailstones showing little of this layering may have been subject to the second process of formation. Instead of being pushed up through the cumulonimbus by updrafts and pulled back through by gravity several times, these hailstones simply fall slowly through the cloud gathering mass as they drop.

The interior of a cumulonimbus cloud is a place of extreme violence. As the hailstones rise and fall, they collide with each other. The result of this can be their breaking up or the formation of large irregular shaped hailstones. Hailstones are categorised according to their size. The Tornado and Storm Research Organisation classifies hailstorms according to their destructive power, ranging from H0 – hard hail composed of hailstones of 5 mm in diameter, which do not cause damage – through H5 storms, destructive enough to damage glass, roofs and injure people, to the most severe – H10 or 'super hailstorms', which cause extensive structural damage and can fatally injure people caught out in the open.

The rate at which they fall varies but can be faster than 160 kph for larger hailstones as they become too heavy for the updraft to support or if a downdraft catches them and blows them violently back to earth. It is estimated that between 40 and 70% of hailstones never reach the earth, melting instead inside the cloud, colliding with and smashing into smaller pieces on their way through the air, or melting in the atmosphere to fall as rain.

Questions 1–8

Do the following statements agree with the information given in Reading Passage 1?
Write

> **TRUE**   *if the statement agrees with the information*
> **FALSE**   *if the statement contradicts the information*
> **NOT GIVEN**   *if there is no information on this*

1   Hailstone storms last a long time and cause considerable damage.

2   The world's largest hailstone had lost volume before it was found.

3   Cumulonimbus clouds hold significant quantities of energy.

4   Cumulonimbus clouds are called 'thunderheads' because they are the cause of thunder and lightening storms.

5   Water always turns to ice when it is under 0°C.

6   A slow freezing rate creates clear ice.

7   Hailstones are classified according to their destructive power.

8   Many hailstones stay within the cloud and do not reach the ground.

Questions 9–16

Label the diagram below using words from the box.

*Write the correct letter, **A–H**, in spaces 9–16.*

A	graupel
B	updraft
C	condensation level
D	accretion
E	heat released into atmosphere
F	downdraft
G	warm air
H	supercooled area

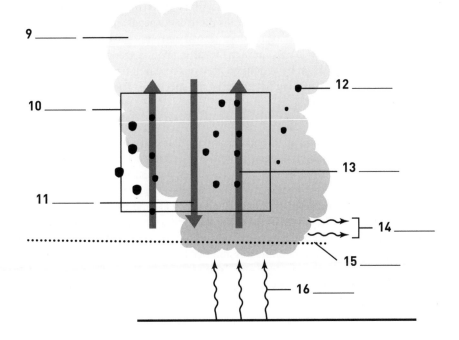

The formation of hailstones in a cloud

READING PASSAGE 2

*You should spend about 20 minutes on **Questions 17–27**, which are based on Reading Passage 2 below.*

Twisted Light

A Why is your mobile phone or wireless signal so slow? If you ask your service provider, they'll tell you that it's the bandwidth. We're running out of signal space on the wireless spectrum. All wireless communications travel through radio or optical frequencies: your TV or radio programmes, your GPS device that helps you find your way, your mobile and smartphone, laptop and wirelessly connected PC. The demands from users and industry on a limited resource, the wireless spectrum, are growing daily and are closely regulated. The reason is that two users cannot use the same signal: think about radio stations, which have to operate on different frequencies otherwise they cause interference with each other. Likewise mobile phone operators cannot transit over the same frequency in the same market at the same time. Government-controlled agencies grant licences to use the wireless spectrum but if a wireless company wants to add more spectrum to its service to boost its capacity, it's likely to be disappointed as there isn't much more available. What is needed is a way of pushing more data through the same amount of bandwidth.

B Now scientists may have found a way of manipulating light waves to carry more information: potentially enough for users to be able to download a film onto a smartphone in a single second. By twisting light waves, scientists could possibly transmit data at speeds of 2.56 terrabits per second: that's 85,000 times faster than the 30 megabits per second currently possible. To put it another way, this is the same as transmitting 70 DVDs through the air in about a second. Researchers based in America, China, Israel and Pakistan have built on previous research from Sweden, which negates the need for more bandwidth by making better use of the spectrum. The basis of the research is to manipulate the properties of light.

C One property of light is wavelength: lasers, radio waves, microwaves are simply different wavelengths of light. Light is made up of photons and photons have two other properties that define a beam of light: spin angular momentum and orbital angular momentum. A good way of thinking about how photons travel is to think of the orbit of a planet: it spins around on its axis (spin angular momentum), and at the same time the planet is also revolving around the sun (orbital angular momentum). The latter force means that light can be twisted around its axis of travel to take the shape of a spiral or a corkscrew. At the centre of the spiral the light waves cancel each other out, leaving darkness in the middle, called an optical vortex. When light travels, it is formed into a spiral shape and it can be manipulated. There are infinite possibilities for ways in which the photon can be made to spiral: clockwise, counterclockwise, tight spirals or loose ones. Each of these spiral states can be uniquely identified but, more importantly for wireless communication, the spirals can be wrapped up within each other – or multiplexed – into a single beam. The beam can be transmitted and unwound at the receiving end to get the data streams back out again, essentially doubling or trebling or even quadrupling the bandwidth.

D Scientists have been twisting light since the 1970s, and the spin angular momentum of waves is already manipulated in standard wireless communication. For years, Bo Thide of the Swedish Institute of Space Physics theorised that the orbital angular momentum could be used to create the spiral signal or as Thide calls it a 'radio vortex'. Then in an experiment in Venice, his team transmitted two signals simultaneously on the same frequency over a distance of 442 metres. Following on from this, researchers in America, China, Israel and Pakistan, led by Alan Wilner, twisted together eight light data streams, each stream with its own level of orbital angular momentum twist. One of the streams was transmitted as a thin stream while the others were transmitted around the outside. The data beam was then sent to a receiver and untwisted to recover the data.

E The achievement is very exciting for developers of wireless network technology as the useful spectrum of frequencies is largely used up. The orbital angular momentum model would allow for an infinite number of data transmissons without taking up any more of the spectrum. There is a problem, however: researchers can only transmit the data stream one metre, which is an insignificant distance for communication purposes. The short transmission range is due to turbulence in the atmosphere, which disrupts the signal as the light hits air molecules. But the scientists are planning to be able to send the beam considerably further. One idea is to create links every kilometre to extend the network. Another is to build high-speed satellite communication links where the atmospheric problems would not affect the signal. Another possibility is to adapt the technology for fibre-optic use, the way data is currently transmitted over the Internet. Unfortunately, at this point standard fibre-optic cables are not capable of carrying multichannel signals and fibre-optic cables that can carry the signal experience problems of interference between channels as they carry data with high bit-rates.

F Nevertheless, exploiting the orbital angular momentum gives scientists options that could lead to significant increases in data transfer; even a modest increase in the existing data transfer rate is worthwhile. Furthermore, very often technology is pulled along by innovative research so a novel solution to carrying the data-rich signal may not be far behind.

Questions 17–22

Reading Passage 2 has six paragraphs, **A–F**.

Which paragraphs contain the following information?

*Write the correct letter, **A–F**, next to Questions 17–22.*

17 changing light waves to increase capacity

18 a practical demonstration of the new technology

19 use of the wireless spectrum needing to be monitored closely

20 overcoming the problem of the short range of the new signal

21 improvements in data transmission possibly leading to technological breakthroughs

22 the prospect of saving people a lot of time

Questions 23–27

*Complete the summary using the list of words, **A–I**, below.*

*Write the correct letter, **A–I**, in spaces 23–27.*

Researchers are looking for a way of using the **23** _____ more efficiently. One option is to transmit signals that are twisted into **24** _____, and wrapping them together, or **25** _____ them. This is still problematic on earth due to **26** _____ but scientists hope that **27** _____ cable technology will catch up with the research breakthrough.

A	bandwidth
B	atmospheric interference
C	fibre-optic
D	light waves
E	multiplexing
F	wireless spectrum
G	spirals
H	data streams
I	novel

READING PASSAGE 3

*You should spend about 20 minutes on **Questions 28–40**, which are based on Reading Passage 3 below.*

Sinking Cities

Looking across the Bund towards Pudong across the Huangpu River in Shanghai, you will see an array of modern world-beating skyscrapers. In contrast, behind you are the magnificent buildings from the nineteenth century. Standing on the high tourist promenade that runs the length of the waterfront, you may also notice that the level of the river is quite a bit higher than that of the buildings on the Bund. It isn't because the river has risen higher than usual due to rainfall; no – Shanghai is sinking. It is an unfortunate problem that Shanghai shares with several other major financial and industrial centres and it is caused by factors most of the cities have in common. Included in the list are New York, Bangkok, Houston and Mexico City, all either built on shaky foundations or low-lying land that is now threatened by rising sea levels.

New York and Bangkok are victims of bad luck. The effect of global warming on the sea levels means that these cities may drown in the oceans that brought them such importance and prosperity. Scientists believe that sea levels in the New York area are expected to rise about twice as quickly as in the rest of the world. The position of the city – situated where the Hudson River flows into the Atlantic Ocean – already puts America's most densely populated city at a higher risk of flooding. But the impact of tropical storms and rising tides poses more dangers than just flooding. Beaches in the area will be swept away followed by the surrounding wetlands eventually becoming part of the sea; surrounding river estuaries will see an increase in the salt levels in the fresh water. All of this will affect the ecosystems in New York's immediate area and damage developments along the coast. Bangkok too will fall victim to rising sea levels. Also situated on swamplands

next to a river, the Chao Phraya, the city is about 50 kilometres north of the Gulf of Thailand. The city is likely to face increasingly severe tropical storms crossing from the Bay as well as threats from coastal erosion and shifting clay soil. It seems unlikely that Bangkok will save itself from drowning under the waters of the Pacific, which are predicted to rise by between 19 and 29 cm by 2050.

Other cities are sinking due to bad planning rather than bad luck. The fourth largest city in America is Houston but it has been built on shaky foundations – and these are now giving way. Houston was literally built on a foundation of sand up to several kilometres deep and loosely packed clay from river deposits formed from the erosion of the Rocky Mountains. In addition to poor foundation materials, Houston has an estimated 300 fault lines running through it. Using GPS data from 24 measuring points throughout the country between 1995 to 2005 a research team were able to monitor the area of subsidence and found an area of Houston measuring 30 kilometres squared was sinking very fast – up to 5 centimetres per year. The reason for the subsidence is quite straightforward: the withdrawal of water from deep beneath the surface. Areas of Houston where water extraction has been stopped have stopped sinking. Similarly, parts of Mexico City are subsiding rapidly due to poor foundations – some areas of the city are sinking up to 20 centimetres a year. The city is built on a dry lake bed in the valley of Mexico, and the council has condemned fifty structures since 2006 because of leaning, and approximately 5,000 homes and buildings are unstable. Some of the heaviest buildings, like the Palace of Fine Arts, have sunk more than three metres over the past one hundred years and its original ground floor is now the basement. Again the reason is the depletion of the water reserve lying under the city. But in this case there is a complicating factor: a vast complex of drains was built under the city to protect it from flooding by water running from the surrounding mountains. As the city sinks, so do the drains and the wastewater they were supposed to carry away is finding its way back to the city. And it's not only water mains and drains that have been affected; as the city sinks the subway network is subsiding with it.

Back in Shanghai, the same problem is causing the city of 13 million people and ultra-modern skyline to sink beneath the waterline of the Huang Pu River. Originally a small fishing village built on swamplands surrounding the mouth of the Yangtze River, Shanghai's population has swollen to around 13 million people. The expansion has been sustained by taking water from wells drilled into the aquifer under the city and by constructing massive skyscrapers. According to China Central Television, Shanghai has sunk up to three metres since the early 1990s mainly due to depletion of underground water but also because of the weight of high-rise buildings situated on areas with soft soil. As a partial solution to the problem, Shanghai is trying to reverse the sinking by pumping 5.2 billion gallons of water a year into the water table with some success – so far the city has risen by almost 11.5 cm.

Questions 28–35

Complete the table below.

*Choose **NO MORE THAN THREE WORDS** from the passage for each answer.*

Write your answers in spaces 28–35.

City	Situated	Cause of sinking	Effect
New York	where the Hudson meets the Atlantic	the effect of **28** _____ and rising tides	increased chance of **29** _____
Bangkok	on swamps near the Gulf of Thailand	increasingly damaging storms, **30** _____ and moving soil	a rise in the level of the Pacific of up to **31** _____ by 2050
Mexico City	on a **32** _____ that has dried out	using up the **33** _____ beneath the city	wastewater drains and subway affected
Shanghai	on wetlands around the **34** _____ of the Yangtze River	wells drilled into aquifer and building **35** _____	sunk up to 3 metres

Questions 36–40

Choose the correct letter, A, B, C or D.

36 The thing that may strike you when you are standing on Shanghai's tourist promenade is

    A the contrasting styles of the buildings.

    B its height.

    C that the river is higher than the buildings behind the promenade.

    D that it runs the length of the waterfront.

37 Which of the following is NOT a predicted effect on New York?

    A wetlands becoming part of the ocean

    B beaches being lost

    C developments along the coastline

    D the increasing saltiness of river mouths

38 Houston has been built on

    A shallow sand.

    B material from the Rocky Mountains.

    C volcanic fault lines.

    D accurate GPS measurements.

39 The sinking in Houston

    A affects the whole city equally.

    B is due to water use and the weight of the buildings.

    C has completely stopped.

    D was measured using historical data.

40 Which of the following is NOT true of Mexico City's drains?

    A They were built to defend the city from flooding.

    B They run back to the surrounding mountains.

    C They are sinking with the city.

    D They are carrying wastewater back to the city instead of away from it.

WRITING

WRITING TASK 1

You should spend about 20 minutes on this task.

The tables below show people's reasons for giving up smoking, and when they intend to give up.

Summarise the information by selecting and reporting the main features, and make comparisons where relevant.

Write at least 150 words.

TOP 5 REASONS FOR WANTING TO GIVE UP SMOKING				
Reasons for wanting to give up	Number of cigarettes smoked per day			
	20+	10–19	Fewer than 10	Total
	%	%	%	%
Better for health in general	64	73	74	71
Less risk of getting smoking-related illnesses	27	28	21	25
Present health problems	19	10	10	12
Financial considerations	31	36	25	31
Family pressure	14	13	20	16

WHEN SMOKERS INTEND TO GIVE UP SMOKING				
When	Number of cigarettes smoked per day			
	20+	10–19	Fewer than 10	Total
	%	%	%	%
Within the next month	8	9	21	12
Within the next 6 months	26	32	46	35
Within the next year	22	23	18	21
Total that intend to give up	60	73	79	71
Do not intend to give up	40	27	21	29

WRITING TASK 2

You should spend about 40 minutes on this task.

Write about the following topic:

> *Many young people choose to take a year out between finishing school and starting university in order to gain work experience or to travel. The experience of non-academic life this offers benefits the individual when they return to education.*
>
> *To what extent do you agree or disagree?*

Give reasons for your answer and include any relevant examples from your knowledge or experience

Write at least 250 words.

PART 1: Introduction and interview

Listen to Track 26, pressing pause after each question to answer.

26

PART 2: Individual long turn

Before you read the task card, listen to Track 27.

27

> Describe a place you would like to live.
>
> You should say:
>> where this place is
>>
>> whether you have been there before
>>
>> what it is like
>
> and explain what it is about this place that you find so appealing.

PART 3: Two-way discussion

Listen to Track 28, pressing pause after each question to answer.

28

General Training Test A

SECTION 1   Questions 1–13

Read the text below and answer Questions 1–7.

Carnival Events Guide

A

Crazy Colin

Children's Entertainer

will be appearing around the Carnival site 9.00–12.00. Free balloon for children and adults. Try balloon modelling and stilt walking! Colin's assistant Kathy will also be available for face-painting.

B

Punch and Judy Show

The Carnival would like to welcome back Punch and Judy after a three-year absence. Come and see everyone's favourite puppets.
Free entry but please feel free to make a donation.
Shows at 1 p.m., 2.30 p.m. and 3.30 p.m.

C

The Carnival Committee

invite you for tea and coffee at the main tent. Browse our second-hand book stalls and buy some of our beautiful homemade cakes and biscuits.
Open throughout the Carnival: 9.00 a.m. Close: 4.00 p.m.
50p Entrance Fee

D

Carnival Procession

This year the theme of our procession is 'fashion through the ages'.
Watch children and adults from the local community model clothes from different periods throughout history.
The procession sets off from St Bartholomew's Church at 12.30 p.m. and arrives at the main Carnival gates at lunchtime (approximately 1.00–1.30 p.m.).

Questions 1–7

*Look at the advertisements for events **A**, **B**, **C** and **D**, on the previous page.*

For which event are the following statements true?

*Write the correct letter, **A**, **B**, **C** or **D**, next to Questions 1–7.*

NB   *You may use any letter more than once.*

Example	*Answer*
People from the community take part	**D**

1   Invites people to make a donation

2   Charges for the service

3   Appears in the morning only

4   Is returning to the Carnival after a break

5   Offers free gifts

6   Appears at the Carnival at lunchtime only

7   Is available all day

Read the text below and answer Questions 8–13.

Dear Sir

Re: Your Physiotherapy Appointment

Following our telephone conversation, this is to confirm that an appointment has been made for you at our Physiotherapy Unit with Sam Major at the following time:

Saturday June 14th 10.30 a.m.

Physiotherapy Unit
Stowerbridge Hospital
Lower Lane
Stowerbridge

Please report to the main reception on arrival. If you are unable to attend please phone 0543 1146 to arrange a new appointment. Patients who fail to notify us may be disqualified from further treatment.

You will be required to carry out some light exercise during your treatment. Please wear loose clothing. You should also avoid eating a heavy meal prior to your appointment.

Please bring a list of all current medication when you attend.

On completion of your treatment please report again to reception to arrange any future sessions and to be signed out of the Physiotherapy Unit.

Parking is available at the hospital. Charges apply except for patients in receipt of benefits (pension, unemployment etc). To claim free parking please supply relevant documents at the reception desk.

We look forward to seeing you at your appointment.

Physiotherapy unit

Questions 8–13

Look at the letter relating to a physiotherapy appointment on the previous page.

Do the following statements agree with the information given in the text? *Write*

TRUE	*if the statement agrees with the information*
FALSE	*if the statement contradicts the information*
NOT GIVEN	*if there is no information on this*

Example	*Answer*
The clinic has been in communication with the patient before	**TRUE**

8   Patients must go to the reception when they arrive.

9   Patients may be fined for not keeping an appointment.

10 It is possible to arrange an alternative appointment if necessary.

11 Patients should bring with them all medicines they are currently taking.

12 There is a limit to the number of sessions available.

13 All patients must pay for parking.

SECTION 2   Questions 14–26

Read the text below and answer Questions 14–20.

Sports Centre

Terms of membership – *Clarenden Engineering employees*

- We offer three levels of membership to Clarenden Engineering employees – Platinum, Gold and Silver. The level of membership will determine when you are able to use the facilities. Please refer to the brochure available from reception for further details.

- Discounts are only available to those employed with Clarenden Engineering. Applicants must show evidence of their employment with the company.

- Subscriptions must be paid in advance. This can be in full or by monthly direct debit. Please note that membership is for the period of one year. Refunds will only be made under special circumstances. Should you cancel your membership, cards must be returned immediately.

- All new members are required to undertake an induction session during which use of the equipment and facilities is explained. Non-attendance at an induction session will result in you being refused entry to the facilities. The centre reserves the right to withdraw membership from, and take appropriate action against, any person found to have wilfully misused the equipment or facilities within the centre.

- Squash and badminton courts must be booked in advance. Bookings can be made up to 7 days in advance by calling 0773 2139 or in person at reception. In order to ensure optimum use of our facilities, members must inform the centre if they do not intend to keep an appointment. Failure to notify us can result in staff refusing to make further reservations. The gymnasium and swimming pool can be used without the need to book a session.

- Members will not be given access to the facilities without the presentation of a valid membership card.

- Please note that we cannot be held responsible for any personal injury you may suffer whilst using our facilities. Should you believe you have an existing medical condition that may be affected by the use of our facilities, we strongly recommend you seek medical advice before using the centre.

Questions 14–20

Look at the text on the previous page.

Do the following statements agree with the information given in the text? *Write*

TRUE	*if the statement agrees with the information*
FALSE	*if the statement contradicts the information*
NOT GIVEN	*if there is no information on this*

14 All members are free to use the centre whenever they wish.

15 Membership is only available to employees at the company.

16 Membership fees are paid in advance.

17 Induction sessions are not compulsory.

18 Members must pay for any damage they cause to the equipment.

19 Members must reserve a court if they want to play squash or badminton.

20 Employees with a medical condition should ask the centre for medical advice.

Questions 21–26

*The text below has seven sections, **A–G**.*

*Choose the correct heading for sections **B–G** from the list of headings below.*

*Write the correct number, **i–ix**, next to Questions 21–26.*

List of Headings
i Our guarantee to you
ii The application process
iii A wide choice
iv Having friends to stay
v On arrival
vi A warm welcome from Melborough
vii Sources of information
viii Meeting our representatives
ix Family applicants

Example	*Answer*
Section **A**	**vi**

21 Section **B**

22 Section **C**

23 Section **D**

24 Section **E**

25 Section **F**

26 Section **G**

A home from home at Melborough University!

A Our relationship with Bechamp Logistics has been a long and fruitful one and we continue to welcome its employees to Melborough University for an education that is second to none. Whether you are about to start a full-time MBA or joining one of our part-time courses, we look forward to welcoming you to the university. We appreciate how important it is that you quickly and easily find somewhere to live during your time here. This leaflet will outline how we work with you to choose the right accommodation.

B Obtaining suitable accommodation is a priority for those who are leaving their friends, colleagues and family to spend a period of time away from home. For this reason we promise that all Bechamp Logistics employees who have been accepted on a course with us will receive help with accommodation should they need it.

C If you are planning on relocating during your studies or just renting during the week, we recommend you live on campus as experience has shown this will help you settle into your studies more quickly. We have economy single rooms in our halls of residence, or for those looking for a little more luxury we have Soho House, our dedicated hall for company-sponsored students. Should you prefer to live off campus we can offer you a single-room apartment or rooms in a shared house in the city centre or suburbs.

D To help you make your choice you will find extensive information on our website with detailed descriptions of all our accommodation including photos and video tours of rooms and halls. You will also find a full price list for the various accommodation types. For people who are able to visit the university before the application deadline, you are welcome to contact our accommodation office for help with viewing places.

E Students with dependent children can apply for accommodation in any of our dedicated family-friendly halls. There are limited spaces available and you will need to contact us quickly to be sure of obtaining a place on campus. Should these not be available we are always able to help with accommodation off campus. You should go through the application process as usual and be sure to complete the section marked 'dependents'. This will alert our staff to your requirements so they can prioritise your application.

F Once you have been offered a place at the university you are advised to apply for accommodation immediately. All applications are made online. Once we have received your application we will arrange a time for you to be called by our accommodation office where we will talk to you about your options. Following this conversation, we will either reserve your campus accommodation or represent you should you be looking for a place to live off campus in private accommodation. You will receive written confirmation of your residence no later than two weeks before the start of term.

G Our accommodation office will be pleased to answer any questions you may have when you arrive at university. Before handing over the keys we ask you to sign a contract outlining your responsibilities. Please note that included in these terms is a commitment to pay for your accommodation for the full academic year.

Please visit the accommodation section of our website for further details.

SECTION 3   *Questions 27–40*

Questions 27–34

*The text below has eight paragraphs, **A–H**.*

*Choose the correct heading for sections **A–H** from the list of headings below.*

*Write the correct number, **i–x**, next to Questions 27–34.*

List of Headings
i   Surprising navigational achievements
ii   Inconsistent data
iii   Setting up the experiment
iv   The bees in action
v   Theories rejected
vi   Achievements explained
vii   Can larger brained creatures achieve the same?
viii   The challenge for previous researchers
ix   Bees versus computers
x   The bees' natural environment

27 Paragraph **A**

28 Paragraph **B**

29 Paragraph **C**

30 Paragraph **D**

31 Paragraph **E**

32 Paragraph **F**

33 Paragraph **G**

34 Paragraph **H**

Understanding the Flight of the Bumblebee

A Bumblebees are remarkable navigators. While their flight paths may look scattered to the casual eye, all that buzzing about is anything but random. Like the travelling salesman in the famous mathematical problem of how to take the shortest path along multiple stops, bumblebees quickly find efficient routes among flowers. And once they find a good route, they stick to it. The same goes for other animals, from hummingbirds to bats to primates, that depend on patchy resources such as nectar and fruit. Perhaps this is not such a surprising feat for animals with relatively high brain power. But how do bumblebees, with their tiny brains, manage it? As new research in this issue of *PLOS Biology* by Lars Chittka and colleagues shows, a simple strategy may be enough for a real-world solution to this complex problem.

B For computers, solving the travelling salesman problem means methodically calculating and comparing the lengths of all possible routes. But such an exhaustive approach isn't feasible in practice, and indeed animals can find a near-optimal foraging route, or trapline, without trying them all. Determining exactly how they do this, however, has been stymied by the difficulties of tracking animals as they forage in the wild. Chittka and colleagues got around this problem by tracking bumblebees (Bombus terrestris) on five artificial flowers set in a mown pasture. The "flowers" had landing platforms with drops of sucrose in the middle, and were fitted with motion-triggered webcams.

C To keep the bees' focus on the artificial flowers, the experiments were done in October, when natural sources of nectar and pollen were scarce. To make the bees want to find all five flowers, each sucrose drop was only enough to fill one-fifth of a bumblebee's crop. And to keep the bees from finding one foraging site from another visually, the flowers were arranged in a pentagon that was 50 m on each side, which is more than three times farther than bumblebees can see.

D The researchers released bees individually from a nest box that was about 60 m from the nearest flower, and used the webcams to track the sequence of flower visits during consecutive foraging bouts. The bees found the closest flowers first and added new flowers during subsequent bouts. With experience, they repeated segments of the visitation sequence that shortened the overall route while abandoning those that did not. Traplines linking all five flowers in a short route were established after an average of 26 foraging bouts, which entailed trying only about 20 of the 120 possible routes.

E In addition, the researchers fitted five bees with transponders and tracked them with radar as they developed traplines. This revealed that flight paths between trapline segments were relatively straight and that, between their first and last bouts, bees cut their total travel distance by 80% (from 1,953 to 458 m). In contrast to computers, bees did not find the absolute shortest route of 312 m even in this simple experimental arrangement. But they came very close, which is remarkable considering that they explored only a small fraction of the possible routes, and established traplines relatively rapidly. This tradeoff between perfection and speed highlights the differences between mathematical and biological solutions to the travelling salesman problem.

F How do bees develop such efficient routes so fast? The researchers assessed three possibilities: that bees optimize foraging routes by visiting flowers in the order of discovery, by shuffling them randomly, or by visiting those that are closest together. But they found that the first two failed to fit their observations while the third did not fully explain them.

G Rather, the researchers propose that bees optimize foraging routes by combining exploration with learning from previous bouts, which enables the bees to adjust their routes as they find shorter paths. Based on the bees' movements during trapline establishment, the researchers developed a model linking experience to the likelihood of visiting particular flowers. Bees are well known to be able to compute and memorize distances between locations, and the model assumes that they remember the length of the shortest route so far, compare it to the length of the current route, and then choose the shorter of the two. Over time, choosing the more efficient route favours shorter segments over longer ones. The model is a good fit with the researchers' observations, predicting, for example, that bees will develop and stick to optimal routes in 20–25 bouts.

H Besides shedding light on how bees develop traplines, this work suggests that small-brained animals can use simple methods to solve complex routing problems without the need for cognitive maps of spatial relationships, as has been suggested. It remains to be seen whether big-brained animals can also develop traplines with such elementary tools. But if so, that would free up their brain power for other tasks.

Questions 35–40

Choose the correct letter, A, B, C or D.

35 What does the writer say about bumble bees?

   A They have similar levels of intelligence to other nectar-eating creatures.

   B Their method for finding the shortest route isn't obvious to the casual observer.

   C They compete with other creatures for a scarce resource.

   D Their ability to find the shortest route isn't surprising.

36 What does the writer tell us about how these creatures find the quickest route between sources of food?

   A They would exhaust themselves if they carried out the process like a computer.

   B They calculate the length of all possible routes.

   C It is impossible to track their methods in the wild.

   D They are able to estimate one of the shortest routes without testing all possible options.

37 The experiment entailed

   A attempting to control the bees' movements.

   B the bees collecting one-fifth of a day's food.

   C discovering the role that sight plays in finding the best route.

   D picking a time when there was plenty of nectar.

38 The experiment showed that the bees

   A found the shortest route on their first flight.

   B went to the nearest flowers first.

   C tested 120 possible options.

   D abandoned flowers that didn't have nectar.

39 The writer thinks that

   A the bees aren't as efficient as computers at finding the shortest route.

   B the experiment was too simple to draw any conclusions.

   C there are benefits to be gained for the bees by not exploring every possible route.

   D mathematical solutions are superior to solve problems like this.

40 The researchers

   A have identified a pattern that the bees will follow on every flight path.

   B believe the bees find a short route through a process of trial and error.

   C were the first to discover that bees are able to memorise distances between locations.

   D are proposing to carry our further research in this area.

WRITING TASK 1

You should spend about 20 minutes on this task.

> *A restaurant has placed an advertisement for waiters and waitresses in your local newspaper.*
>
> *Write a letter to the restaurant, applying for the job. In the letter*
>
> - *explain what you are currently doing*
> - *describe your suitability for this area of work*
> - *say when you can attend an interview.*

Write at least 150 words.

You do NOT need to write any addresses.

Begin your letter as follows:

Dear Sir or Madam,

WRITING TASK 2

You should spend about 40 minutes on this task.

Write about the following topic:

> *Many cities around the world have seen an explosion in the number of supermarkets appearing on the high street and in out-of-town shopping centres. This development has led to increased choice for the consumer, ensured prices are kept low and made the shopping experience a lot easier for busy working families.*
>
> *To what extent do you agree or disagree?*

Give reasons for your answer and include any relevant examples from your knowledge or experience.

Write at least 250 words.

General Training Test B

SECTION 1   Questions 1–13

Read the text below and answer Questions 1–6.

Manor Road Primary School

Dear Parents

It will soon be Literacy Week here at school and as in previous years we intend to deal with your child's reading and writing skills in the context of a motivational theme. And the theme for this year's literacy week is 'superheroes'!

During the week your child will carry out a variety of tasks to help them develop their reading and writing skills. Children will produce artwork, videos, podcasts, drama performances, pictures, books and DVDs. They will also create imaginative pieces of writing full of interesting characters and plots. We can't wait to see all their work on show in the school reception and main school hall in the coming weeks. There will also be a competition for which prizes will be awarded.

What can you do to help? Please get involved with what your child is doing. At the end of the day ask them what they've been involved in and, if you have the chance, help them with their superhero homework tasks like finding information on the Internet or from books in the library.

Friday 19th October is 'Dressing-Up Day' and your child can come into school dressed as their favourite superhero.

The week will end with parents being invited into the school hall on Friday 19th to view the children's work. Classes end at 3.00 as usual but the school will be open from 2.00 p.m. and parents will be able to take their child home early if they wish.

We look forward to what we think will be a very creative week!

With best regards
Margaret Maclean
Principal

Questions 1–6

Look at the letter to parents on the previous page.

Do the following statements agree with the information given in the text? Write

TRUE	*if the statement agrees with the information*
FALSE	*if the statement contradicts the information*
NOT GIVEN	*if there is no information on this*

Example	*Answer*
This is the first time the school has had a literacy week.	**FALSE**

1   Children will be able to watch films and go to the theatre.

2   The school will be putting the children's work on show.

3   There will be three prizes for the best work.

4   Parents should try not to help their child too much with their homework.

5   The children don't have to wear school uniform on the final day.

6   Children must stay in school until 3.00 on Friday 19th October.

Support Away Day

Away Day relies on generous donations from sympathetic supporters like you to be able to offer disadvantaged children invaluable experiences and lifelong memories, doing things that that are financially out of the reach of their parents.

How can your donation help?

- £10 will pay for the cost of petrol for a trip to London.
- £20 will pay for the cost of a picnic for four children on a day out in the countryside.
- £50 will pay for the hire of eight uniforms for a fancy dress party.
- £100 will pay for the cost of a ticket to the seaside with parents or a guardian.
- £150 will pay for a trip to the theatre at Christmas for two families of four with a chance to see the children's favourite pantomime characters.
- £500 will buy accommodation at Disneyland Paris for two children.

Almost £7 out of every £10 we raise comes from the general public so your contributions are essential if we are to be able to continue offering this valued service.

How to donate

Why not set up a direct debit? If you live in the UK you could make a small monthly or annual donation.

If you prefer to make a single donation you can do so using any of the following options:

- Donate by text message – It's free and very easy. Just text AWAYDAY and an amount to 71117111.
- Donate by post – Send a cheque or postal order to the address at the bottom of this leaflet.
- To make a donation over the phone by credit or debit card, please call 03318 463219.

Gift Aid your donation

Add Gift Aid to your donation and help us benefit even more from your generosity. For every £1 you give, we are able to claim 25p more from the government. If you donate by text, watch out for our 'thank you' message. We'll supply a link to a webpage where you can fill in details to allow us to claim Gift Aid.

Questions 7–13

Look at the leaflet on the previous page.

Complete the notes below.

Write **NO MORE THAN THREE WORDS AND/OR A NUMBER** *for each answer.*

The charity enables children to do things that their parents would have difficulty
7 _____.

Donations of **8** _____ and **9** _____ will enable the charity to organise events for the whole family.

Children can go and watch their **10** _____ at the theatre.

70% of donations the charity receives come from **11** _____.

People can make a regular donation by setting up a **12** _____.

If people Gift Aid their donation the charity can get **13** _____ money from the government.

Read the text below and answer Questions 14–20.

Expenses Policy

All candidates invited for interview at Masons Finance are invited to claim back expenses for costs that are, by the HM Revenue and Customs definition, WHOLLY, NECESSARILY AND EXCLUSIVELY incurred during the process of attending the interview.

In general, for candidates travelling from within the UK, expenses covered include those for travel such as mileage or train tickets. Expenses are paid on the basis of the cost of second-class rail travel or 25p per mile for car travel. Mileage will be paid up to but not more than the equivalent cost of second-class rail travel. We request that when travelling by train an off-peak service is used whenever possible. Candidates can also claim taxi fares to and from Shamfield Station to the company head office. In exceptional circumstances the company is prepared to reimburse candidates from the UK requiring hotel accommodation. However, this must be agreed with our HR department first.

For candidates travelling from overseas, subsistence and hotel costs can be reimbursed in addition to travel expenses. Candidates should contact our HR department regarding accommodation as we will pre-book and pay for a room at a local hotel. Please note that the company will not normally reimburse the costs of accommodation that has been booked independently by the candidate. As a general guide, candidates travelling from overseas can claim the cost of an economy airfare. Meals and refreshments consumed during travel can be claimed to a maximum of £20 per day. In exceptional cases we understand that further nights of accommodation might be required for candidates travelling from overseas. In such cases additional expenses may be claimed but only after written agreement has been received from our HR department.

Candidates must retain all receipts and submit these with the expense report we ask you to fill in when making a claim. Please note that the company will not reimburse any costs the candidate incurs in the form of tips paid nor will it pay for fines such as parking tickets or speeding tickets issued during travel.

If you have a question regarding an expense, please contact your interview contact or our HR team.

Questions 14–16

Look at the text on the previous page.

Choose THREE letters, A–G.

Which **THREE** of the following are true?

    A The company uses an official definition for allowable expenses.

    B Candidates can claim more than the cost of a second-class ticket if they travel by car.

    C Candidates should try to avoid travelling at busy times of the day.

    D The company has special rates with a local taxi firm.

    E Accommodation expenses for UK candidates are not usually paid.

    F UK candidates must agree all expenses with HR before travelling.

    G Candidates must choose a hotel close to the company offices.

Questions 17–20

*Choose the correct letter, **A, B, C** or **D**.*

17 Candidates from overseas

    A find travel in the UK expensive.

    B always need hotel accommodation.

    C are allowed to claim for more items than candidates from the UK.

    D should contact HR about travel expenses.

18 Candidates from overseas can claim for food and drinks

    A if they were consumed in a hotel.

    B up to the value of £20 in total.

    C for more than one day.

    D on the outward journey only.

19 The company believe that candidates from overseas

    A sometimes need accommodation for more than one night.

    B should avoid booking additional nights' accommodation.

    C may find it difficult to reach agreement for expenses.

    D are likely to need accommodation for several nights.

20 When claiming expenses candidates should

    A include any additional expenses such as fines incurred during the trip.

    B notify HR about motoring offences.

    C report to the HR department on arrival.

    D supply evidence of things they have purchased.

Questions 21–26

The text below has seven paragraphs, A–G.

Choose the correct heading for sections B–G from the list of headings below.

Write the correct number, i–ix, next to Questions 21–26.

List of Headings
i Help improve our working practices
ii Become an ambassador
iii How to get involved
iv Get to know your colleagues
v No need to work up a sweat
vi The equipment you need
vii Discover our fascinating town
viii A time to suit everyone
ix Get back to nature

Example	*Answer*
Paragraph **A**	**iv**

21 Paragraph **B**

22 Paragraph **C**

23 Paragraph **D**

24 Paragraph **E**

25 Paragraph **F**

26 Paragraph **G**

Join a Workplace Walking Group

A   Several members of staff have been busy planning a series of lunchtime walks that we are sure you and your colleagues will soon become addicted to. Why join? The reasons are endless. You'll get the chance to chat with close friends and colleagues who participate as you would if you were stuck in your office. But what about all those other people you are on nodding terms with but have yet to get into conversation with? A lunchtime walk will be the perfect opportunity to get to know each other better.

B   We rarely get the chance to experience work outside of our own department, which obviously isn't healthy for an organisation like ours. So apart form the pleasure you'll get from talking to new people, these lunchtime walks will also give you the chance to get an insight into how other teams and departments work and share experiences of how teams work together, including situations where problems sometimes arise. This may hopefully lead to better communication and more efficient internal systems.

C   We also appreciate that many of you may want to completely switch off from work during your lunch break so we've tried to organise walks that will appeal to everyone. We are situated close to many historical landmarks and one of our walks takes in several of these sites. We've already had one or two employees with an interest in local history volunteer to act as guides, so now's your chance to discover more about where you work.

D   For those who prefer a gentle stroll through the great outdoors we have countryside walks taking in some of the beautiful lanes and fields at the back of the building. You'll be amazed at how tranquil this area can be – experience some lovely views and the sound of birdsong to help you relax before returning to work fully revitalised after lunch. By the way, these walks take in a stop at the local café for those who'd like to end with a tea or coffee. And there's no need for walking boots as we'll follow landscaped routes.

E   Of course an added benefit is the chance to get away from your desk, clear your head and keep fit. Walking, even at a gentle pace, is regarded as a great way to get into shape and help reduce stress. We also like to think it a pleasurable way to do this for those who don't like the idea of a gym or an aerobics session.

F   We appreciate that people take their lunch breaks at different times and so have organised a staggered timetable so there will always be a spot at least once a week for everyone. However, please feel free to organise a walk independently if you'd like to make it a daily event.

G   All departmental secretaries and managers have signed up already and will be more than pleased to give you any information you need. We also have a 'walking ambassador' in each department who will be able to answer any questions. See the departmental notice board to check for names or watch out for our next email on the subject. If you're convinced and are ready to sign up see if you can encourage some of your colleagues to join you. The more the merrier!

SECTION 3   *Questions 27–40*

Read the text below and answer Questions 27–40.

The Carvers of Bukittinggi

The world is becoming increasingly familiar with the products of Indonesia's talented artists. The beautiful batik paintings from Java, the slender wood statues from Bali and the local jewellery from Sulawasi can be found in shops in New York and Paris. Fortunately, the natural wealth and beauty of the area around the Minangkabau town of Bukittinggi allowed both time and inspiration for the development of crafts, especially weaving, silverwork and wood-carving. Although the wood-carvers of the Minangkabau may not be as well known as some other Indonesian artisans, their strong sense of tradition and of dedication to detail makes for a fascinating story.

Nestled in a high valley between the two volcanic mountains of Merapi and Singgalang is the small village of Pandai Sikek, better known as the "Wood Carving Village." The village is south of Bukittinggi, the cultural centre of the Minangkabau, and east of Padang, the capital of west Sumatra. The terraced rice fields, lush tropical vegetation, cool breezes and abundant water of the Anai Valley have made it an ideal spot for creativity and an inspiration for centuries of wood-carvers. The neighbouring forest provides an abundance of the wood called suriyan, a hard but workable medium for the carvers. Today, more than one hundred carvers claim Pandai Sikek as their home, though only a few can be found at work in the village. Many are away on contract assignments in Malaysia and in major Indonesian cities.

In the village, carvers knee-deep in wood shavings work in little huts along the roadside. Many have two or three apprentices carving repetitive patterns on small items to supplement their incomes. Cigarette boxes, jewellery boxes, ashtrays, bookholders – all can be purchased for sums that seem very modest in relation to the skill involved in making them. Most large items, such as chairs, tables and bed frames, are done on a custom-order basis, and all the shops were busy filling orders, evidence of both the continual need for their craft and the appreciation of their handiwork.

The village's Handicraft Centre is a large framed hall whose outside and inside walls display a wide variety of the wood-carvers' work. The hall is also used as a centre to train future wood-carvers: recently, 19 students from Sekolah Menengah Seni Rupa, a fine-arts school in Padang, were being instructed, carving the letters of the alphabet and the numbers one to nine. Each student first stencilled a number or letter on a block of wood, which he or she then chiselled, carved and sanded into a finished product. The village craftsmen took turns inspecting, advising and encouraging the trainees.

"Pandai" translates as "clever" and Sikek, according to one of several local traditions, is a contraction of *Si Ikek*, the name of a cultural hero who introduced wood-carving in the area centuries ago. There are many "pandai" carvers in the village of Pandai Sikek today, such as one known as Bapak (*Father* or *Uncle*) Fauzi. His skill was developed through 20 years of memorizing, manipulating and mastering the styles and motifs his uncle taught him. As a young boy, Fauzi would intently watch his uncle's hands as they felt, touched, explored and worked the block of wood until an ornately carved treasure was created. Several years ago, Fauzi was chosen along with many of the other village carvers to work on the Minangkabau Palace of Pagaruyung. It was to be an exact replica of the royal palace destroyed by fire during the early days of Dutch colonial rule, and would be used as a museum to recall the wealth and artistry of the Minangkabau at the peak of their power.

Fauzi jumped at the opportunity, because he would be able to see, learn and recreate many of the historical patterns used in wood-carving.

The patterns used on many Minangkabau wood carvings are believed by anthropologists to have been adapted from stone carvings found scattered about the Anai Valley. The original settlers of the valley, probably Hindus, believed strongly in ancestral and natural spirits, and portrayed these beliefs on the stones. Other patterns came from the artistic interpretation of the carvers as they observed the local flora and fauna. The designs taken from nature, such as the bamboo shoot, fern tendrils and sirih leaf, have been passed down from generation to generation, and have symbolic social and cultural meanings for the Minangkabau.

The early inhabitants arrived in elaborately carved boats, so it was to be expected that they would also carve their houses, and indeed the gables on each end of the roof are decorated with intricately carved wood panels. On these panels adorning the inside walls of their traditional houses, the bamboo-shoot motif is usually placed on the border and is representative of the three male leaders in the Minangkabau culture: the clan chief, the religious leader and the intellectual leader. The fern tendril is thought to represent man as the Father and Uncle, symbolically signifying flexibility to turn inward and outward in dealing with the family unit. The sirih leaf is symbolic of male fertility. The traditional colours painted on the wood carvings of Minangkabau houses also have significance in the culture: red symbolizes life, black stands for independence and yellow for wisdom.

The Minangkabau can be proud of their past and look forward to new generations of master craftsmen following in the footsteps of present-day masters. Bapak Fauzi and his fellow carvers now have the responsibility to pass on to the younger generation the traditions and skills they were taught by their elders.

Questions 27–32

Look at the article on the previous pages.

Do the following statements agree with the information given in the text? *Write*

TRUE	*if the statement agrees with the information*
FALSE	*if the statement contradicts the information*
NOT GIVEN	*if there is no information on this*

27 Indonesia is famous for its wood-carvers.

28 Wood is hard to find near the village.

29 The majority of the wood-carvers work away from their village.

30 It is difficult to become an apprentice.

31 Smaller items are cheap in relation to the skill involved in making them.

32 Craftsmen make some items to suit the requirements of customers.

Questions 33–36

Complete the notes below.

*Write **NO MORE THAN THREE WORDS** for each answer.*

The Handicraft Centre also functions as a training centre for aspiring **33** _____.

Students are given feedback on their work by **34** _____.

Pandai Sikek gets its name from the word 'clever' and the name of a **35** _____.

Working on an exact copy of a royal palace enabled Fauzi to learn a number of the

36 _____ used by carvers in the past.

Questions 37–40

*Choose the correct letter, **A, B, C** or **D**.*

37 Wood carvings

    A were originally found all over the Anai Valley.

    B are based on images found on ancient stone carvings.

    C are made out of respect for local spirits.

    D are the same as those found on stone carvings.

38 Designs featuring local plants and wildlife

    A appear in carvings created by several generations of craftsmen.

    B have less symbolic significance than in the past.

    C are interpreted in unusual ways by the wood-carvers.

    D are painted by local artists.

39 The carvings in the houses

    A are copies of designs that originally appeared on boats.

    B feature leaders of the community.

    C are in the form of wall panels.

    D are made from recycled panels from old boats.

40 The fern and sirih leaves

    A represent particular qualities.

    B are painted in different colours.

    C are worn by men who feature in the carvings.

    D only serve a decorative purpose.

WRITING

WRITING TASK 1

You should spend about 20 minutes on this task.

> *You recently spent a night in a hotel and had to put up with a great deal of noise very early in the morning because of a faulty central heating system. The manager promised to contact you regarding compensation but you still haven't heard from him.*
>
> *Write a letter to the hotel. In the letter*
>
> - *describe the problem at the hotel*
> - *explain what the manager had said at the time*
> - *say what you want the manager to do.*

Write at least 150 words.

You do NOT need to write any addresses.

Begin your letter as follows:

Dear Sir,

WRITING TASK 2

You should spend about 40 minutes on this task.

Write about the following topic:

> *What distinguishes young people from their parents' or grandparents' generation is a lack of physical exercise. Today's generation are spending far too long playing computer games, chatting aimlessly on social networking sites or simply watching TV, and too little time being active.*
>
> *To what extent do you agree or disagree?*

Give reasons for your answer and include any relevant examples from your knowledge or experience.

Write at least 250 words.

Mini-dictionary

 Some of the more difficult words from each of the Reading and Listening passages are defined here in this mini-dictionary. The definitions focus on the meanings of the words in the context in which they appear in the text. Definitions and examples are from *Collins COBUILD Key Words for IELTS (Advanced)*, and from *Collins COBUILD Advanced Dictionary*.

TEST 1: LISTENING

Section 1

courier /ˈkuriə/ (couriers) NOUN If you send something by **courier**, you pass it on to someone whose job is to deliver letters and parcels.
• *Confidential reports are sent to ministers by courier.*

incident /ˈɪnsɪdənt/ (incidents) NOUN An **incident** is something that happens, often something that is unpleasant. [FORMAL] • *These incidents were the latest in a series of disputes between the two nations.*

trace /treɪs/ (traces, tracing, traced) VERB If you **trace** something, you find it after looking for it. • *Police are anxious to trace two men seen leaving the house just before 8am.*

unattended /ˌʌnəˈtendɪd/ ADJECTIVE When people or things are left **unattended**, they are not being watched or looked after. • *The mob broke into the family house while it was unattended and started four fires.*

Section 2

age profiling /ˈeɪdʒ ˈprəʊˌfaɪlɪŋ/ UNCOUNTABLE NOUN **Age profiling** is the practice of categorizing people and predicting their behaviour according to their age. • *Age profiling isn't always accurate, but it can benefit your organization.*

axe /æks/ NOUN If a person or institution is facing **the axe**, that person is likely to lose their job or that institution is likely to be closed, usually in order to save money. • *St Bartholomew's is one of four London hospitals facing the axe.*

cater to /ˈkeɪtə/ (caters to, catering to, catered to) VERB To **cater to** a group of people means to provide all the things that they need or want. • *We cater to an exclusive clientele.*

cutback /ˈkʌtbæk/ (cutbacks) NOUN A **cutback** is a reduction that is made in something. • *...the 200-person staff cutback announced yesterday.*

intent /ɪnˈtent/ ADJECTIVE If you are **intent on** doing something, you are eager and determined to do it.
• *The rebels are obviously intent on keeping up the pressure.*

niche /niːʃ/ ADJECTIVE A **niche** product is very specialized, and appeals to a relatively small number of people. • *Our radio show caters to listeners who appreciate niche musical genres such as Celtic-World Beat fusion.*

washout /ˈwɒʃaut/ (washouts) NOUN If an event or plan is a **washout**, it fails completely. [INFORMAL] • *The mission was a washout.*

Section 3

evangelical /ˌiːvænˈdʒelɪkəl/ ADJECTIVE If you describe someone's behaviour as **evangelical**, you mean that it is very enthusiastic. • *With almost evangelical fervour, Marks warns against deliberately seeking a tan.*

factor in /ˌfæktər ɪn/ PHRASAL VERB If you **factor** a particular cost or element **in** a calculation you are making, you include it. [mainly US] • *Using a computer model they factored in the costs of transplants for those women who die.*

interfere /ˌɪntəˈfɪə/ (interferes, interfering, interfered) VERB Something that **interferes with** a situation, activity, or process has a damaging effect on it. • *Drug problems frequently interfered with his work.*

loom /luːm/ (looms, looming, loomed) VERB If a worrying or threatening situation or event **is looming**, it seems likely to happen soon. • *Another government spending crisis is looming in the United States.*

misleading /ˌmɪsˈliːdɪŋ/ ADJECTIVE If you describe something as **misleading**, you mean that it gives you a wrong idea or impression. • *The article contains several misleading statements.*

prevaricate /prɪˈværɪkeɪt/ (prevaricates, prevaricating, prevaricated) VERB If you **prevaricate**, you avoid giving a direct answer or making a firm decision. • *British ministers continued to prevaricate.*

regime /reɪˈʒiːm/ (regimes) NOUN A **regime** is the way that something such as an institution, company, or economy is run, especially when it involves tough or severe action. • *The authorities moved him to the less rigid regime of an open prison.*

TEST 1: READING

Passage 1

breed /briːd/ (breeds, breeding, bred) VERB When animals **breed**, they have babies. • *Frogs will usually breed in any convenient pond.*

colony /ˈkɒləni/ (colonies) NOUN A **colony** of birds, insects, or animals is a group of them that live together. • *The caterpillars feed in large colonies.*

cull /kʌl/ (culls, culling, culled) VERB To **cull** animals means to kill the weaker animals in a group in order to reduce their numbers. • *To save remaining herds and habitat, the national parks department is planning to cull two thousand elephants.*

ecosystem /ˈiːkəʊsɪstəm/ (ecosystems) NOUN An **ecosystem** is all the plants and animals that live in a particular area together with the complex relationship that exists between them and their environment. • *Human overfishing has destabilised marine ecosystems.*

estuary /ˈestjuri/ (estuaries) NOUN An **estuary** is the wide part of a river where it joins the sea. • *...naval manoeuvres in the Clyde estuary.*

graze /greɪz/ (grazes, grazing, grazed) VERB When animals **graze** or **are grazed**, they eat the grass or other plants that are growing in a particular place. You can also say that a field **is grazed** by animals. • *Several horses grazed the meadowland.*

hurricane /ˈhʌrɪkən/ (hurricanes) NOUN A **hurricane** is an extremely violent wind or storm. • *Around eight hurricanes are predicted to strike America this year.*

livestock /ˈlaɪvstɒk/ UNCOUNTABLE NOUN Animals such as cattle and sheep which are kept on a farm are referred to as **livestock**. • *The heavy rains and flooding killed scores of livestock.*

myriad /ˈmɪriəd/ ADJECTIVE **Myriad** means having a large number or great variety. • *...the myriad tiny animals and plants living in the ice.*

erosion /ɪˈrəʊʒən/ NOUN **Erosion** is the process by which layers of a substance such as soil on the earth's surface are gradually worn away by the action of wind, water or ice. • *Running water, including rivers, is a common agent of soil erosion.*

thrive /θraɪv/ (thrives, thriving, thrived) ADJECTIVE A **thriving**, business, economy or place is financially strong and very successful. • *In the past, this town was a thriving centre for the fur trade.*

underestimate /ˌʌndərˈestɪmeɪt/ (underestimates, underestimating, underestimated) VERB If you **underestimate** something, you do not realize how large or great it is or will be. • *Marx clearly underestimated the importance of population growth.*

Passage 2

aerodynamics /ˌeərəʊdaɪˈnæmɪks/ UNCOUNTABLE NOUN **Aerodynamics** is the study of the way in which objects move through the air. • *...a bird aerodynamics expert from the University of Bristol.*

analogy /əˈnælədʒi/ (analogies) NOUN If you make or draw an **analogy between** two things, you show that they are similar in some way. • *It is probably easier to make an analogy between the courses of the planets, and two trains travelling in the same direction.*

automate /ˈɔːtəmeɪt/ (automates, automating, automated) VERB To **automate** a factory, office, or industrial process means to put in machines which can do the work instead of people. • *an initiative that involved automating a manual process.*

aviation /ˌeɪviˈeɪʃən/ UNCOUNTABLE NOUN **Aviation** is the operation and production of aircraft. • *He went to the University of Wisconsin to study engineering, but was more interested in the new, exciting field of aviation.*

back /bæk/ (backs, backing, backed) VERB If you **back** a person or a course of action, you support them, for example by voting for them or giving them money. • *... if France cannot persuade all five permanent members of the Security Council to back the plan.*

break-even point /breɪkˈiːvən ˌpɔɪnt/ (break-even points) NOUN In business and commerce, the **break-even point** is the level at which the total cost and the total revenue of a business enterprise are equal. • *Above break-even point a profit is made; below break-even point a loss is made.*

commission /kəˈmɪʃən/ (commissions, commissioning, commissioned) VERB If you **commission** something or **commission** someone **to** do something, you formally arrange for someone to do a piece of work for you. • *The Ministry of Agriculture commissioned a study into low-input farming.*

delegate /ˈdelɪˌgeɪt/ (delegates, delegating, delegated) VERB If you **delegate** duties, responsibilities, or power **to** someone, you give them those duties, those responsibilities, or that power so that they can act on your behalf. • *He plans to delegate more authority to his deputies.*

enterprise /ˈentəpraɪz/ (enterprises) NOUN An **enterprise** is a company or business, often a small one. • *There are plenty of small industrial enterprises.*

envision /ɪnˈvɪʒən/ (envisions, envisioning, envisioned) VERB If you **envision** something, you envisage it. [LITERARY] • *In the future we envision a federation of companies.*

initiative /ɪˈnɪʃətɪv/ (initiatives) NOUN An **initiative** is an important act or statement that is intended to solve a problem. • *Government initiatives to help young people have been inadequate.*

milestone /ˈmaɪlstəʊn/ (milestones) NOUN A **milestone** is an important event in the history or development of something or someone. • *He said the launch of the party represented a milestone in Zambian history.*

mine /maɪn/ (mines, mining, mined) VERB When a mineral such as coal, diamonds, or gold **is mined**, it is obtained from the ground by digging deep holes and tunnels. • *...the finest gems, mined from all corners of the world.*

orbit /ˈɔːbɪt/ (orbits) NOUN An **orbit** is the curved path in space that is followed by an object going round and round a planet, moon, or star. • *Mars and Earth have orbits which change with time.*

outsource /ˌaʊtˈsɔːs/ **(outsources, outsourcing, outsourced)** VERB If a company **outsources** work or things, it pays workers from outside the company to do the work or supply the things. • *Increasingly, corporate clients are seeking to outsource the management of their facilities.*

payoff /ˈpeɪɒf/ **(payoffs)** NOUN The **payoff from** an action is the advantage or benefit that you get from it. • *If such materials became generally available to the optics industry, the payoffs from such a breakthrough would be enormous.*

pose /pəʊz/ **(poses, posing, posed)** VERB If something **poses** a problem or a danger, it is the cause of that problem or danger. • *This could pose a threat to jobs in the coal industry.*

sound /saʊnd/ ADJECTIVE **Sound** advice, reasoning, or evidence is reliable and sensible. • *His reasoning is perfectly sound, but he misses the point.*

vindicate /ˈvɪndɪkeɪt/ **(vindicates, vindicating, vindicated)** VERB If a person or their decisions, actions, or ideas **are vindicated**, they are proved to be correct, after people have said that they were wrong. [FORMAL] • *Ministers and officials are confident their decision will be vindicated.*

Passage 3

adverse /ˈædvɜːs/ ADJECTIVE **Adverse** decisions, conditions, or effects are unfavourable to you. • *Despite the adverse conditions, the road was finished in just eight months.*

catastrophic /ˌkætəˈstrɒfɪk/ ADJECTIVE Something that is **catastrophic** involves or causes a sudden terrible disaster. • *A tidal wave caused by the earthquake hit the coast causing catastrophic damage.*

counteract /ˈkaʊntərækt/ **(counteracts, counteracting, counteracted)** VERB To **counteract** something means to reduce its effect by doing something that produces an opposite effect. • *The vitamin counteracts the harmful effect of allergens in the body.*

deplete /dɪˈpliːt/ **(depletes, depleting, depleted)** VERB To **deplete** a stock or amount of something means to reduce it. [FORMAL] • *substances that deplete the ozone layer*

glacier /ˈɡlæsiə/ **(glaciers)** NOUN A **glacier** is an extremely large mass of ice which moves very slowly, often down a mountain valley. • *University of Alaska scientists report that the state's glaciers are melting faster than expected.*

mirror /ˈmɪrə/ **(mirrors)** NOUN A **mirror** is a flat piece of glass which reflects light, so that when you look at it you can see yourself reflected in it. • *He checked his mirror and saw that a dark coloured van was immediately behind him.*

mundane /ˌmʌnˈdeɪn/ NOUN You can refer to mundane things as **the mundane**. • *It's an attitude that turns the mundane into something rather more interesting and exciting.*

orbit See Test 1 Reading Passage 2

plankton /ˈplæŋktən/ UNCOUNTABLE NOUN **Plankton** is a mass of tiny animals and plants that live in the surface layer of the sea. • *...its usual diet of plankton and other small organisms.*

proponent /prəˈpəʊnənt/ **(proponents)** NOUN If you are a **proponent of** a particular idea or course of action, you actively support it. [FORMAL] • *Halsey was identified as a leading proponent of the values of progressive education.*

replicate /ˈreplɪkeɪt/ **(replicates, replicating, replicated)** VERB If you **replicate** someone's experiment, work, or research, you do it yourself in exactly the same way. [FORMAL] • *Tests elsewhere have not replicated the findings.*

unforeseen /ˌʌnfɔːˈsiːn/ ADJECTIVE If something that has happened was **unforeseen**, it was not expected to happen or known about beforehand. • *Radiation may damage cells in a way that was previously unforeseen.*

TEST 2: LISTENING

Section 1

host family /ˌhəʊst ˈfæmli/ **(host families)** NOUN A **host family** is a family that provides accommodation and meals for students, usually in return for a fee. • *When I studied in Brazil, I stayed with a host family.*

Section 2

induction /ɪnˈdʌkʃən/ **(inductions)** NOUN **Induction** is a procedure or ceremony for introducing someone to a new job, organization, or way of life. • *...an induction course for new members.*

Section 3

make out /ˌmeɪk ˈaʊt/ **(makes out, making out, made out)** VERB If you **make** something **out**, you manage with difficulty to see or hear it. • *I could just make out a tall, pale, shadowy figure tramping through the undergrowth.*

Section 4

clinical /ˈklɪnɪkəl/ ADJECTIVE **Clinical** means involving or relating to the direct medical treatment or testing of patients. • *The first clinical trials were expected to begin next year.*

CRB check /ˌsiːɑːˈbiː ˌtʃek/ **(CRB checks)** NOUN In Britain, a **CRB check** is an investigation by the Criminal Records Bureau to see if a person has a criminal record. • *All applicants will be subject to a CRB check.*

enrolment /ɪnˈrəʊlmənt/ UNCOUNTABLE NOUN **Enrolment** is the act of registering at an institution or on a course. • *A fee is charged for each year of study and is payable at enrolment.*

forensic /fəˈrensɪk/ ADJECTIVE **Forensic** means relating to the legal profession. • *He won admiration for his forensic skills in cross-examining ministers.*

opt /ɒpt/ (opts, opting, opted) VERB If you **opt for** something, or **opt to** do something, you choose it or decide to do it in preference to anything else. • *Depending on your circumstances you may wish to opt for one method or the other.*

placement /ˈpleɪsmənt/ (placements) NOUN If someone who is training gets a **placement**, they get a job for a period of time which is intended to give them experience in the work they are training for. • *He had a six-month work placement with the Japanese government.*

qualitative /ˈkwɒlɪtətɪv/ ADJECTIVE **Qualitative** means relating to the nature or standard of something, rather than to its quantity. [FORMAL] • *There are qualitative differences in the way children and adults think.*

quantitative /ˈkwɒntɪtətɪv/ ADJECTIVE **Quantitative** means relating to different sizes or amounts of things. [FORMAL] • *...the quantitative analysis of migration.*

rehabilitation unit /ˌriːəˌbɪlɪˈteɪʃən juːnɪt/ (rehabilitation units) NOUN A **rehabilitation unit** is a place where people with an alcohol or drug addiction are helped to give up, so that they can return to normal life. • *I worked in a rehabilitation unit for a year to conduct research on drug addiction.*

stroke /strəʊk/ (strokes) NOUN If someone has a **stroke**, a blood vessel in their brain bursts or becomes blocked, which may kill them or make them unable to move one side of their body. • *He had a minor stroke in 1987, which left him partly paralysed.*

trauma /ˈtrɔːmə/ (traumas) NOUN **Trauma** is a very severe shock or very upsetting experience, which may cause psychological damage. • *The officers are claiming compensation for trauma after the disaster.*

workshop /ˈwɜːkʃɒp/ (workshops) NOUN A **workshop** is a period of discussion or practical work on a particular subject in which a group of people share their knowledge or experience. • *Trumpeter Marcus Belgrave ran a jazz workshop for young artists.*

TEST 2: READING

Passage 1

antibiotics /ˌæntibaɪˈɒtɪks/ (antibiotics) NOUN **Antibiotics** are medical drugs used to kill bacteria and treat infections. • *Approximately 60 per cent of antibiotics are prescribed for respiratory infections.*

breed /briːd/ (breeds, breeding, bred) VERB If you **breed** animals or plants, you keep them for the purpose of producing more animals or plants with particular qualities, in a controlled way. • *Australians must now focus on breeding sheep for three specific purposes: wool, meat and maternal traits.*

cholesterol /kəˈlestərɒl/ UNCOUNTABLE NOUN **Cholesterol** is a substance that exists in the fat,

tissues, and blood of all animals. Too much cholesterol in a person's blood can cause heart disease. • *a dangerously high cholesterol level*

excavation /ˌekskəˈveɪʃən/ UNCOUNTABLE NOUN **Excavation** is the activity of digging into the ground to find buried objects from the past. • *It was hoped that further excavation might even reveal other skeletons.*

fibre /ˈfaɪbə/ UNCOUNTABLE NOUN **Fibre** consists of the parts of plants or seeds that your body cannot digest. Fibre is useful because it makes food pass quickly through your body. • *Most vegetables contain fibre.*

foliage /ˈfəʊliɪdʒ/ UNCOUNTABLE NOUN The leaves of a plant are referred to as its **foliage**. • *shrubs with grey or silver foliage.*

forage /ˈfɒrɪdʒ/ UNCOUNTABLE NOUN **Forage** is crops that are grown as food for cattle and horses. • *...the amount of forage needed to feed one cow and its calf.*

gene /dʒiːn/ (genes) NOUN A **gene** is the part of a cell in a living thing which controls its physical characteristics, growth, and development. • *a change in a single DNA letter that appears in 70 per cent of defective genes.*

germinate /ˈdʒɜːmɪneɪt/ (germinates, germinating, germinated) VERB If a seed **germinates** or if it **is germinated**, it starts to grow. • *First, the researchers germinated the seeds.*

marked /mɑːkt/ ADJECTIVE A **marked** change or difference is very obvious and easily noticed. • *There has been a marked increase in crimes against property.*

nourishment /ˈnʌrɪʃmənt/ UNCOUNTABLE NOUN If something provides a person, animal, or plant with **nourishment**, it provides them with the food that is necessary for life, growth, and good health. • *The mother provides the embryo with nourishment and a place to grow.*

nutrient /ˈnjuːtriənt/ (nutrients) NOUN **Nutrients** are substances that help plants and animals to grow. • *the role of vegetable fibres, vitamins, minerals and other essential nutrients.*

parasitic /ˌpærəˈsɪtɪk/ ADJECTIVE **Parasitic** animals and plants live on or inside larger animals or plants and get their food from them. • *...tiny parasitic insects.*

pest /pest/ (pests) NOUN **Pests** are insects or small animals which damage crops or food supplies. • *...crops which are resistant to some of the major insect pests and diseases.*

pollinate /ˈpɒlɪneɪt/ (pollinates, pollinating, pollinated) VERB To **pollinate** a plant or tree means to fertilize it with pollen. This is often done by insects. • *Many of the indigenous insects are needed to pollinate the local plants.*

protein /ˈprəʊtiːn/ (proteins) NOUN **Protein** is a substance found in food and drink such as meat, eggs, and milk. You need protein in order to grow and be healthy. • *Fish was a major source of protein for the working man.*

resist /rɪˈzɪst/ (resists, resisting, resisted) VERB If someone or something **resists** damage of some kind, they are not damaged. • *Chemicals form a protective layer that resists both oil and water-based stains.*

resistance /rɪˈzɪstəns/ UNCOUNTABLE NOUN **Resistance to** something is the ability not to be affected or harmed by it. • *Many of these crops lack resistance to disease.*

resistant /rɪˈzɪstənt/ ADJECTIVE If something is **resistant to** a particular thing, it is not harmed by it. • *how to improve plants to make them more resistant to disease.*

yield /jiːld/ (yields, yielding, yielded) VERB If an area of land **yields** a particular amount of a crop, this is the amount that is produced. You can also say that a number of animals **yield** a particular amount of meat. • *Last year 400,000 acres of land yielded a crop worth $1.75 billion.*

Passage 2

abstract /ˈæbstrækt/ ADJECTIVE An **abstract** idea or way of thinking is based on general ideas rather than on real things and events. • *The author takes the abstract concept of power and defines it in terms of familiar relationship-types.*

cognition /kɒgˈnɪʃən/ UNCOUNTABLE NOUN **Cognition** is the mental process involved in knowing, learning, and understanding things. [FORMAL] • *...processes of perception and cognition.*

genetic /dʒɪˈnetɪk/ ADJECTIVE You use **genetic** to describe something that is concerned with genetics or with genes. • *Cystic fibrosis is the most common fatal genetic disease in the United States.*

predator /ˈpredətə/ (predators) NOUN A **predator** is an animal that kills and eats other animals. • *The mites in turn were eaten by other arachnid predators.*

prevalence /ˈprevələns/ UNCOUNTABLE NOUN When you refer to the **prevalence** of an illness or, you are talking about how common it is. • *The report focuses on the prevalence of asthma in Britain and western Europe.*

prey /preɪ/ UNCOUNTABLE NOUN A creature's **prey** are the creatures that it hunts and eats in order to live. • *Electric rays stun their prey with huge electrical discharges.*

property /ˈprɒpəti/ (properties) NOUN The **properties** of a substance or object are the ways in which it behaves in particular conditions. • *A radio signal has both electrical and magnetic properties.*

syndrome /ˈsɪndrəum/ (syndromes) NOUN A **syndrome** is a medical condition that is characterized by a particular group of signs and symptoms. • *The syndrome is more likely to strike those whose immune systems are already below par.*

Passage 3

bug /bʌg/ (bugs) NOUN If there is a **bug** in a computer program, there is a mistake in it. • *There is a bug in the software.*

collaborate /kəˈlæbəreɪt/ (collaborates, collaborating, collaborated) VERB When one person or group **collaborates with** another, they work together, especially on a book or on some research. • *He collaborated with his son Michael on the English translation of a text on food production.*

collate /kəˈleɪt/ (collates, collating, collated) VERB When you **collate** pieces of information, you gather them all together and examine them. • *They have begun to collate their own statistics on racial abuse.*

compromise /ˈkɒmprəmaɪz/ (compromises, compromising, compromised) VERB If you **compromise** something or if it is **compromised**, there is a risk that it will be harmed or damaged.. • *His behaviour compromised our chances.*

escalating /ˈeskəleɪtɪŋ/ ADJECTIVE An **escalating** situation is increasing or becoming more serious in a way that causes problems. • *the escalating cost of health care.*

feed /fiːd/ (feeds) NOUN In computing, a **feed** is a facility for notifying the user of a website that new content has been added to it. • *Most news sites offer RSS feeds of their latest content.*

flaw /flɔː/ (flaws) NOUN A **flaw in** something such as a theory or argument is a mistake in it, which causes it to be less effective or valid. • *There were, however, a number of crucial flaws in his monetary theory.*

functionality /ˌfʌŋkʃəˈnælɪti/ UNCOUNTABLE NOUN The **functionality** of a computer or other machine is how useful it is or how many functions it can perform. • *It is significantly more compact than any comparable laptop, with no loss in functionality.*

hostile /ˈhɒstaɪl/ ADJECTIVE **Hostile** situations and conditions make it difficult for you to achieve something. • *If this round of talks fails, the world's trading environment is likely to become increasingly hostile.*

humanitarian /hjuːˌmænɪˈteərɪən/ ADJECTIVE If a person or society has **humanitarian** ideas or behaviour, they try to avoid making people suffer or they help people who are suffering. • *The UN also orchestrated humanitarian aid though there was much criticism at the lack of competence revealed that winter.*

maturation /ˌmætjuˈreɪʃən/ UNCOUNTABLE NOUN **Maturation** is the process of developing or improving. • *Despite the continued maturation of his singing voice, he opted to study history at university.*

meltdown /ˈmeltdaʊn/ (meltdowns) NOUN If there is a **meltdown** in a nuclear reactor, the fuel rods start melting because of a failure in the system, and radiation starts to escape. • *Emergency cooling systems could fail and a reactor meltdown could occur.*

operational /ˌɒpəˈreɪʃənəl/ ADJECTIVE A machine or piece of equipment that is **operational** is in use or is ready for use. • *The whole system will be fully operational by December.*

patch /pætʃ/ (patches, patching, patched) VERB In computing, if you **patch** a program, you correct or improve it by adding a small set of instructions. • *The security flaw has highlighted the need to patch servers before hackers can mount attacks.*

platform /ˈplætfɔːm/ (platforms) NOUN A **platform** is a type of computer system. • *By 1991, programmers had produced HTML browsers for numerous computing platforms.*

plot /plɒt/ (plots, plotting, plotted) VERB When someone **plots** something on a graph, they mark certain points on it and then join the points up. • *We plot about eight points on the graph.*

scale /skeɪl/ NOUN If you refer to the **scale** of something, you are referring to its size or extent, especially when it is very big. • *However, he underestimates the scale of the problem.*

shun /ʃʌn/ (shuns, shunning, shunned) VERB If you **shun** someone or something, you deliberately avoid them or keep away from them. • *This extremist organization has shunned conventional politics.*

surveillance /səˈveɪləns/ UNCOUNTABLE NOUN **Surveillance** is the careful watching of someone, especially by an organization such as the police or the army. • *He was arrested after being kept under constant surveillance.*

track /træk/ (tracks, tracking, tracked) VERB To **track** someone or something means to follow their movements by means of a special device, such as a satellite or radar. • *Our radar began tracking the jets.*

TEST 3: LISTENING

Section 1

mileage /ˈmaɪlɪdʒ/ UNCOUNTABLE NOUN **Mileage** refers to the total number of miles that a motor vehicle has travelled. • *Considering the mileage it had done, the car had lasted very well.*

no claims bonus /nəʊ ˈkleɪmz ˌbəʊnəs/ (no claims bonuses) NOUN In Britain, a **no claims bonus** is a reduction on an insurance premium, especially one covering a motor vehicle, if no claims have been made within a specified period. • *Most no claims bonus schemes have a clause which allows drivers a limited number of claims before the discount is reduced.*

Section 2

acclimatise also **acclimatize** /əˈklaɪmətaɪz/ (acclimatises, acclimatising, acclimatised) VERB When you **acclimatise** or **are acclimatised to** a new situation, place, or climate, you become used to it. [FORMAL] • *This year he has left for St Louis early to acclimatise himself.*

feat /fiːt/ (feats) NOUN If you refer to an action, or the result of an action, as a **feat**, you admire it because it is an impressive and difficult achievement. • *A racing car is an extraordinary feat of engineering.*

iconic /aɪˈkɒnɪk/ ADJECTIVE An **iconic** image or thing is important or impressive because it seems to be a symbol of something. [FORMAL] • *The ads helped Nike to achieve iconic status.*

intrepid /ɪnˈtrepɪd/ ADJECTIVE An **intrepid** person acts in a brave way. • *...an intrepid space traveller.*

summit /ˈsʌmɪt/ (summits, summiting, summited; summits) 1 VERB To **summit** a mountain or hill means to reach the top of it. • *We summited the mountain after a long day of climbing.* 2 NOUN The **summit** of a mountain is the top of it. • *I reached the summit of the mountain before sunset.*

Section 3

critique /krɪˈtiːk/ (critiques, critiquing, critiqued) VERB When you **critique** a person's work or ideas, you provide a written or spoken examination and judgment of it. • *The director critiqued their performance, and offered suggestions on how to improve it.*

mind map /ˈmaɪnd ˌmæp/ (mind maps) NOUN A **mind map** is a diagram that is used to represent ideas, with related concepts arranged around a central key word or concept. • *Mind maps can help you become a faster, more fluent and effective learner.*

spidergram /ˈspaɪdəˌɡræm/ (spidergrams) NOUN A **spidergram** is a diagram used to represent ideas, with related concepts arranged around a central key word or concept. • *Spidergrams are used to get a quick visual representation of the main issues.*

Section 4

aesthetic /iːsˈθetɪk/ ADJECTIVE **Aesthetic** is used to talk about beauty or art, and people's appreciation of beautiful things. • *...products chosen for their aesthetic appeal as well as their durability and quality.*

congregate /ˈkɒŋɡrɪɡeɪt/ (congregates, congregating, congregated) VERB When people **congregate**, they gather together and form a group. • *Youngsters love to congregate here in the evenings outside cinemas showing American films.*

demarcation /ˌdiːmɑːˈkeɪʃən/ (demarcations) NOUN A **demarcation** is a boundary or limit separating two areas, groups, or things. • *The two countries had reached an agreement on demarcation of the border.*

employ /ɪmˈplɔɪ/ (employs, employing, employed) VERB To **employ** something is to use it. • *The painting technique was much employed by artists such as Picasso.*

inclined /ɪnˈklaɪnd/ ADJECTIVE If you are **inclined to** behave in a particular way, you often behave in that way, or you want to do so. • *Nobody felt inclined to argue with Smith.*

kerb /kɜːb/ (kerbs) NOUN The **kerb** is the raised edge of a pavement or sidewalk which separates it from the road. • *Stewart stepped off the kerb.*

negotiate /nɪˈɡəʊʃieɪt/ (negotiates, negotiating, negotiated) VERB If you **negotiate** an area of land, a place, or an obstacle, you successfully travel across it or around it. • *I negotiated the corner on my motorbike and pulled to a stop.*

thriving /ˈθraɪvɪŋ/ ADJECTIVE If you describe something as **thriving**, you mean it is doing well. • *They have a thriving business, despite the economy.*

unsightly /ʌnˈsaɪtli/ ADJECTIVE If you describe something as **unsightly**, you mean that it is unattractive to look at. • *My mother has had unsightly varicose veins for years.*

TEST 3: READING

Passage 1

absolutist /ˌæbsəˈluːtɪst/ ADJECTIVE An **absolutist** approach to an issue is one where a particular principle, belief, or rule must always be upheld, without exception. • *If you take the absolutist position, you do not have to decide what constitutes 'acceptable' animal research.*

atom /ˈætəm/ (atoms) NOUN An **atom** is the smallest amount of a substance that can take part in a chemical reaction. • *A methane molecule is composed of one carbon atom attached to four hydrogens.*

bore /bɔː/ (bores) NOUN A **bore** is a hole or tunnel in the ground, especially one that has been drilled order to find minerals, oil, etc. • *The flexible dredging pipe was marked with yellow bands, giving an indication of how deep it had penetrated the bore.*

cite /saɪt/ (cites, citing, cited) VERB If you **cite** something, you quote it or mention it, especially as an example or proof of what you are saying. [FORMAL] • *The author cites just one example.*

clay /kleɪ/ UNCOUNTABLE NOUN **Clay** is a kind of earth that is soft when it is wet and hard when it is dry. Clay is shaped and baked to make things such as pots and bricks. • *...the heavy clay soils of Cambridgeshire.*

deplete See Test 1 Reading Passage 3

dynamic level /daɪˈnæmɪk ˌlevəl/ (dynamic levels) NOUN In hydrology, the **dynamic level** is the level to which water in a well falls when it is being pumped out. • *Engineers need to test the water level in a well at both the static level (when the pump is not running) and the dynamic level (when the pump is running).*

evacuate /ɪˈvækjueɪt/ (evacuates, evacuating, evacuated) VERB To **evacuate** something from a place means to take it out. • *There is no way to evacuate water from the system, and so it accumulates under the floor.*

extraction /ɪkˈstrækʃən/ UNCOUNTABLE NOUN **Extraction** is the processs of removing a substance from the substance around it, especially using effort or force. • *The environmental effects of quarrying and mineral extraction must be rigorously assessed.*

fossil /ˈfɒsəl/ (fossils) NOUN A **fossil** is the hard remains of a prehistoric animal or plant that are found inside a rock. • *a newly discovered 425 million-year-old fossil*

gravel /ˈɡrævəl/ UNCOUNTABLE NOUN **Gravel** consists of very small stones. It is often used to make paths. • *...a gravel path leading to the front door.*

hydrology /haɪˈdrɒlədʒi/ UNCOUNTABLE NOUN **Hydrology** is the study of the distribution, conservation, and use of the earth's water. • *scientific work on forest hydrology*

motto /ˈmɒtəʊ/ (mottoes or mottos) NOUN A **motto** is a short sentence or phrase that expresses a rule for sensible behaviour, especially a way of behaving in a particular situation. • *Our motto is 'Plan for the worst and hope for the best'.*

operational See Test 2 Reading Passage 3

peer /pɪə/ (peers, peering, peered) VERB If you **peer at** something, you look at it very hard, usually because it is difficult to see clearly. • *He watched the Customs official peer into the driver's window.*

penetrate /ˈpenɪtreɪt/ (penetrates, penetrating, penetrated) VERB If something or someone **penetrates** a physical object or an area, they succeed in getting into it or passing through it. • *X-rays can penetrate many objects.*

pore /pɔː/ (pores) NOUN **Pores** are very small holes in the surface of rock, soil, etc. • *The membranes have tiny pores which allow the rapid passage of small water molecules.*

practitioner /prækˈtɪʃənə/ (practitioners) NOUN A **practitioner** is a person who practises a particular profession or art. • *In the past, the condition was not recognized by medical practitioners.*

profile /ˈprəʊfaɪl/ (profiles) NOUN The **profile** of a person, place, or thing is a detailed description of their characteristics. • *The marketing software gathers and analyses our customers' profiles, allowing us to design appropriate products and services.*

recharge /ˌriːˈtʃɑːdʒ/ (recharges, recharging, recharged) VERB If an aquifer **is recharged** it fills with water again. • *Aquifers may be artificially recharged in two main ways.*

saturated /ˈsætʃureɪtɪd/ ADJECTIVE If something is **saturated** it has absorbed as much water as it can. • *Saturated soils increase the danger of trees uprooting.*

shale /ʃeɪl/ UNCOUNTABLE NOUN **Shale** is smooth soft rock that breaks easily into thin layers. • *The soil here is very poor - it's shallow, with rock and shale underneath.*

shallow /ˈʃæləʊ/ ADJECTIVE A **shallow** container, hole, or area of water measures only a short distance from the top to the bottom. • *The water is quite shallow for some distance.*

the stakes are high /steɪks/ PHRASE If you say **the stakes are high**, you mean that someone risks losing a lot if they do not achieve their aim. • *Risk taking is essential to success in any goal where the stakes are high.*

static level /ˈstætɪk ˌlevəl/ (static levels) NOUN In hydrology, the **static level** is the level at which water naturally stands in a well. • *The static level will vary with the season of the year and may be affected by how much ground water is being used in the surrounding area.*

stratum /ˈstrɑːtəm/ (strata) NOUN Strata are different layers of rock. • *Contained within the rock strata is evidence that the region was intensely dry 15,000 years ago.*

trace /treɪs/ (traces, tracing, traced) VERB If you **trace** the origin or development of something, you find out or describe how it started or developed. • *The exhibition traces the history of graphic design in America from the 19th century to the present.*

velocity /vɪˈlɒsɪti/ (velocities) NOUN Velocity is the speed at which something moves in a particular direction. • *...the velocity of light.*

Passage 2

abdomen /ˈæbdəmən/ (abdomens) NOUN Your **abdomen** is the part of your body below your chest where your stomach and intestines are. [FORMAL] • *He was suffering from pains in his abdomen.*

burst /bɜːst/ (bursts) NOUN A **burst of** something is a sudden short period of it. • *It is easier to cope with short bursts of activity than with prolonged exercise.*

cite See Test 3 Reading Passage 1

conduct /kənˈdʌkt/ (conducts, conducting, conducted) VERB When you **conduct** an activity or task, you organize it and carry it out. • *The council conducted a survey of the uses to which farm buildings are put.*

contract /kənˈtrækt/ (contracts, contracting, contracted) VERB If you **contract** a serious illness, you become ill with it. [FORMAL] • *He contracted AIDS from a blood transfusion.*

endurance /ɪnˈdjʊərəns/ UNCOUNTABLE NOUN **Endurance** is the ability to continue with an unpleasant or difficult situation, experience, or activity over a long period of time. • *The exercise obviously will improve strength and endurance.*

glucose /ˈgluːkəʊz, -əʊs/ UNCOUNTABLE NOUN Glucose is a type of sugar that gives you energy. • *Diabetics suffer from a lack of insulin, a hormone produced by the pancreas that stimulates cells to take up glucose from the blood.*

index /ˈɪndeks/ (indices or indexes) NOUN An **index** is a system by which changes in the value of something and the rate at which it changes can be recorded, measured, or interpreted. • *...economic indices.*

insulin /ˈɪnsjʊlɪn/ UNCOUNTABLE NOUN Insulin is a substance that most people produce naturally in their body and which controls the level of sugar in their blood. • *In diabetes the body produces insufficient insulin.*

intake /ˈɪnteɪk/ (intakes) NOUN Your **intake** of a particular kind of food, drink, or air is the amount that you eat, drink, or breathe in. • *Your intake of alcohol should not exceed two units per day.*

metabolism /mɪˈtæbəlɪzəm/ (metabolisms) NOUN Your **metabolism** is the way that chemical processes in your body cause food to be used in an efficient way, for example to make new cells and to give you energy. • *He says reducing carbohydrates and eating more fat*

and protein will alter your metabolism and stimulate weight loss.*

physiology /ˌfɪziˈɒlədʒi/ UNCOUNTABLE NOUN **Physiology** is the scientific study of how people's and animals' bodies function, and of how plants function. • *...the Nobel Prize for Medicine and Physiology.*

proponent See Test 1 Reading Passage 3

sprint-and-recover cycle /ˌsprɪntənrɪˈkʌvə saɪkəl/ (sprint-and-recover cycles) NOUN A **sprint-and-recover cycle** is a method of improving fitness that involves an athlete running a series of short sprints followed by short rests. • *Repeat this sprint-and-recover cycle 3-5 times during your workout.*

startling /ˈstɑːtəlɪŋ/ ADJECTIVE Something that is **startling** is so different, unexpected, or remarkable that people react to it with surprise. • *Sometimes the results may be rather startling.*

time-consuming /ˈtaɪmkənˌsjuːmɪŋ/ ADJECTIVE If something is **time-consuming**, it takes a lot of time. • *Starting a new business, however small, is a time-consuming exercise.*

Passage 3

adjacent /əˈdʒeɪsənt/ ADJECTIVE If one thing is **adjacent to** another, the two things are next to each other. • *surveys to monitor toxin levels in the areas adjacent to the incinerators*

anatomically /ˌænəˈtɒmɪkli/ ADVERB **Anatomically** means relating to the structure of the body of people or animals. • *Homo sapiens became anatomically modern in Africa about 100,000 years ago.*

anatomy /əˈnætəmi/ (anatomies) NOUN An animal's **anatomy** is the structure of its body. • *It is hard to determine whether an animal's anatomy or physiology has been altered by environmental problems.*

ancestor /ˈænsestə/ (ancestors) NOUN Your **ancestors** are the people from whom you are descended. • *Modern humans and great apes both descend from one common ancestor.*

artifact /ˈɑːtɪfækt/ (artifacts) NOUN An **artifact** is an ornament, tool, or other object that is made by a human being, especially one that is historically or culturally interesting. • *a sacred Ethiopian artifact, seized 130 years ago by British soldiers*

attribute /ˈætrɪˌbjuːt/ (attributes) NOUN An **attribute** is a quality or feature that someone or something has. • *Cruelty is a normal attribute of human behaviour.*

cognitive /ˈkɒgnɪtɪv/ ADJECTIVE **Cognitive** means relating to the mental process involved in knowing, learning, and understanding things. [FORMAL] • *As children grow older, their cognitive processes become sharper.*

curtail /kɜːˈteɪl/ (curtails, curtailing, curtailed) VERB If you **curtail** something, you reduce or limit it. [FORMAL] • *NATO plans to curtail the number of troops being sent to the region.*

demise /dɪˈmaɪz/ NOUN The **demise** of something or someone is their end or death. [FORMAL] • *Smoking, rather than genetics, was the cause of his early demise.*

displace /dɪsˈpleɪs/ **(displaces, displacing, displaced)** VERB If a person or group of people **is displaced**, they are forced to moved away from the area where they live. • *Most of the civilians displaced by the war will be unable to return to their homes.*

distinction /dɪˈstɪŋkʃən/ NOUN If you say that someone or something has **the distinction of** being something, you are drawing attention to the fact that they have the special quality of being that thing. **Distinction** is normally used to refer to good qualities, but can sometimes also be used to refer to bad qualities. • *He has the distinction of being regarded as the Federal Republic's greatest living writer.*

DNA /ˌdiː en ˈeɪ/ UNCOUNTABLE NOUN **DNA** is an acid in the chromosomes in the centre of the cells of living things. DNA determines the particular structure and functions of every cell and is responsible for characteristics being passed on from parents to their children. DNA is an abbreviation for 'deoxyribonucleic acid'. • *techniques of extracting DNA from ancient bones*

edge /edʒ/ **(edges)** NOUN If someone or something has an **edge**, they have an advantage that makes them stronger or more likely to be successful than another thing or person. • *Through superior production techniques they were able to gain the competitive edge.*

excavate /ˈekskəveɪt/ **(excavates, excavating, excavated)** VERB When archaeologists or other people **excavate** a piece of land, they remove earth carefully from it and look for things such as pots, bones, or buildings which are buried there, in order to discover information about the past. • *Archaeologists excavated the skeletal remains in Indonesia.*

exodus /ˈeksədəs/ NOUN If there is an **exodus of** people from a place, a lot of people leave that place at the same time. • *Lieutenant Malcolm said she saw no sign that the exodus from Haiti was abating.*

fossil See Test 3 Reading Passage 1

gene See Test 2 Reading Passage 1

genetic See Test 2 Reading Passage 2

geneticist /dʒɪˈnetɪsɪst/ **(geneticists)** NOUN A **geneticist** is a person who studies or specializes in genetics. • *Hugo de Vries was one of the first geneticists.*

genome /ˈdʒiːnəʊm/ **(genomes)** NOUN In biology and genetics, a **genome** is the particular number and combination of certain chromosomes necessary to form the single nucleus of a living cell. • *Conventional gene therapy relies on modified viruses to insert the desired bit of DNA into a cell's genome.*

hands down /ˌhændz ˈdaʊn/ ADVERB If you win something **hands down** you win very easily. • *They won the match hands down.*

heritage /ˈherɪtɪdʒ/ UNCOUNTABLE NOUN A person's or society's **heritage** consists of characteristics that are important in their history, and that can be seen in the way that they are today. • *Scotland's cultural heritage.*

locomotion /ˌləʊkəˈməʊʃən/ UNCOUNTABLE NOUN **Locomotion** is the ability to move and the act of moving from one place to another. [FORMAL] • *Flight is the form of locomotion that puts the greatest demands on muscles.*

marginalize /ˈmɑːdʒɪnəlaɪz/ **(marginalizes, marginalizing, marginalized)** VERB To **marginalize** a group of people means to make them feel isolated and unimportant. • *We've always been marginalized, exploited, and constantly threatened.*

molecular /məˈlekjʊlə/ ADJECTIVE **Molecular** means relating to or involving molecules. • *...the molecular structure of fuel.*

navigable /ˈnævɪɡəbəl/ ADJECTIVE A **navigable** river is wide and deep enough for a boat to travel along safely. [FORMAL] • *...the navigable portion of the Nile.*

paleoanthropologist /ˌpælɪəʊˌænθrəˈpɒlədʒɪʃt/ **(paleoanthropologists)** NOUN A **paleoanthropologist** is a person who studies the origins of the human race using fossils and other remains. • *Paleoanthropologists have played a major role in discovering what we know about evolution today.*

pronounced /prəˈnaʊnst/ ADJECTIVE Something that is **pronounced** is very noticeable. • *Most of the art exhibitions have a pronounced Scottish theme.*

proponent See Test 1 Reading Passage 3

refugee /ˌrefjuːˈdʒiː/ **(refugees)** NOUN **Refugees** are people who have been forced to leave their homes or their country, either because there is a war there or because of their political or religious beliefs. • *Thousands of Hungarian refugees fled to the West, and armed resistance in Hungary was soon crushed.*

relegate /ˈrelɪɡeɪt/ **(relegates, relegating, relegated)** VERB If you **relegate** someone or something **to** a less important position, you give them this position. • *Other newspapers relegated the item to the middle pages.*

robust /rəʊˈbʌst, ˈrəʊbʌst/ ADJECTIVE Someone or something that is **robust** is very strong or healthy. • *More women than men go to the doctor. Perhaps men are more robust or worry less?.*

skull /skʌl/ **(skulls)** NOUN Your **skull** is the bony part of your head which encloses your brain. • *I discovered two human skulls, obviously very old and half disintegrated.*

sole /səʊl/ ADJECTIVE The **sole** thing or person of a particular type is the only one of that type. • *It's the sole survivor of an ancient family of plants.*

stature /ˈstætʃə/ UNCOUNTABLE NOUN Someone's **stature** is their height. • *She was a little short in stature.*

stem /stem/ **(stems, stemming, stemmed)** VERB If a condition or problem **stems from** something, it was caused originally by that thing. • *Much of the instability stems from the economic effects of the war.*

strait /streɪt/ **(straits)** NOUN You can refer to a narrow strip of sea which joins two large areas of sea as a **strait** or **the straits**. • *...the Straits of Gibraltar.*

trace See Test 3 Reading Passage 1

track /træk/ (tracks, tracking, tracked) VERB If you **track** animals or people, you try to follow them by looking for the signs that they have left behind, for example the marks left by their feet. • *He thought he had better track this wolf and kill it.*

watercraft /ˈwɔːtəˌkrɑːft, -ˌkræft/ (watercrafts) NOUN A **watercraft** is a boat or a ship. • *Numerous watercraft sailed down the Thames that day.*

TEST 4: LISTENING

Section 1

commission /kəˈmɪʃən/ UNCOUNTABLE NOUN If a bank or other company charges **commission**, they charge a fee for providing a service, for example for exchanging money or issuing an insurance policy. • *Travel agents charge 1 per cent commission on sterling cheques.*

Section 2

donate /dəʊˈneɪt/ (donates, donating, donated) VERB If you **donate** something **to** a charity or other organization, you give it to them. • *He frequently donates large sums to charity.*

mount up /ˌmaʊnt ˈʌp/ (mounts up, mounting up, mounted up) VERB If something **mounts up**, it increases in quantity. • *The uncollected rubbish mounts up in city streets.*

roaring trade /ˌrɔːrɪŋ ˈtreɪd/ PHRASE If someone **does a roaring trade** in a type of goods, they sell a lot of them. • *Salesmen of unofficial souvenirs have also been doing a roaring trade.*

Section 3

authentic /ɔːˈθentɪk/ ADJECTIVE An **authentic** person, object, or emotion is genuine. • *...authentic Italian food.*

ICT /ˌaɪ siː ˈtiː/ UNCOUNTABLE NOUN **ICT** refers to activities or studies involving computers and other electronic technology. **ICT** is an abbreviation for 'Information and Communications Technology'. • *English, Maths, ICT and science are compulsory subjects.*

syllabus /ˈsɪləbəs/ (syllabuses) NOUN You can refer to the subjects that are studied in a particular course as the **syllabus**. [mainly BRIT] • *...the GCSE history syllabus.*

track /træk/ (tracks, tracking, tracked) VERB If you **track** something, you make sure that you have the newest and most accurate information about it all the time. • *It's hard to track the books I've read in the past year because I've read so many!*

Section 4

acknowledge /ækˈnɒlɪdʒ/ (acknowledges, acknowledging, acknowledged) VERB If a fact is

acknowledged, it is accepted to be true. • *The problem has finally been acknowledged by the government.*

craving /ˈkreɪvɪŋ/ (cravings) NOUN If you have a **craving** for something, you want to have it very much. • *I have a craving for sugar.*

obesity /əʊˈbiːsɪti/ UNCOUNTABLE NOUN **Obesity** is a condition in which a person is extremely fat. • *Obesity is on the rise in many countries.*

sedentary /ˈsedəntəri/ ADJECTIVE Someone who has a **sedentary** lifestyle or job sits down a lot of the time and does not take much exercise. • *Obesity and a sedentary lifestyle have been linked with an increased risk of heart disease.*

stimulus /ˈstɪmjʊləs/ (stimuli) NOUN A **stimulus** is something that encourages activity in people or things. • *Interest rates could fall soon and be a stimulus to the U.S. economy.*

susceptible /səˈseptɪbəl/ ADJECTIVE If you are **susceptible** to something, you are likely to do it or be affected by it. • *Young people are susceptible to buying cheap airline tickets.*

TEST 4: READING

Passage 1

accrete /əˈkriːt/ (accretes, accreting, accreted) VERB When something **accretes** new layers or parts, they are added to it so that it increases in size. • *During each cycle the hailstone accretes ice crystals.*

accumulation /əˌkjuːmjuˈleɪʃən/ UNCOUNTABLE NOUN **Accumulation** is the collecting together of things over a period of time. • *The rate of accumulation decreases with time.*

collide /kəˈlaɪd/ (collides, colliding, collided) VERB If two or more moving people or objects **collide**, they crash into one another. If a moving person or object **collides with** a person or object that is not moving, they crash into them. • *Two trains collided head-on in northeastern Germany early this morning.*

concentric /kənˈsentrɪk/ ADJECTIVE **Concentric** circles or rings have the same centre. • *On a blackboard, he drew five concentric circles.*

condensation /ˌkɒndenˈseɪʃən/ UNCOUNTABLE NOUN **Condensation** consists of small drops of water which form when warm water vapour or steam touches a cold surface such as a window. • *Silicon carbide crystals are formed by the condensation of supersaturated vapour.*

condense /kənˈdens/ (condenses, condensing, condensed) VERB When a gas or vapour **condenses**, or **is condensed**, it changes into a liquid. • *Water vapour condenses to form clouds.*

dense /dens/ ADJECTIVE In science, a **dense** substance is very heavy in relation to its volume. • *The densest ocean water is the coldest and most saline.*

distinguishable /dɪˈstɪŋgwɪʃəbəl/ **ADJECTIVE** If something is **distinguishable from** other things, it has a quality or feature which makes it possible for you to recognize it and see that it is different. • *...features that make their products distinguishable from those of their rivals.*

evacuate /ɪˈvækjueɪt/ **(evacuates, evacuating, evacuated) VERB** To **evacuate** someone means to send them to a place of safety, away from a dangerous building, town, or area. • *Since 1951, 18,000 people have been evacuated from the area.*

opaque /əʊˈpeɪk/ **ADJECTIVE** If an object or substance is **opaque**, you cannot see through it. • *You can always use opaque glass if you need to block a street view.*

particle /ˈpɑːtɪkəl/ **(particles) NOUN** A **particle of** something is a very small piece or amount of it. • *a particle of hot metal*

precipitation /prɪˌsɪpɪˈteɪʃən/ **UNCOUNTABLE NOUN** **Precipitation** is rain, snow, or hail. • *Halfway through the year, it feels like we have had our full yearly complement of precipitation already.*

sizeable /ˈsaɪzəbəl/ **ADJECTIVE** **Sizeable** means fairly large. • *Harry inherited the house and a sizeable chunk of land.*

span /spæn/ **(spans) NOUN** A **span** is the period of time between two dates or events during which something exists, functions, or happens. • *Gradually the time span between sessions will increase.*

Passage 2

axis /ˈæksɪs/ **(axes) NOUN** An **axis** is an imaginary line through the middle of something. • *The reason for the solstice is the 23.5 degrees tilt of the Earth's axis towards the Sun.*

bandwidth /ˈbændwɪdθ/ **(bandwidths) NOUN** A **bandwidth** is the range of frequencies used for a particular telecommunications signal, radio transmission, or computer network. • *To cope with this amount of data, the system will need a bandwidth of around 100mhz.*

beam /biːm/ **(beams) NOUN** A **beam** is a line of energy, radiation, or particles sent in a particular direction. • *... high-energy laser beams.*

force /fɔːs/ **(forces) NOUN** In physics, a **force** is the pulling or pushing effect that something has on something else. • *interactions between the forces of gravity and electromagnetism*

frequency /ˈfriːkwənsi/ **(frequencies) NOUN** In physics, the **frequency** of a sound wave or a radio wave is the number of times it vibrates within a specified period of time. • *You can't hear waves of such a high frequency.*

grant /grɑːnt, grænt/ **(grants, granting, granted) VERB** If someone in authority **grants** you something, or if something **is granted to** you, you are allowed to have it. [FORMAL] • *France has agreed to grant him political asylum.*

interference /ˌɪntəˈfɪərəns/ **UNCOUNTABLE NOUN** When there is **interference**, a radio signal is affected by other radio waves or electrical activity so that it cannot be received properly. • *They have been accused of deliberately causing interference to transmissions.*

laser /ˈleɪzə/ **(lasers) NOUN** A **laser** is a narrow beam of concentrated light produced by a special machine. It is used for cutting very hard materials, and in many technical fields such as surgery and telecommunications. • *Therapies currently under investigation include laser surgery and bone marrow transplants.*

manipulate /məˈnɪpjuˌleɪt/ **(manipulates, manipulating, manipulated) VERB** If you **manipulate** something that requires skill, such as a complicated piece of equipment or a difficult idea, you operate it or process it. • *The technology uses a pen to manipulate a computer.*

molecule /ˈmɒlɪkjuːl/ **(molecules) NOUN** A **molecule** is the smallest amount of a chemical substance which can exist by itself. • *At high temperatures, the two strands of the famous double helix that constitutes a DNA molecule come apart.*

momentum /məʊˈmentəm/ **UNCOUNTABLE NOUN** In physics, **momentum** is the mass of a moving object multiplied by its speed in a particular direction. • *The position, energy, and momentum of particles vary over time in an unpredictable manner.*

negate /nɪˈgeɪt/ **(negates, negating, negated) VERB** If one thing **negates** another, it causes that other thing to lose the effect or value that it had. • *An amendment to the bill effectively negated federal regulations that require organic feed for farm animals.*

optical /ˈɒptɪkəl/ **ADJECTIVE** **Optical** devices, processes, and effects involve or relate to vision, light, or images. • *the optical effects of volcanic dust in the stratosphere*

orbit See Test 1 Reading Passage 2

revolve /rɪˈvɒlv/ **(revolves, revolving, revolved) VERB** If one object **revolves around** another object, the first object turns in a circle around the second object. • *The satellite revolves around the Earth once every hundred minutes.*

spectrum /ˈspektrəm/ **(spectra or spectrums) NOUN** A **spectrum** is a range of light waves or radio waves. • *Vast amounts of energy, from X-rays right through the spectrum down to radio waves, are escaping into space.*

transmit /trænzˈmɪt/ **(transmits, transmitting, transmitted) VERB** If an object or substance **transmits** something such as sound or electrical signals, the sound or signals are able to pass through it. • *These thin crystals transmit much of the power.*

turbulence /ˈtɜːbjʊləns/ **UNCOUNTABLE NOUN** **Turbulence** is violent and uneven movement within a particular area of air, liquid, or gas. • *His plane encountered severe turbulence and winds of nearly two hundred miles an hour.*

vortex /ˈvɔːteks/ (**vortexes** or **vortices**) NOUN A **vortex** is a mass of wind or water that spins round so fast that it pulls objects down into its empty centre. • *The polar vortex is a system of wintertime winds.*

Passage 3

clay See Test 3 Reading Passage 1

condemn /kənˈdem/ (**condemns, condemning, condemned**) VERB If authorities **condemn** a building, they officially decide that it is not safe and must be pulled down or repaired. • *State officials said the court's ruling clears the way for proceedings to condemn buildings in the area.*

densely /ˈdensli/ ADVERB A **densely** populated place contains a lot of people in a small area. • *Java is a densely populated island.*

depletion /dɪˈpliːʃən/ UNCOUNTABLE NOUN **Depletion** is the act of using up or reducing something. • *...the problem of ozone depletion.*

drain /dreɪn/ (**drains**) NOUN A **drain** is a pipe that carries water or sewage away from a place, or an opening in a surface that leads to the pipe. • *Tony built his own house and laid his own drains.*

ecosystem See Test 1 Reading Passage 1

erosion See Test 1 Reading Passage 1

estuary See Test 1 Reading Passage 1

extraction See Test 3 Reading Passage 1

fault line /ˈfɔːlt ˌlaɪn/ (**fault lines**) NOUN A **fault line** is a long crack in the surface of the earth. Earthquakes usually occur along fault lines. • *It can be dangerous to build a house near a fault line.*

foundation /faʊnˈdeɪʃən/ (**foundations**) NOUN A structure's **foundations** are the parts under the ground on which it stands. • *Tenants feared that the renovation work would damage the building's foundations.*

give way /ˌgɪv ˈweɪ/ PHRASAL VERB If an object that is supporting something **gives way**, it breaks or collapses, so that it can no longer support that thing. • *The hook in the ceiling had given way and the lamp had fallen blazing on to the table.*

literally /ˈlɪtərəli/ ADVERB You use **literally** to emphasize that what you are saying is true, even though it seems exaggerated or surprising. • *Putting on an opera is a tremendous enterprise involving literally hundreds of people.*

main /meɪn/ (**mains**) NOUN The **mains** are the pipes which supply gas or water to buildings, or which take sewage away from them. • *The capital has been without mains water since Wednesday night.*

pose See Test 1 Reading Passage 2

promenade /ˌprɒməˈnɑːd/ (**promenades**) NOUN In a seaside town, the **promenade** is the road by the sea where people go for a walk. • *The promenade has been closed for the weekend due to flooding.*

prosperity /prɒˈsperɪti/ UNCOUNTABLE NOUN **Prosperity** is a condition in which a person or community is doing well financially. • *...Japan's economic prosperity.*

subside /səbˈsaɪd/ (**subsides, subsiding, subsided**) VERB If the ground or a building **is subsiding**, it is very slowly sinking to a lower level. • *Does that mean the whole house is subsiding?*

subsidence /səbˈsaɪdəns, ˈsʌbsɪdəns/ UNCOUNTABLE NOUN When there is **subsidence** in a place, the ground there sinks to a lower level. • *A surveyor said that the problems were caused by subsidence and the house needed to be underpinned.*

swampland /ˈswɒmplænd/ (**swamplands**) NOUN **Swampland** is an area of land that is always very wet. • *The golf course was built on a reclaimed swampland.*

swell /swel/ (**swells, swelling, swollen**) VERB If the amount or size of something **swells** or if something **swells** it, it becomes larger than it was before. • *The human population swelled, at least temporarily, as migrants moved south.*

tide /taɪd/ (**tides**) NOUN The **tide** is the regular change in the level of the sea on the shore. • *Scientists have found proof that strong tides can trigger earthquakes.*

GENERAL TRAINING TEST A: READING

Section 1

browse /braʊz/ (**browses, browsing, browsed**) VERB If you **browse** in a shop, you look at things in a fairly casual way, in the hope that you might find something you like. • *She browsed in an upmarket antiques shop.*

donation /dəʊˈneɪʃən/ (**donations**) NOUN A **donation** is something which someone gives to a charity or other organization. • *Charities appealed for donations of food and clothing for victims of the hurricane.*

physiotherapy /ˌfɪziəʊˈθerəpi/ UNCOUNTABLE NOUN **Physiotherapy** is medical treatment for problems of the joints, muscles, or nerves, which involves doing exercises or having part of your body massaged or warmed. • *An alternative is to visit an osteopathy or physiotherapy clinic at an NHS health centre.*

stilt /stɪlt/ (**stilts**) NOUN **Stilts** are two long pieces of wood with pieces for the feet fixed high up on the sides so that people can stand on them and walk high above the ground. • *I have successfully taught several people how to walk on stilts.*

Section 2

applicant /ˈæplɪkənt/ (**applicants**) NOUN An **applicant for** something such as a job or a place at a college is someone who makes a formal written request to be given it. • *How many applicants will I be interviewing today?.*

bout /baʊt/ (**bouts**) NOUN A **bout** is a period of time spent doing something. • *I managed to get a bit of sleep between bouts of partying last weekend.*

to the casual eye /ˈkæʒʊəl aɪ/ PHRASE You say that something looks a certain way **to the casual eye** if it appears that way first but it is different when you examine it more closely. • *To the casual eye, these figures may not seem very significant.*

cognitive See Test 3 Reading Passage 3

consecutive /kənˈsekjutɪv/ ADJECTIVE **Consecutive** periods of time or events happen one after the other without interruption. • *This is the third consecutive year that these countries achieved economic growth.*

dedicated /ˈdedɪkeɪtɪd/ ADJECTIVE You use **dedicated** to describe something that is made, built, or designed for one particular purpose or thing. • *Such areas should also be served by dedicated cycle routes.*

elementary /ˌelɪˈmentri/ ADJECTIVE Something that is **elementary** is very simple and basic. • *...elementary computer skills.*

entail /ɪnˈteɪl/ (entails, entailing, entailed) VERB If one thing **entails** another, it involves it or causes it. [FORMAL] • *The changed outlook entails higher economic growth than was previously assumed.*

exhaustive /ɪgˈzɔːstɪv/ ADJECTIVE If you describe a study, search, or list as **exhaustive**, you mean that it is very thorough and complete. • *The author's treatment of the subject is exhaustive.*

extensive /ɪkˈstensɪv/ ADJECTIVE Something that is **extensive** covers a wide range of details, ideas, or items. • *Developments in South Africa receive extensive coverage in The Sunday Telegraph.*

feat See Test 3 Listening Section 2

forage /ˈfɒrɪdʒ/ (forages, foraging, foraged) VERB When animals **forage**, they search for food. • *We disturbed a wild boar that had been foraging by the roadside.*

fruitful /ˈfruːtful/ ADJECTIVE Something that is **fruitful** produces good and useful results. • *The talks had been fruitful, but much remained to be done.*

induction See Test 2 Listening Section 2

mow /məʊ/ (mows, mowing, mowed, mown) VERB If you **mow** an area of grass, you cut it using a machine called a lawnmower. • *He continued to mow the lawn and do other routine chores.*

navigator /ˈnævɪgeɪtə/ (navigators) NOUN A **navigator** is a person or thing that is skilled at finding the way to a specific place. • *Howcroft was a confident driver and a talented navigator.*

nectar /ˈnektə/ UNCOUNTABLE NOUN **Nectar** is a sweet liquid produced by flowers, which bees and other insects collect. • *Honey bees are believed to have evolved from hunting wasps who liked the taste of nectar and decided to become vegetarian.*

optimal /ˈɒptɪməl/ ADJECTIVE The **optimal** way of doing something is the best one, taking into account the circumstances. • *The program examines hundreds of strategies to find the optimal solution using the least effort.*

optimize /ˈɒptɪmaɪz/ (optimizes, optimizing, optimized) VERB To **optimize** a situation or opportunity means to get as much advantage or benefit from it as you can. [FORMAL] • *What can you do to optimize your family situation?.*

optimum /ˈɒptɪməm/ ADJECTIVE The **optimum** level or state of something is the best level or state that it could achieve. [FORMAL] • *Aim to do some physical activity three times a week for optimum health.*

pasture /ˈpɑːstʃə, ˈpæs-/ (pastures) NOUN **Pasture** is land with grass growing on it for farm animals to eat. • *The cows are out now, grazing in the pasture.*

patchy /ˈpætʃi/ ADJECTIVE If something is **patchy**, it is not completely reliable or satisfactory because it is not always good. • *Transport is difficult, communications are patchy.*

pentagon /ˈpentəgən/ (pentagons) NOUN A **pentagon** is a shape with five sides. • *Workspace for each module of the spacecraft is physically arranged as a pentagon seating five persons.*

pollen /ˈpɒlən/ UNCOUNTABLE NOUN **Pollen** is a fine powder produced by flowers. It fertilizes other flowers of the same species so that they produce seeds. • *Your susceptibility to pollen allergy or other sensitivities can be increased by emotional stresses.*

primate /ˈpraɪmət, -meɪt/ (primates) NOUN A **primate** is a member of the group of mammals which includes humans, monkeys, and apes. • *The woolly spider monkey is the largest primate in the Americas.*

scarce /skeəs/ ADJECTIVE If something is **scarce**, there is not enough of it. • *Jobs are becoming increasingly scarce.*

scattered /ˈskætəd/ ADJECTIVE **Scattered** things are spread over an area in an untidy or irregular way. • *Tomorrow there will be a few scattered showers.*

shed light /ʃed/ (sheds light, shedding light, shed light) PHRASAL VERB To **shed light on** something means to make it easier to understand, because more information is known about it. • *A new approach offers an answer, and may shed light on an even bigger question.*

spatial /ˈspeɪʃəl/ ADJECTIVE **Spatial** is used to describe things relating to areas. • *...the spatial distribution of black employment and population in South Africa.*

stymie /ˈstaɪmi/ (stymies, stymieing, stymied) VERB If you **are stymied by** something, you find it very difficult to take action or to continue what you are doing. [INFORMAL] • *Companies have been stymied by the length of time it takes to reach an agreement.*

subscription /səbˈskrɪpʃən/ (subscriptions) NOUN A **subscription** is an amount of money that you pay regularly in order to belong to an organization, to help a charity or campaign, or to receive copies of a magazine or newspaper. • *You can become a member by paying the yearly subscription.*

sucrose /ˈsuːkrəʊs/ UNCOUNTABLE NOUN **Sucrose** is a common type of sugar. • ...*simple sugars like sucrose, glucose and fructose.*

track See Test 3 Reading Passage 3

tradeoff /ˈtreɪdɒf/ (**tradeoffs**) NOUN A **tradeoff** is a situation where you make a compromise between two things, or where you exchange all or part of one thing for another. • *The newspaper's headline indicates that there was a tradeoff at the summit.*

wilfully /ˈwɪlfʊli/ ADVERB If you do something **wilfully**, you do it deliberately, often causing harm as a result. • *It seems that ministers are wilfully ignoring the evidence.*

GENERAL TRAINING TEST B: READING

Section 1

direct debit /ˌdaɪˈrekt ˈdebɪt/ (**direct debits**) NOUN If you set up a **direct debit**, you instruct your bank to pay a certain sum from your bank account to a specified organization, usually every month. • *I finally phoned my bank to cancel the direct debit on Wednesday.*

disadvantaged /ˌdɪsədˈvɑːntɪdʒd, -ˈvæn-/ ADJECTIVE People who are **disadvantaged** or live in **disadvantaged** areas live in bad conditions and tend not to get a good education or have a reasonable standard of living. • *The centre aims to help disadvantaged areas of Europe, mainly by fostering new businesses.*

donate See Test 4 Listening Section 2

donation See General Training Test A Reading Section 1

invaluable /ɪnˈvæljəbəl/ ADJECTIVE If you describe something as **invaluable**, you mean that it is extremely useful. • *The research should prove invaluable in the study of linguistics.*

literacy /ˈlɪtərəsi/ UNCOUNTABLE NOUN **Literacy** is the ability to read and write. • *The literacy rate there is the highest in Central America.*

motivational /ˌməʊtɪˈveɪʃənəl/ ADJECTIVE Someone or something that is **motivational** makes people feel enthusiastic and interested. • *Steve is an inspirational and motivational speaker.*

postal order /ˈpəʊstəl ˌɔːdə/ (**postal orders**) NOUN A **postal order** is a piece of paper representing a sum of money which you can buy at a post office and send to someone as a way of sending them money by post. [BRIT] • *I would like to renew my subscription by paying £30 by postal order.*

Section 2

expense /ɪkˈspens/ (**expenses**) NOUN **Expenses** are amounts of money that you spend while doing something in the course of your work, which will be paid back to you afterwards. • *As a member of the International Olympic Committee her fares and hotel expenses were paid by the IOC.*

HR /eɪtʃ ˈɑːr/ ABBREVIATION In a company or other organization, the **HR** department is the department with responsibility for the recruiting, training, and welfare of the staff. **HR** is an abbreviation for 'human resources'. • *Most HR departments monitor your holidays.*

incur /ɪnˈkɜː/ (**incurs, incurring, incurred**) VERB If you **incur** something unpleasant, it happens to you because of something you have done. [WRITTEN] • *The government had also incurred huge debts.*

mileage See Test 3 Listening Section 1

reimburse /ˌriːɪmˈbɜːs/ (**reimburses, reimbursing, reimbursed**) VERB If you **reimburse** someone **for** something, you pay them back the money that they have spent or lost because of it. [FORMAL] • *I'll be happy to reimburse you for any expenses you might have incurred.*

revenue /ˈrevənjuː/ UNCOUNTABLE NOUN **Revenue** is money that a company, organization, or government receives from people. • *Fishing is the main industry, with seal-hunting in season an additional source of revenue.*

revitalize /ˌriːˈvaɪtəlaɪz/ (**revitalizes, revitalizing, revitalized**) VERB To **revitalize** something that has lost its activity or its health means to make it active or healthy again. • *...the revitalized Democratic Party.*

stagger /ˈstægə/ (**staggers, staggering, staggered**) VERB To **stagger** things such as people's holidays or hours of work means to arrange them so that they do not all happen at the same time. • *During the past few years the government has staggered the summer vacation periods for students.*

stroll /strəʊl/ (**strolls**) NOUN A **stroll** is a slow walk that you take for pleasure. • *We went for a stroll along the beach.*

subsistence /səbˈsɪstəns/ UNCOUNTABLE NOUN **Subsistence** is the condition of just having enough food or money to stay alive. • *The standard of living today is on the edge of subsistence.*

tranquil /ˈtræŋkwɪl/ ADJECTIVE Something that is **tranquil** is calm and peaceful. • *The tranquil atmosphere of The Connaught allows guests to feel totally at home.*

Section 3

abundant /əˈbʌndənt/ ADJECTIVE Something that is **abundant** is present in large quantities. • *There is an abundant supply of cheap labour.*

adorn /əˈdɔːn/ (**adorns, adorning, adorned**) VERB If something **adorns** a place or an object, it makes it look more beautiful. • *His watercolour designs adorn a wide range of books.*

artisan /ˌɑːtɪˈzæn/ (**artisans**) NOUN An **artisan** is someone whose job requires skill with their hands. • *The 55-year-old New York-based artisan has made everything from wine bottles to lipstick holders.*

breeze /briːz/ NOUN breezes A **breeze** is a gentle wind. • *...a cool summer breeze.*

chisel /ˈtʃɪzəl/ **(chisels, chiselling, chiselled)** VERB If you **chisel** wood or stone, you cut and shape it using a tool with a long metal blade and a sharp edge, known as a chisel. • *They sit and chisel the stone to size.*

clan /klæn/ **(clans)** NOUN A **clan** is a group which consists of families that are related to each other. • *...rival clans.*

contraction /kənˈtrækʃən/ **(contractions)** NOUN A **contraction** is a shortened form of a word or words. • *'It's' (with an apostrophe) should be used only as a contraction for 'it is'.*

dedication /ˌdedɪˈkeɪʃən/ UNCOUNTABLE NOUN Someone who shows **dedication to** a particular activity puts a lot of time and effort into it. • *An indication of Sir Ferrers's modern approach is his dedication to environmentalism.*

fauna /ˈfɔːnə/ **(faunas)** NOUN Animals, especially the animals in a particular area, can be referred to as **fauna**. • *Brackish waters generally support only a small range of faunas.*

flora /ˈflɔːrə/ UNCOUNTABLE NOUN You can refer to plants as **flora**, especially the plants growing in a particular area. [FORMAL] • *...the variety of food crops and flora which now exists in Dominica.*

handiwork /ˈhændiwɜːk/ UNCOUNTABLE NOUN A person's **handiwork** is something special that they have made. • *She stood back and proudly surveyed her handiwork.*

intently /ɪnˈtentli/ ADVERB If you watch or listen to someone or something **intently**, you concentrate very hard on them. • *Nick watched intently, absorbing every detail.*

lush /lʌʃ/ ADJECTIVE **Lush** fields or gardens have a lot of very healthy grass or plants. • *The beautifully landscaped gardens sprawl with lush vegetation.*

manipulate See Test 4 Reading Passage 2

medium /ˈmiːdiəm/ **(mediums** or **media)** NOUN A **medium** is a substance or material which is used for a particular purpose or in order to produce a particular effect. • *Hyatt has found a way of creating these qualities using the more permanent medium of oil paint.*

motif /məʊˈtiːf/ **(motifs)** NOUN A **motif** is a design which is used as a decoration or as part of an artistic pattern. • *...a rose motif.*

nestle /ˈnesəl/ **(nestles, nestling, nestled)** VERB If something such as a building **nestles** somewhere or if it **is nestled** somewhere, it is in that place and seems safe or sheltered. • *Nearby, nestling in the hills, was the children's home.*

ornately /ɔːˈneɪtli/ ADVERB Something that is decorated **ornately** is decorated with lots of complicated patterns and details. • *The ornately carved doors were made in the 17th century.*

portray /pɔːˈtreɪ/ **(portrays, portraying, portrayed)** VERB When a writer or artist **portrays** something, he or she writes a description or produces a painting of it. • *...the landscape as portrayed by painters such as Claude and Poussin.*

recall /rɪˈkɔːl/ **(recalls, recalling, recalled)** VERB If a thing a place or an event **recalls** something from the past it reminds you of it. • *Waddell's paintings recall a time when men and women could wander freely through the Capitol's halls.*

replica /ˈreplɪkə/ **(replicas)** NOUN A **replica of** something such as a statue, building, or weapon is an accurate copy of it. • *Royce Hall was an exact replica of the basilica of Sant'Ambrogio in Milan.*

sand /sænd/ **(sands, sanding, sanded)** VERB If you **sand** a wood or metal surface, you rub sandpaper over it in order to make it smooth or clean. • *Sand the surface softly and carefully.*

scattered See General Training Test A Reading Passage 2

shoot /ʃuːt/ **(shoots)** NOUN **Shoots** are plants that are beginning to grow, or new parts growing from a plant or tree. • *Pandas feed mainly on bamboo shoots and leaves.*

signify /ˈsɪɡnɪfaɪ/ **(signifies, signifying, signified)** VERB If an event, a sign, or a symbol **signifies** something, it is a sign of that thing or represents that thing. • *The contrasting approaches to Europe signified a sharp difference between the major parties.*

stencil /ˈstensəl/ **(stencils, stencilling, stencilled)** VERB If you **stencil** a surface **with** a design, you put a design on it using a piece of paper, plastic, or metal which has a design cut out of it. • *He then stencilled the ceiling with a moon and stars motif.*

terraced /ˈterɪst/ ADJECTIVE A **terraced** slope or side of a hill has flat areas like steps cut into it, where crops or other plants can be grown. • *Terraced rice paddies lay below engraved into the hill.*

vegetation /ˌvedʒɪˈteɪʃən/ UNCOUNTABLE NOUN Plants, trees, and flowers can be referred to as **vegetation**. [FORMAL] • *The inn has a garden of semitropical vegetation.*

Audio script

Track 01

TEST 1   LISTENING SECTION 1

Operator:	Good morning. z-Mobile Services. This is Tess speaking. How can I help?
Caller:	I want to report a stolen mobile phone.
Operator:	Could you confirm your postcode please sir?
Caller:	It's CN2 1EB.
Operator:	Thanks. And your house number?
Caller:	34.
Operator:	Okay. Can you give me the telephone number of the phone that was stolen?
Caller:	Yes, it's ... wait a minute ... it's 07890 ...
Operator:	07890 ...
Caller:	623 ...
Operator:	623 ...
Caller:	570.
Operator:	570. Okay. So, it's 07890 623570.
Caller:	Yes, that's right.
Operator:	Can you just confirm your name?
Caller:	Yes, it's Tomas Green.
Operator:	Is that Thomas spelt T-H-O-M-A-S?
Caller:	No, there's no 'h'. It's just Tomas. T-O-M-A-S.
Operator:	Okay. So you said your phone was stolen?
Caller:	That's right. I reported it to the police this morning.
Operator:	That's good. I'll need to take down your crime reference number.
Caller:	I've got it here. It's CZ ...
Operator:	CZ ...
Caller:	Dash 17624 ...
Operator:	17624 ...
Caller:	Dash 5.
Operator:	5. Thank you. Let me run through that again. CZ dash 17624 dash 5.
Caller:	That's it.
Operator:	Just a few more details. Can I have your IMEI number?
Caller:	Oh, what's that?
Operator:	It's the International Mobile Equipment Identity number. It's a—
Caller:	Sorry, I don't have it.
Operator:	Not to worry – we'll deal with that in a moment. I just need to have the date and time your mobile was stolen.
Caller:	That's easy. Between 1 and 2 o'clock yesterday.
Operator:	That's 1 to 2pm on 16th August. Thank you. Now, I just need a few details of the incident if you wouldn't mind.
Caller:	Sure. I was in the Bangs Coffee Bar in the city centre. I definitely had my phone with me when I sat down. In fact I remember checking to see if I had any text messages. But when I came to leave it wasn't on the table.
Operator:	Did you leave the phone unattended at any time, perhaps to go to the toilet?
Caller:	No, that's the funny thing. Like I told the police, it was very busy in there because it was lunchtime and all the tables and chairs were pushed really close together. There were a couple of other people at my table. Someone must have leaned across when I wasn't looking and slipped my phone into their pocket.
Operator:	Oh dear.
Caller:	I know. It's such a pain. I suppose I'll have to pay for a replacement?

Operator:	Fortunately you're covered by our 12-month Care Plan so there won't be a charge for replacing it this time. But I have to tell you if it happens again within the next three months you may have to pay a fee.
Caller:	Fair enough. How soon can you send me a new one?
Operator:	We've got two options. You can get it sent by courier for next-day delivery for a small fee or we can send it in the standard post free of charge. You should allow about five days for it to arrive.
Caller:	That's a bit difficult. I'm gong back to Australia the day after tomorrow to see my parents for a month. Any chance you could send it to their address?
Operator:	No, I'm sorry. We can only send replacements to UK addresses.
Caller:	In that case I'd better have next-day delivery then.
Operator:	Okay, so just to confirm the delivery address ... Is it 34 Solent Gardens?
Caller:	That's it.
Operator:	The final thing we need to do is to put a block on your phone.
Caller:	You mean to stop the thief from using it? I was wondering about that.
Operator:	What I need to do is put your IMEI number into the Central Register, which will essentially prevent anyone else from making calls from your phone. Now the IMEI number is a 15-digit number that you can see underneath the phone's battery. Do you have a record of it?
Caller:	No, sorry. Is there any other way to find the number?
Operator:	Yes. We usually trace it from a call you've recently made. In a moment I'll put you through to my colleague who deals with that. By the time you've finished with him your mobile will no longer operate.
Caller:	Good.
Operator:	And with your new phone I'll also send you a Crime Prevention leaflet, which will give you some tips on how to protect your phone from being stolen again.
Caller:	Thanks, you've been really helpful.
Operator:	Don't mention it. Just putting you through to my colleague now ...

Track 02

TEST 1   LISTENING SECTION 2

Hi, you're listening to Marc Ambrose and I'll be with you through to midday on Talk Back, the show where you tell us what you think about Radio Western. I'm sure you've all heard we have a new boss here at Radio Western and she's very keen to get your feedback. Well, you've certainly taken her invitation seriously. We'll be dipping into the postbag for your feedback in just a moment and speaking to a surprise guest or two later in the show.

I must start by saying a big 'thank you' to Tony Marsons – judging by your letters, he did a great job of covering the show last week whilst I was away. Thanks Tony, if you're listening. And thanks for all the emails asking about my holiday. I had a long, rather boring flight home late last night but I must say I had a wonderful time. The food was absolutely delicious and the locals we spoke to were really friendly. Shame about the weather, which was an absolute washout, but you can't have everything I suppose. And the kids loved it, so everyone was happy.

Anyway, on to the first of your letters ... Sally from Liverpool is very concerned about the consequences of the cutbacks we've been experiencing here at Radio Western, in particular whether some of our late-night music shows could be facing the axe. 'We're force-fed a great deal of pop music throughout the day,' writes Sally, 'and some of your listeners look forward to the more niche musical genres you cover in the evening. Are these in danger when you rearrange the schedule?' Not at all Sally. In fact look out for one or two exciting new shows over the coming weeks. We've got a brand new classical music show coming soon and the return of the ever-popular Chris Greene with his show on international folk music. And of course there's Carol Whittaker's History of Jazz every Friday night. Hopefully this will put your mind at rest, Sally.

John from Leicester writes in to point out that many of our guests on Talk Back and other shows seem to run out of time before they have the chance to finish the interview. 'It happens again and again,' writes John. 'As the programmes draw to a close guests get rushed and many questions go unanswered. Why don't you offer some kind of after-show online channel where the guest can continue answering listeners' questions?' I think that's a great idea John. And as you go on to say, if it were recorded, people who don't get the chance to hear the live show could catch up later. We'll certainly pass this one up to management. I'm sure a service like this would go down really well on our website.

Now Clive has a question that will be of interest to all us over-50s fans of Radio Western. Clive wants to know why we don't feature more issues related to this age group and cater more to this group's taste in music. As Clive explains, 'As a regular listener I'm concerned about your age profiling. Presenters seem intent on covering topics that appeal very much to the 30-somethings, which is great for them, but what about people of other ages?' Clive would like to see music shows aimed at the older generation and more on problems facing the over-50s in our consumer affairs shows. Well Clive, we'd certainly hate to think you're feeling excluded from our schedule. What about other listeners? Do you think we're getting it about right or is there room for improvement?

Track 03

TEST 1   LISTENING SECTION 3

Simon:	Hi Kelly. How are you?
Kelly:	Fine thanks. Do you still have time to talk about our presentation?
Simon:	Yeah, for sure. We need to get going on this, don't we?
Kelly:	Well, it's next Wednesday, so yes.
Simon:	I thought it was Thursday.
Kelly:	No that's the other group. We're doing ours the day before. I've just seen Fiona. She's going to be a bit late so shall we just get started?
Simon:	Yes, fine. We're definitely doing it on women in education, aren't we? I know we talked about women in politics but are we going for education?
Kelly:	Yes, that's right. Now it's not too long is it, the presentation? They said to keep it to about half an hour. Maybe we can sort out who's doing what today.
Simon:	Yes, good idea. One thing we do need to sort out is a projector and laptop. We're going to use PowerPoint or something like that for the talk, aren't we?
Kelly:	Yes. They said we could book a projector and laptop from technical services if we needed them. Because it's not in the lecture theatre, is it? I know there's already one set up in there but …
Simon:	No, the lecture theatre was booked. We're in the seminar room.
Kelly:	Okay. So what's the next step? We need to work out who's doing what, don't we?
Simon:	Well, we all know the subject, seeing as our last essay was on this topic.
Kelly:	Yes, but we can't just stand up and ramble on; it'll need to be structured. I've got an idea. Fiona's essay was brilliant, wasn't it? Why don't we base the talk on that? We can always add bits here and there if we think it needs padding out anywhere.
Simon:	That's a good idea. Shall we ask her to get a copy of it for both of us?
Kelly:	Yes, I'm sure she won't mind. We can always let everyone know at the start of the presentation that it's Fiona's work. But we don't want to just read it out. That'll be really boring. It's probably best to make notes from it so that we can improvise a bit on the day.
Simon:	Why don't we break the essay down into sections and the three of us can each take on one section. We can all make notes on our own part and add to it where we think it needs it. That way we can try to make it our own.
Kelly:	Yes, I like it. So let's ask Fiona to start the talk off and bring it to a close. She can take on the introduction and conclusion. I know she divided the essay into the situation for woman in the past and then compared it to how things are now. So why don't I take the bit on the past and you talk about the situation for women as it is now?
Simon:	Okay. If we give ourselves till the weekend to work on it we can get together on Saturday to see how it's looking. Now what about the presentation itself? Someone will need to build that and find images. We don't just want to fill each slide with a load of text, do we?
Kelly:	No we don't. Before I forget, I can sort out the laptop and projector. I've got to go down to technical services to get them to have a look at my laptop. They reckon they can get it to run a bit faster. But the presentation … who's good with computers? Do you fancy having a go?
Simon:	I don't mind. But I'll wait until we've met up on Saturday just to make sure we've all got our notes.
Kelly:	We'll need images, won't we? Shall we all search for our own to fit our section of the talk?
Simon:	Yes, and then if you and Fiona email them to me I'll add them to the presentation.
Kelly:	Right, that was easy wasn't it? And look, here comes Fiona. Let's ask her about her essay.

Track 04

TEST 1   **LISTENING SECTION 4**

Tanya: Hi everyone. Today Mark has come in to talk to you about time management strategies. If you remember, in the introductory session I told you the difference it can make to your studies so this is an incredibly important session. Thanks Mark.

Mark: Hello. Yes, I'm Mark. I lecture over in the Business School but I have a bit of a reputation for being rather evangelical about time management and I'm often invited in to other courses to talk about it. So here I am!

You've now come to the end of your first week at university and you've probably noticed how different it is from school or college. For some people this step up comes very naturally but, in our experience, many students find this new regime a challenge. People aren't watching over you anywhere near as much and you're expected to be far more responsible for your own learning. Research I've carried out shows that 65% of male students have poor time management skills. It's not quite so high for females but still a majority of 55% would benefit from developing these skills. Students who don't will see their grades and general progress suffer as deadlines are missed or work gets rushed, with a decline in the quality of work as a result.

In a nutshell, you need to be aware of the big picture, to know what's coming down the line at any given time and what needs prioritising. Start by creating that big picture, using our yearly academic planner. And don't hide it away in a drawer somewhere. Give it pride of place somewhere like on the bedroom wall so you'll have daily reminders of what's approaching. During this first week you'll have been given seminar and lecture times, essay deadlines, exams dates and so on. Add these dates to your planner and add any new deadlines such as seminar presentations or tutorial dates as you get them. Those important non-academic occasions shouldn't be ignored either. Trips back home for family celebrations need to be factored in.

Looking at your planner, the first thing that will strike you is how much time you have on your hands. Just a few seminars here and there, a couple of lectures on Tuesday and Thursday. Easy, you think. But this is very misleading indeed. Your planner only looks empty because it doesn't show all that essential self-study you'll need to do. And as there's no-one else structuring this time for you you'll need to manage this yourself. You don't want to waste those hours between lectures or seminars in the café. Use this time to read through your lecture notes, prepare for the next seminar or do some research for that next assignment. Essentially, structure your days on a 9–5 basis as if you were a full-time employee and start to calculate how you're going to fill those gaps efficiently.

Start by considering how you're going to meet all these deadlines. If there are any cooks amongst you you'll know that putting a nice meal on the table requires more than just ... well, cooking. You need to research the ingredients, buy them, chop, slice, mix and so on. Cooking itself is a long way into the process. It's the same with that essay you have to write or that presentation you might have to make. They need careful planning beforehand and that time needs to be built into your preparation. Start prioritising what needs doing and when. Download our monthly and weekly planners to help you map it all out.

And here's an important point: when you're planning what to do, be task-orientated rather than time-orientated and set achievable goals. 'Finding images for a presentation' for example, is measurable. Simply writing 'research 10 a.m.–11 a.m.' isn't. This task-orientated approach will be immensely helpful, forcing you to break your preparation down into individual, achievable steps.

Try to assess when busy periods are likely to occur such as the week leading up to an assignment deadline. Are there any evenings during the week you could put aside for extra work? And, just as importantly, make a note of any times you won't want to be working. You'll need time for you, sessions in the gym, evenings when your favourite programmes are on TV. Don't forget to schedule in time for non-academic activities like going shopping or doing the laundry. It's best to have a fixed time each week for jobs like these so they don't interfere with your academic work.

Finally, decide where you're going to do your self-study. Will you be distracted by the TV, the Internet or friends if you stay in your room? Perhaps the library will be a better place. Anywhere that encourages you to prevaricate should be avoided at all costs.

Starting with the big picture and then working towards individual goals will leave you feeling in control rather than being pulled here and there, firefighting as the next deadline looms ...

Track 05
TEST 1   SPEAKING PART 1

In this first part of the exam I'd like to ask you some general questions about yourself.

Where do you live?

Is it a nice place to live?

Do you have many tourists visit your area?

Let's talk about your interests. Do you have any hobbies or interests?

Have you seen a good film recently?

How often do you go out with friends?

Track 06
TEST 1   SPEAKING PART 2

I'm going to give you a topic and I'd like you to talk about it for one to two minutes. Before you talk, you have one minute to think about what you are going to say. You can make some notes if you wish. Here is your topic.

Track 07
TEST 1   SPEAKING PART 3

We've been talking about the subject of fame and celebrity. I'd like to discuss this subject with you with some more questions.

Do you think being famous is a worthwhile ambition?

Who are currently some of the biggest celebrities in your country?

Do celebrities deserve the attention they get from the media?

Does fame generally bring happiness to the individual?

Do well-known people suffer a loss of personal privacy?

If you could be famous for doing something, what would it be?

Track 08
TEST 2   LISTENING SECTION 1

Seb:	Hi Lydia. How was your French class?
Lydia:	I enjoyed it. Françoise, the teacher, she's really nice and friendly. What about you? You're in the exam class, aren't you?
Seb:	Yes. It was good. There's a lot of work but I think I'm going to enjoy it. Anyway, we were going to meet up later, weren't we? To see what the city centre's like. Do you still want to go?
Lydia:	Definitely, yes. Some of the people in my class went out last night and had a great time. Where would you like to go? What would you like to do?
Seb:	I'm not that bothered really. We could walk around for a while, do some window shopping, see some local sights. I wouldn't mind seeing a film later in the evening if you'd like to. My host family are cooking so I don't think I'll be hungry for a meal or anything like that. I don't really want to stay out too late, no clubs or anything. What about you?
Lydia:	Let's just see how we feel when we get there, shall we? My teacher told me it's late night shopping so there should be lots to do. Shall I meet you after school?
Seb:	Well, I need to go back to my host family first. As I said, they're cooking me a meal and it'll be a chance to meet all their family. Shall I come to your house when I've finished. You're with a host family as well, aren't you?
Lydia:	Yes. I haven't memorised the address yet ... Wait a minute ... Where's that card they gave me earlier? ... Here it is. Have you got a pen?
Seb:	Hang on .... Right ... yes, what is it?
Lydia:	Okay, it's Mr and Mrs Andrews ... You don't need that, do you? Here we are ... the address, it's 60 Mayweather Road. It's in Coldfield, not far from the city centre actually. My house is on the 14 bus route. It's easy to find; it's just across the road from the police station. If you get lost, here's the telephone number ... 01764 38864. Shall we say about 6.00?
Seb:	Okay, that'll give me time to get ready.

Lydia:	I'd like to find somewhere that sells paper and pens if possible.
Seb:	I'm sure you'll find somewhere. I'm hoping there's a bookshop. The teacher has recommended a good grammar practice book for the course.
Lydia:	If we've got time I could use this voucher the school gave us for a free coffee in the library café.
Seb:	Oh yes, I've got one of them too. Good idea.

Track 09

TEST 2   LISTENING SECTION 2

Tutor: OK, so here were are on the first floor. The self-access centre is just along here on the left. This room's very popular with students and can get quite busy. When it's quiet you can come here as often as you want but if there's a lot of demand, such as coming up to exam time, we have to limit sessions to make sure everyone gets a chance to use the resources.

If you'd like to follow me in. So, here we are. As you can see, it's a lovely bright room with lots of resources to help you with your English studies. Over there against the wall we have a row of Internet-connected computers. As you can imagine these get taken very quickly with students wanting to check their email, Facebook, that kind of thing. Because of the demand we ask students to try and stick to about 30 minutes maximum.

You'll need to log in with your username and password. You should have created these already during your induction. Please do not share your details with anyone else and please make sure you read our policy on using the Internet.

I mentioned the help desk earlier and that's it over there just past the computers in the corner. There are usually two members of staff available to help you and these will often be teachers so if you have any language questions that's where you can go.

Now, over there you can see the reference section. You'll find dictionaries, exam practice tests, vocabulary and grammar books. I should point out that these books are for reference only and we don't offer a loan service. We are allowed to make photocopies of one or two pages so if there's an exercise you need a copy of ask the staff to help.

Now these computers on the oval table here, they're our high-spec PCs. You'll find programmes to help you with your English but also opportunities to practise other languages such as Spanish, Chinese, German; several languages in fact. Some of them require a CD-ROM ... You can collect them from the help desk. By the way, there's no Internet connection on these computers nor any office software for the time being. If you want to do any word processing you'll need to use one of the laptops we keep for this purpose. Again, see the staff if you need one of these.

Some of you were asking earlier about extra listening practice and these small rooms here are dedicated language labs. If you want to use this resource see a member of staff to buy a set of headphones. And finally here on the left we have two stands with our large collection of readers. These are simplified novels by well-known British authors like Charlotte Brontë, Charles Dickens and Shakespeare. The books are graded and you'll find lots that will be appropriate to your level. Unlike the reference books you can take these readers home and keep them for up to 14 days.

I think that's everything. The centre is open from 8.30 till 5.30 during the week so, as your classes start at 9.00, those of you who get here early can use the resource before your lesson. Although it's open all day long, it's booked by a tutor for their class now and again so you might not be able to gain access if you have any free time during the day. It's best to ask the tutor concerned if it's okay to pop in. Oh, and it's open on Saturday as well, just for a few hours, from 10.00 till 1.00.

Track 10

TEST 2   LISTENING SECTION 3

Tutor:	Hello Jacob. Come in and take a seat. How are you finding the course?
Jacob:	Very good. I'm really enjoying myself.
Tutor:	Good. Well, I've had a look at the first draft of your assignment and it shows a great deal of promise. How well do you think you answered the question?
Jacob:	I think I dealt with the task okay. I spent hours in the library reading up on the subject so I feel confident I answered the question. I'm not sure about my Spanish though.

Tutor:	Well, for a first draft I was very happy with the content ... You've included all the important points and you've given a very balanced argument so I'm pleased with that. I think one area you need to work on is organisation.
Jacob:	Yes, my other tutor said the same thing about another piece of writing. My ideas weren't organised logically, she said.
Tutor:	Well, to be fair, I think the order of your ideas here is fine. It's your paragraphing that's the problem. If you look at this page it's difficult to actually see your organisation. Your ideas are in the right order ... but I can't make the organisation out very well because there aren't any paragraphs.
Jacob:	Yes, I see what you mean. Perhaps if I left a line between paragraphs it would make it clearer.
Tutor:	Yes, that's an excellent idea. Have a look at paragraphs in books, magazines, newspapers ... that kind of thing. There's no need to read everything ... Just pay attention to how paragraphs are presented.
Jacob:	Okay. I'll have a look at some of my friends' work as well. They don't seem to have this problem. What about the style of the writing? Is that okay? I've never really learnt how to write formally so I'm always a bit worried about this when I write an essay.
Tutor:	The register is very good Jacob, no problem at all. You've used lots of nice set expressions we'd expect to find in a piece of writing like this and used them very naturally.
Jacob:	That's good. What about my Spanish?
Tutor:	Your basic grammar is okay; you haven't made many mistakes so that's good. What I would suggest is trying to experiment more with advanced sentence structures. Yours tend to be on the short side. That's okay when short sentences are required but sometimes combining two sentences into one can make the essay flow more naturally.
Jacob:	Have you got anything I can use to practise that? Any books or websites I could visit?
Tutor:	Yes, no problem. I'll give you one of our worksheets in a minute. You can take it away and work on it before you write your second draft. Finally, another thing you could think about is using more advanced vocabulary. Again, the words you've used are fine but there are more advanced synonyms that would fit more appropriately in an essay like this.
Jacob:	Well I've bought a thesaurus.
Tutor:	Yes, that's just what you need. As you can see, I've underlined where I think you could make changes but I haven't suggested any synonyms. Use your thesaurus to try and find some alternatives ...

Track 11

TEST 2   LISTENING SECTION 4

Good morning. I'm here today to talk about the placement that's offered to all Psychology students. As you all know this takes place in the third year of the Psychology BSc. I'm here to explain a little about the placement and how the process works. A lot of preparation's involved in getting these placements right so you need to be thinking about this now.

Students taking up a placement year benefit immensely from the experience. To find decent employment in the field of psychology the chances are you'll need to undertake some form of postgraduate training such as one of our Master's courses. These courses invariably demand experience in the field you intend to study so being able to gain this experience during your undergraduate degree is a great advantage.

There's a lot to be gained from joining the scheme. Of course it will help you identify the areas of psychology you may or may not be interested in. And you'll develop transferable skills such as problem solving, team working, communication skills – skills that employers demand and that graduates often lack. Also remember that the placement will offer you networking opportunities to become acquainted with key players in your field.

Many of our students who've completed a placement year take up a position with the same employer after graduation or after successfully completing postgraduate training. In fact many of our students from previous years now hold influential positions in the police, the health service and the private sector as a direct result of their placements.

The placement you choose will depend very much on your own area of interest. Those of you who have a particular interest in research can opt for a placement in a hospital unit here or abroad, working in areas of forensic and clinical psychology. A post here can be very rewarding and allows you to contribute to qualitative and quantitative research data and learn practical research skills you can use in your coursework.

For those who prefer hands-on experience of working with patients there are a wide range of options available. We have links with several charitable and public-sector organisations that support stroke patients and people recovering from serious physical trauma, for example due to motoring or industrial accidents. You will have the opportunity to help them deal with long-term clinical treatment and pain management.

There are several opportunities to work with addiction and rehabilitation units. The kind of experience you'll gain here can be very wide-ranging, for example offering you the chance to observe group therapy and one-to-one counselling sessions for anxiety and anger management classes. Students are encouraged to give their reaction to sessions during regular team meetings, which can often be of benefit to both the student and the organisation.

For those of you interested in the application of psychology in education, we have a number of students who take placements working with children with special educational needs. Students in the past have worked as teaching assistants and contributed to teacher-training workshops.

There's a lot more information about this on the website including case studies written by some of our previous students. These will give you a much wider and richer picture of our placements.

As I said earlier, you should already be giving this some serious thought. Our placement tutor, Greg Smith, will be able to advise you about the organisations we have contacts with and we've worked with in the past. Once you've discussed the opportunities available we ask you to contact the organisation concerned to investigate potential positions and to arrange an interview. Your personal tutor will be able to help you with updating your CV and interview skills.

During the enrolment process you'll have been notified of the need to obtain a CRB check. In cases where you're working with vulnerable people it's a legal requirement that you've had a Criminal Records Bureau check carried out. Without this we won't be able to approve the placement. If you haven't yet arranged this you must notify the placement officer of this during your first meeting. He'll give you the necessary paperwork to make your application. Once you have the certificate, please supply a photocopy to the placement officer.

Track 12

TEST 2   SPEAKING PART 1

In this first part of the exam I'd like to ask you some general questions about yourself.
How long have you been studying English?
Do you enjoy learning another language?
What subjects do / did you enjoy studying at school?
Let's talk about travel. Have you been on holiday recently?
What is your favourite form of transport?
Where would you like to spend a two-week holiday if you could go anywhere?

Track 13

TEST 2   SPEAKING PART 2

I'm going to give you a topic and I'd like you to talk about it for one to two minutes. Before you talk, you have one minute to think about what you are going to say. You can make some notes if you wish. Here is your topic.

Track 14

TEST 2   SPEAKING PART 3

We've been talking about the subject of hobbies and interests. I'd like to discuss this subject with you with some more questions.
What are the benefits of having a hobby or an interest?
Do hobbies change from generation to generation?
In what ways can hobbies or interests bring people together?
Are there any hobbies that can lead to work in the same area?
Has the use of technology in the home led to a decline in hobbies?
Are some people put off taking up some hobbies because of the cost involved?

Track 15

TEST 3   LISTENING SECTION 1

Debbie:	Good afternoon, Hartline Car Insurance. How can I help you?
Liam:	Hello. I'd like to speak to someone about car insurance.
Debbie:	Certainly sir. Can I take your name please?
Liam:	It's Liam. Liam Byrd.

Debbie:	Okay Mr Byrd. Is the policy for you?
Liam:	Yes, I bought the car last night. It's still with the original owner though ... until I get the insurance sorted out. Will I be able to do this over the phone now?
Debbie:	Of course sir. If you have all the information we need to process the application, we should be able to sort it out for you immediately. Could you tell me the make and model Mr Byrd.
Liam:	Yes, it's a Ford Fiesta.
Debbie:	And can I have the registration number please?
Liam:	Yes, it's 3R1 JTW.
Debbie:	Okay ... I can see it's a 2002 model, is that right?
Liam:	That's right, yes.
Debbie:	And what's the current mileage Mr Byrd?
Liam:	Very high unfortunately! 90,000 miles.
Debbie:	Okay. It's obviously very reliable!
Liam:	Hopefully, yes.
Debbie:	And how many miles will you be driving per year?
Liam:	Erm, probably about 6,000 a year.
Debbie:	Okay. And where will the car be kept overnight?
Liam:	Well, I don't have a garage or a driveway so it'll be on the road.
Debbie:	Okay, nearly there. When would you like the policy to be effective from? Immediately I suppose?
Liam:	Yes. I'm hoping to drive the car home this evening so could I be covered from today?
Debbie:	Yes, that's fine. Now, do you want fully comprehensive cover or third party fire and theft?
Liam:	Just third party fire and theft. It's only an old car.
Debbie:	And how much no claims bonus have you got, sir?
Liam:	6 years.
Debbie:	Okay. Have you decided to take up any of our additional cover options? We have legal cover, for a small fee each month. And we can offer a very competitive rate for driver injury insurance or—
Liam:	No, no thanks ... Sorry but I've already looked through what's available on your website and how much it all costs. I've got breakdown cover with another company and the car comes with a spare set of keys so I should be okay there. I'd like to take out the 14-day courtesy car though, and keep my no claims bonus ... so I'll protect that and I'd like to have the windscreen cover as well.
Debbie:	Okay Mr Byrd. So that's third party fire and theft, with additional cover for a courtesy car, protected no claims bonus and windscreen cover. That comes to £425. We'll need to see proof of your no claims bonus. Can you send this to us?
Liam:	Yes, no problem at all.
Debbie:	Okay, I just need your payment details and I can process this for you. So can I have your full name please?
Liam:	It's Liam Byrd. That's B-Y-R-D.
Debbie:	And your address?
Liam:	35 Bottiville Crescent, Birmingham, B56 1ED.
Debbie:	And your date of birth?
Liam:	The 11th of November 1969.
Debbie:	And your telephone number Mr Byrd?
Liam:	0121 677 9887.
Debbie:	How will you be paying Mr Byrd? By credit card?
Liam:	By debit card if that's OK.
Debbie:	Yes, that's fine. What kind of card is it?
Liam:	It's a Visa card.
Debbie:	Okay. Can you give me the full number that runs across the centre of the card?
Liam:	Yes, it's 2337 4006 2005 1551.
Debbie:	And the three-digit security number on the reverse of the card?
Liam:	Okay ... hang on ... Yes, it's 426.
Debbie:	Thank you. Finally, can I just ask how you got to hear about our company?
Liam:	Yes, sure. I found you on the Internet.
Debbie:	Thanks. Okay, your payment has been processed successfully. You're now covered Mr Byrd. Would you like us to send your documents to you or are you happy to download them from the website?

| Liam: | Would you mind posting them to me please? I'd like a paper copy and my printer's not working. |
| Debbie: | No problem Mr Byrd. |

Track 16

TEST 3　　LISTENING SECTION 2

Presenter:	Welcome back to B.U.R.S., your independent student union radio station. We're looking at some of the incredible feats one or two of you have been up to during your summer break. I'm with Katherine who's going to tell us about her successful climb of one of the most iconic mountains in the world – Mont Blanc. Katherine, tell us a little about your achievement.
Katherine:	Well, actually it was the second time I've reached the summit – the first was in 2007, the year before I came to university. People are often surprised to hear how popular the mountain is with climbers – I've read somewhere over 30,000 people attempt the climb each year and around 200 people a day summit during the summer season so it's very crowded up there. Unfortunately it's also potentially very dangerous. In July 2007, the month before I did my first climb, the death toll reached 30, mainly due to bad weather conditions. The sheer number of people can cause falling rocks, which only adds to the danger.
Presenter:	So why did you do the same climb twice? And was it easier the second time around?
Katherine:	In many ways they were totally different experiences. The first time I went as part of an organised group. There were about 20 of us and we took four days to summit. It was much more of a sociable experience compared to the second climb. This year I decided to go solo with just one overnight stop. I felt more confident having already summited once and I wanted to face the challenge of being in control. Actually, you're never really alone – there are other climbers and groups around all the time but I suppose being alone made me feel more intrepid. The first climb was quite difficult as the weather was very changeable and we found ourselves climbing in very cold, windy conditions. We were in a group so we offered each other encouragement but it was still very difficult. The weather this time was wonderful. Plus I also spent a few days beforehand in Chamonix and acclimatised myself more to the altitude – this certainly made it easier. You can achieve the same thing by climbing some of the smaller peaks in the area first but I wanted a more leisurely start. It was fantastic. I thoroughly enjoyed it.
Presenter:	Did your experiences on the first climb help you the second time around? I'm wondering if you have any useful advice for others planning on doing something similar.
Katherine:	Well, because the climb's becoming so popular I think people don't always give it the respect it deserves. And I'm not talking here about the physical condition you need to be in to take on a challenge like this or having the right equipment. That goes without saying. I think what took me by surprise more than anything else was the extreme weather conditions, even in the summer. For those who want to summit in a single day or two the climb will often start early in the morning so you'll need to make sure you're wearing enough layers to protect yourself from the cold and wind. You'll be glad of this when you hit queues and find yourself standing around waiting to move on. Then at the other extreme around midday you must make sure you're fully protected from the sun or you're likely to get very badly burnt. Whether you climb alone, in a group or a with a guide, that will depend on your own experience but however you decide to go it's essential that you take your time and get used to the altitude.
Presenter:	Okay, many thanks for taking the time to come in and tell us all about it!

Track 17

TEST 3　　LISTENING SECTION 3

Adam:	Elaine. Have you seen the exam timetable? They've just put it up on the department noticeboard.
Elaine:	Yeah, I've just come from there. I must be honest, I'd put the thought of exams to the back of my mind. Now the dates are there it all seems a little scary. Have you been revising much?
Adam:	No, not really. We've got a month so I'm going to really get going on it now. Why don't we try and work together?
Elaine:	Yes, let's meet a few times a week. I don't like working on my own; I never seem to be able to focus properly. What about Tuesday and Thursday? Oh no ... I have a late seminar on Tuesday. Monday and Thursday? What about that?

Adam:	Yes, that'll be okay. How do you go about revising? Have you got any tips?
Elaine:	Well, our tutor said we shouldn't start background reading or writing notes until we're clear in our mind what we need to revise. He said start with a revision timetable so we know what to revise and when.
Adam:	That sounds sensible. Then we can use the timetable to work independently ... It'll help us to make sure we're both working on the same subjects ... We can make that the first thing to do in our first session – write up a timetable.
Elaine:	Okay. I reckon the kinds of things we can do on our own in between meetings are things like arranging our materials – lecture and seminars notes, handouts, feedback from our tutors, that kind of thing. If we arrange all these by subject, according to the timetable, it will help us get organised.
Adam:	Good idea. Once we have all the content I suppose we could make notes based on past exam papers. We had a talk about note taking in one of the seminars. They reckon you shouldn't copy word for word. It helps to learn things if you paraphrase main points. And don't just copy loads of facts either ... try to get a feel for the main arguments or theories and match any facts to these.
Elaine:	I also like using mind maps or spidergrams when I make notes. It means you can put down a lot of information but so that it's nicely organised. It also means you can add new notes after. And bullet points ... they really help you focus on main points rather than trying to link them together in sentences.
Adam:	We also need to remember to make a note of where the information comes from – the author, publisher that kind of thing.
Elaine:	That's really important ... otherwise when you're writing the assignment you can never remember where you got a particular quote from.
ADAM:	I know I said earlier about testing each other when we get together but, now I think about it, do you think it would be a better idea to talk through our notes on a particular subject, have a kind of discussion between ourselves? We could use the questions in the past papers to base the discussion on.
Elaine:	Yes, so basically the timetable can be a discussion schedule. Then after each session we could go away and do a timed essay on the subject ... maybe swap and mark each other's essays. That's a good way to learn, I think; critique each other's work.
Adam:	Great idea. So we'll start next Monday with the timetable ...

Track 18

TEST 3   LISTENING SECTION 4

Tutor:	Okay everyone. This week it's the turn of Carol to talk about the progress of her research project. Over to you Carol.
Carol:	Thanks. Yes, hello everybody. I'm going to talk about something called 'shared space' and the research I'm in the process of carrying out into people's attitudes to this as it might affect them in their local community.
	First I'd best explain what shared space is. In essence, shared space is an approach to urban design that attempts to open up main street junctions more to pedestrians by reducing the dominance of motor vehicles. It's a form of planning associated with a Dutch road traffic engineer called Hans Monderman, who believed that by sharing the space available drivers become more aware of pedestrians and drive more carefully. Pedestrians are able to move more freely in this shared space and the number of accidents is reduced.
	Shared space design is usually employed in urban centres where pedestrians congregate, such as in shopping areas. It usually results in demarcations between vehicle traffic and pedestrians being reduced or removed altogether. This includes features like kerbs, road surface markings and traffic signs. There are many examples of shared space in operation abroad and in the UK, for example in Kensington High Street in London and Giles Circus in Ipswich.
	In addition to a decline in accidents, those in favour of shared space also claim additional benefits such as a reduction in unsightly street furniture like signs and metal guard rails, which can be replaced with more trees, planters, seating areas, and other aesthetic improvements determined by local people. With these urban centres easier to get around

in, supporters claim that people are more inclined to shop there and as a consequence the centre can become a more thriving area for local people and businesses. Here are some before-and-after photographs of shared space developments to give you an idea of what it looks like …

Despite all its advantages, shared space is opposed by various interest groups. Some motorist organisations claim that the system means drivers lose important information through the reduction of signage. Those representing blind people argue that removing features such as kerbs, railings and barriers between pavements and roads takes away familiar support and means this group of people cannot negotiate their way as easily as other road users. Cyclist representatives have also criticised some aspects of the scheme arguing that despite benefits some cyclists feel more bullied by motorists and consequently less safe. Supporters of shared space themselves also point out that a lack of experience and understanding of shared space by planners can lead to negative experiences for all these groups.

To carry out my research I approached a local campaigning group in my area who are interested in adopting shared space in our local shopping centre. I discovered that they were very keen to get feedback from local residents on shared space and because of the experience I'd gained in research methods they were keen for me to construct a questionnaire for them. The focus group have a website and an active social media presence and they decided that the questionnaire will be available as an online survey. Hard-copy questionnaires will also be used for face-to-face interviews. There were plans to leave paper questionnaires in the local library but this is still under discussion. Interviews using the questionnaires will be carried out with pedestrians in the area itself. The group don't have the resources to deliver additional questionnaires to the homes of local residents so this option was dropped.

We have met on several occasions to agree on the data the focus group need. I've pointed out that, if they want valid results, the questions must be totally unbiased and not in any way loaded to encourage participants to give the 'preferred' answer. Also we mustn't assume that participants have sufficient information to answer these questions. We're currently looking into how we can best present the concept of shared space during interviews.

I've designed some of the questionnaire and I'd just like to spend a few minutes going through it with you. I'd be grateful for any feedback you have …

Track 19
TEST 3   SPEAKING PART 1

In this first part of the exam I'd like to ask you some general questions about yourself.
Are you currently studying at a school or college?
Why are you taking the IELTS exam?
What do you hope to do after you finish your studies?
Let's talk about food. What kind of food do you like to eat?
Can you cook?
Are there any regional specialities in your country you would recommend to visitors?

Track 20
TEST 3   SPEAKING PART 2

I'm going to give you a topic and I'd like you to talk about it for one to two minutes. Before you talk, you have one minute to think about what you are going to say. You can make some notes if you wish. Here is your topic.

Track 21
TEST 3   SPEAKING PART 3

We've been talking about personal possessions. I'd like to discuss this subject with you with some more questions.
Do our important possessions these days tend to be technology based?
What kind of possessions often have sentimental value?
Does the advertising industry lead to us buying things we don't really need?

How should parents deal with demands from their children for things they have seen advertised?

Are we happier the more things we own?

Is there anything you don't have that you would like to buy?

Track 22

TEST 4   LISTENING SECTION 1

Cashier: Good morning, how can I help you?

Sandra: Yes, hello. I'm going away on holiday next month and I was wondering if you could give me some advice about traveller's cheques.

Cashier: Yes, of course. Where are you off to? Anywhere nice?

Sandra: To France, to Paris for a week.

Cashier: Ooh, lovely! So how many cheques would you like to order?

Sandra: Well, before I do, are they the best option, traveller's cheques?

Cashier: Well, they're certainly safer than taking cash. If they get lost or stolen they can be replaced, usually within 24 hours. It's a good idea to have a small amount of cash though, for snacks and taxis, that sort of thing.

Sandra: Yes, that's what I was thinking. What about my credit card? Are there any charges for using it abroad?

Cashier: No, it's debit cards that get charged for ATM withdrawals not credit cards. And remember anything you buy with the card might be covered by insurance so if something you buy turns out to be faulty or—

Sandra: So it's probably a good idea to do all three then – traveller's cheques, credit card ... some cash, yes?

Cashier: Yes. So how many traveller's cheques would you like?

Sandra: I was thinking about £300. How long will they take to arrive?

Cashier: It depends. If you order before 2.30 between Monday and Thursday you'll have them the next day by 10.00 a.m. in the branch or if we post them to you, you'll have them by 5.00 p.m.

Sandra: Oh, but I was hoping I could order them today?

Cashier: That's okay. Orders taken anytime on Saturday will be here in the branch at 10.00 a.m. on Tuesday or delivered to your home by Tuesday at 1.30.

Sandra: Okay, that's alright. I don't mind waiting until then. Can I order them now?

Cashier: Yes. Have you got an account with us?

Sandra: Yes. Here's my credit card.

Cashier: Thanks. Let's just log in and I can place an order for you. Could you confirm your date of birth?

Sandra: 15th of the 3rd, 1975. What's the commission on the cheques, by the way?

Cashier: It's 1.5 per cent. That's pretty standard, I think you'll find.

Sandra: And what happens if I don't spend them all. Will I be able to bring them back?

Cashier: Yes, no problem. We buy them back and there are no additional charges or conditions of return. So would you like me to go ahead and place an order?

Sandra: Yes. Yes please.

Cashier: Will you be coming in to collect them?

Sandra: I don't think I'll have the chance to come into the branch on Tuesday. Could you send them to my house?

Cashier: No problem. Can I just check your address? 54 Tavistock Road?

Sandra: Yes, that's right.

Cashier: Postcode CB1 3LR?

Sandra: That's it, yes.

Cashier: Okay. So that's £300-worth of traveller's cheques.

Sandra: Yes please.

Cashier: Now what about Euros? Would you like to order any?

Sandra: No. No thank you. I still have some at home from the last holiday. I forgot to change them at the airport when we got back. I was going to give them to our daughter but I'll treat myself for a change I think.

Cashier:	Good idea. So, £300 in traveller's cheques. Could I ask you to sign here to confirm the order? … Thank you. Okay. That's done for you. Your cheques will be with you by 1.30 Tuesday. Someone will need to be at home to sign for them. Will that be okay?
Sandra:	Yes. I'll be at work but my husband will be in. Is that okay?
Cashier:	Yes, that's fine. Have a lovely holiday!

Track 23

TEST 4   LISTENING SECTION 2

Presenter:	Welcome to our monthly podcast for overseas students planning to study in the UK. This month we're looking at how to make your money last longer whilst studying here. And to help us find some bargains I have Jenny Lubeck from the student union. Jenny, students are renowned for being hard up but there are lots of savings to be made, aren't there?
Jenny:	Well, as soon as students start their course at university or college they'll be able to buy their NUS extra card. This will enable them to get a wide range of discounts on essentials like books, clothes and eating out. The card only costs about £12 for one year and for about the same amount you can include an ISIC card. The ISIC is an internationally recognised discount card for full-time students. Discount offerings vary and usually include things like travel, guidebooks, music, eating out – that kind of thing. Students are told all about this when they start their studies but if your listeners want to find out more about these cards before they arrive I've put some details of websites on the podcast page.
Presenter:	Now travel costs can mount up for students, can't they? I know the ISIC card is useful here but are there any other things students should be aware of?
Jenny:	Understandably lots of overseas students like to take the opportunity to travel around the country whilst they're in the UK and for this reason I'd strongly recommend they invest in a Young Person's railcard. To be eligible you need to be between 16 and 25 … mature students over the age of 25 can also apply so long as they're in full-time education. You can buy a one-year or three-year card, and it gives you a third off rail journeys across the UK. The card also gives you access to competitions and things like theatre discounts and holiday offers. At the moment, a one-year card costs £28, and it's £65 for a three-year card.
Presenter:	And what about buses?
Jenny:	Erm, well, as well as the railcard, it's also more than likely the local bus operators will offer discounted bus travel with their own travel cards. These aren't aimed specifically at students but can still save you a lot of money if you use the buses regularly. You can usually get these cards for a week, a month, a term or a whole year with bigger savings the longer the period. Another advantage of these cards is that as well as making it cheaper to commute to and from university you'll also find them very handy free transport whenever you need to do some shopping or visit friends in your area.
Presenter:	Are there any cultural things that students coming to the UK might not be aware of that can save them money?
Jenny:	Some overseas students are surprised by the amount of recycling that goes on in the UK and how much money can be saved in the process. They'll be a roaring trade in used coursebooks in the student union on campus. Lots of students who were on the same course as you the year before will be selling their books at the end of their course – they'll be a lot cheaper than buying them new. Off campus you'll find lots of charity shops in your local town centre with a good selection of novels and you'll often get some really nice clothes, CDs and DVDs that people have donated and all at very cheap prices. Of course, shopping in this way means you're contributing to a worthwhile cause as well. And check your local paper frequently for car boot sales. Car boot sales are a very British style of market where private individuals come together to sell home and garden goods. In fact they're a great way of recycling some of your own unwanted stuff and can help you make some money in the process. Finally there are websites and mailing lists where local people offer up items they no longer want, for free – as long as you agree to collect them …

Track 24

TEST 4   LISTENING SECTION 3

Tutor: Hi everyone. I know you have lots of questions about the college intranet – my inbox is full of messages! I thought it would be quicker and more useful to come in and talk to you rather than respond to all the messages. I'm happy to answer or try and answer any questions you have – about how to use it, when we'll be making things available online ... I'm the ICT champion for the department so hopefully I'll be able to help. Yes Mark – fire away.

Mark: Can you tell us when the assignments are going to be put online?

Tutor: If you're talking about your second assignment, that should be on already. I uploaded it last Monday .... Wait a minute – let me check the schedule ... Here we are ... No, tell a lie – it was the following day, the 14ᵗʰ, Tuesday 14ᵗʰ October. Have you logged into the intranet yet?

Mark: No. If the assignment's there I'll download it after we've finished. Are you putting all the assignments up?

Tutor: Yes. I've been waiting for your subject tutors to email them to me. As soon as I have them all I'll put them online. There's a deadline of 24ᵗʰ November ... all course assignments need to be online by then. That's college policy for all staff so they'll be there then for sure.

Mark: Will there be anything else? Timetables, trip information ... that kind of thing? Only there wasn't much online for our course last term.

Tutor: I know. But we're making more of an effort this time. We'll be releasing your marks for the first assignment soon – that'll be 17ᵗʰ November. You'll find them in your 'My Grades' area. Again, the timetables are already there, Mark. You need to log in! I made these available at the beginning of term in September. According to the schedule here, the booking forms for those who want to go on the Belgium trip will be available next week on 29ᵗʰ October, so don't forget to check then. You need to get these back to us quickly if you want to go ... the trip's coming up soon, isn't it? Let's see ... yes 19ᵗʰ November. Now, remember there are lots of learning materials on the intranet as well ... quizzes, weblinks ...

Claire: Sir, wouldn't it be easier if we were just given the documents ... so we don't have to go online to get them?

Tutor: I know it seems a little frustrating Claire but we're doing it this way for a good reason. We're trying to cut down drastically on the amount of paper we get through. I'm afraid that students are always losing documents we give out in class so we've decided to stop doing this. You have a limited printing allowance, which means you'll probably be more careful with any documents you have to print off. Besides, it means you'll always know where the information is when you need it. If you're at home and you forget an important date or need a document urgently you can always log in to the intranet and get it.

Claire: You said something about quizzes sir ...

Tutor: Yes, we've had permission from the exam board to put some of their past papers online in an interactive form. That means you'll be able to get answers immediately with some feedback .... They'll make a nice change from using the paper copies. Most of them are already online and I'll be putting the rest on over the next couple of weeks. As I said, these are authentic past papers so you'll get a really clear idea of your progress. Just to let you know, the technology tracks your scores so your tutors will be able to tell who's having problems and what areas of the syllabus you might need help with, so it's definitely worth spending some time doing them.

Track 25

TEST 4   LISTENING SECTION 4

Good afternoon. Today we're continuing our investigation into obesity. We've looked at several factors causing obesity including lack of exercise and a general sedentary lifestyle and the role the media plays in promoting the consumption of high-calorific food. In the coming weeks we'll go on to examine serious eating disorders such as anorexia nervosa and bulimia nervosa.

The decline in formal eating times within the family and the subsequent increase in the degree of 'snacking' that takes place have had a significant effect on obesity. Today we're going to turn our attention to an example of this, what has been termed 'emotional hunger' or 'emotional eating', as opposed to the consumption of food to satisfy a physical need. Studies have uncovered how our emotional state can lead to us eating more than we physically need. It was originally believed that negative emotions brought on through depression or anxiety were the main cause of this. But it is now acknowledged that positive emotions can have a similar effect on our eating habits.

Not everyone is susceptible to emotional eating, and even those who do suffer have highly individual symptoms. However, there are common themes. It seems that people who are already overweight are more susceptible to emotional eating when suffering negative emotions than those who are underweight. Equally, excessive eating of this kind can happen during or after happy events, when larger meals than normal tend to be eaten.

So what are the signs that someone is eating to satisfy an emotional stimulus? Well, there are several differences between emotional and physical hunger.

Those experiencing emotional hunger will feel the urge to eat all of a sudden. This compares to the gradual sensation of hunger that occurs with a physical stimulus.

Interestingly, and I'm sure many of you will recognise this, when you're eating to satisfy an emotional need for food, the craving will often be for a specific item like a pizza or something sweet like ice cream. In this kind of situation, nothing else will really satisfy the craving. When the urge to eat is driven by a physical need, you're far less bothered about what you eat.

Emotional hunger makes the individual feel the craving must be satisfied immediately by whatever the specific kind of food is. I'm sure we've all experienced that feeling: 'I must have some chocolate … now!' In contrast, the need to satisfy sensations of physical hunger seems less urgent.

Emotional eaters will carry on eating even when they're full. A person eating to satisfy a physical hunger will be more likely to stop.

Finally and probably not surprisingly, feelings of guilt often follow emotional eating but not when eating normally.

This has serious consequences for those working with patients suffering with obesity. One way to deal with this is to educate sufferers into understanding the different symptoms of physical and emotional hunger and to try to help them identify the pressure points during a typical day when daily stresses occur. Being conscious of one's eating habits is the first step in dealing with the problem.

Track 26
TEST 4   SPEAKING PART 1

In this first part of the exam I'd like to ask you some general questions about yourself.
Do you come from a large family?
Have you got a favourite relative?
How often do you get to see your wider family?
Let's talk about work. Do you have any definite career ambitions?
How easy is it to find work where you live?
If you could do any job you liked, what would it be?

Track 27
TEST 4   SPEAKING PART 2

I'm going to give you a topic and I'd like you to talk about it for one to two minutes. Before you talk, you have one minute to think about what you are going to say. You can make some notes if you wish. Here is your topic.

Track 28
TEST 4   SPEAKING PART 3

We've been talking about the subject of places we would like to live. I'd like to discuss this subject with you with some more questions.
What is it about a place that makes it feel like home?
Is it important to live close to your relatives?
What are the main reasons people decide to move to another location?
What are the kind of things a family looks for when deciding where to live?
Why do some people choose to leave their own country and live abroad?
Do you think people who want to move to another country have a realistic idea of what it will be like?

Sample answer sheet: Listening

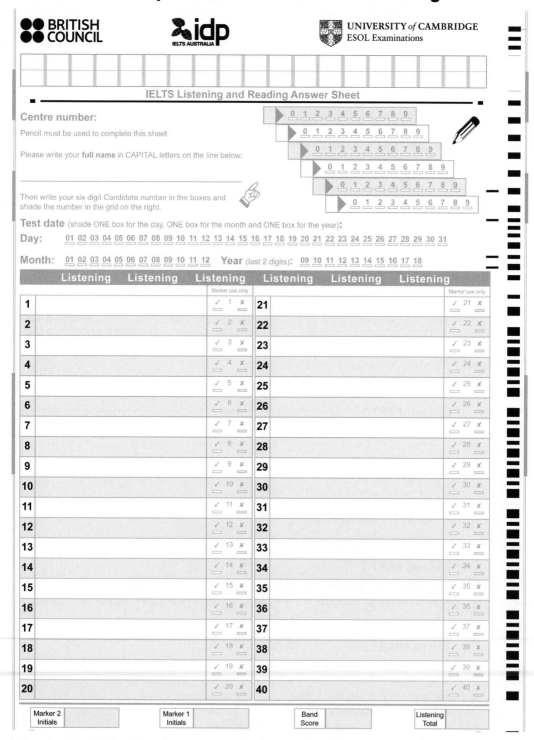

Sample answer sheet: Reading

Please write your **full name** in CAPITAL letters on the line below:

_____

Please write your Candidate number on the line below:

_____

Please write your three digit language code
in the boxes and shade the numbers in the
grid on the right.

0 1 2 3 4 5 6 7 8 9
0 1 2 3 4 5 6 7 8 9
0 1 2 3 4 5 6 7 8 9

Are you: Female? ▭   Male? ▭

| Reading | Reading | Reading | Reading | Reading | Reading |

Module taken (shade one box):   Academic ▭   General Training ▭

	Marker use only			Marker use only
1	✓ 1 ✗	**21**		✓ 21 ✗
2	✓ 2 ✗	**22**		✓ 22 ✗
3	✓ 3 ✗	**23**		✓ 23 ✗
4	✓ 4 ✗	**24**		✓ 24 ✗
5	✓ 5 ✗	**25**		✓ 25 ✗
6	✓ 6 ✗	**26**		✓ 26 ✗
7	✓ 7 ✗	**27**		✓ 27 ✗
8	✓ 8 ✗	**28**		✓ 28 ✗
9	✓ 9 ✗	**29**		✓ 29 ✗
10	✓ 10 ✗	**30**		✓ 30 ✗
11	✓ 11 ✗	**31**		✓ 31 ✗
12	✓ 12 ✗	**32**		✓ 32 ✗
13	✓ 13 ✗	**33**		✓ 33 ✗
14	✓ 14 ✗	**34**		✓ 34 ✗
15	✓ 15 ✗	**35**		✓ 35 ✗
16	✓ 16 ✗	**36**		✓ 36 ✗
17	✓ 17 ✗	**37**		✓ 37 ✗
18	✓ 18 ✗	**38**		✓ 38 ✗
19	✓ 19 ✗	**39**		✓ 39 ✗
20	✓ 20 ✗	**40**		✓ 40 ✗

| Marker 2 Initials | | Marker 1 Initials | | Band Score | | Reading Total | |

© **Cambridge ESOL 2012**

Sample answer sheet: Writing

This is just one page of a longer booklet.

INTERNATIONAL ENGLISH LANGUAGE TESTING SYSTEM

WRITING ANSWER BOOKLET

Candidate Name: ....   Candidate Number: ....

Centre Number: ....   Date: ....

Module: ACADEMIC ☐   GENERAL TRAINING ☐   (Tick as appropriate)

TASK 1

_____

_____

_____

_____

_____

_____

_____

_____

_____

_____

_____

EXAMINER'S USE ONLY

EXAMINER 2 NUMBER: ....

CANDIDATE NUMBER: ....   EXAMINER 1 NUMBER: ....

© Cambridge ESOL 2012

Listening and Reading answer key

TEST 1 Listening

Section 1 Questions 1–10
1 623	6 C
2 Tomas	7 B
3 17624	8 A
4 International	9 B
5 August	10 A

Section 2 Questions 11–20
11,12&13 IN ANY ORDER	History of Jazz
A	17 B
E	18 C
F	19&20 IN EITHER ORDER
14,15&16 IN ANY ORDER	B
classical music show	C
international folk music	

Section 3 Questions 21–30
21 Wednesday	25 (the) seminar room
22 women in education	26 C
23 half an hour /	27 B
30 minutes	28 A
24 projector and laptop /	29 B
computer	30 A

Section 4 Questions 31–40
31 C	37 B
32 A	38,39&40 IN ANY ORDER
33 B	B
34 C	D
35 A	E
36 C	

TEST 1 Reading

Passage 1 Questions 1–12
1 FALSE	7 B
2 FALSE	8 competition
3 TRUE	9 extinction of
4 E	10 land
5 D	11 not known
6 G	12 B

Passage 2 Questions 13–29
13 D	16 B
14 C	17 F
15 A	18 E

19 D	25 risk
20 D	26 accident
21 C	27 ambitions
22 D	28 political
23 B	29 (space) race
24 business model	

Passage 3 Questions 30–40
30 vii	36 B
31 ii	37 C
32 i	38 C
33 v	39 A
34 iv	40 B
35 C	

TEST 2 Listening

Section 1 Questions 1–10
1 B	6 police station
2 B	7 38864
3 C	8 A
4 60	9 bookshop
5 14	10 (library) café

Section 2 Questions 11–20
11 C	17 set / pair of
12 A	headphones
13 C	18 14 days / 2 weeks
14 B	19 5.30
15 B	20 booked / reserved
16 C	

Section 3 Questions 21–30
21 B	26 sentence structures
22 A	27 short
23 B	28 A
24 A	29 C
25 set expressions	30 F

Section 4 Questions 31–40
31 B	38 to arrange
32 A	39 a legal requirement
33 B	40 the placement officer /
34 A	Greg Smith
35,36&37 IN ANY ORDER	
B	
D	
E	

TEST 2 Reading

Passage 1 Questions 1–12

1 iii	7 FALSE
2 iv	8 TRUE
3 vii	9 TRUE
4 viii	10 NOT GIVEN
5 ii	11 FALSE
6 TRUE	12 C

Passage 2 Questions 13–29

13 mathematical	22 TRUE
14 damage	23 D
15 from birth	24 A
16 learning	25 B
17 TRUE	26 C
18 FALSE	27 C
19 FALSE	28 D
20 NOT GIVEN	29 A
21 TRUE	

Passage 3 Questions 30–40

30 B	36 D
31 E	37 C
32 D	38 C
33 A	39 D
34 C	40 C
35 A	

TEST 3 Listening

Section 1 Questions 1–10

1 JTW	D
2 90,000	G
3 on the road	8 B56 1ED
4 fire and theft	9 debit card / Visa card
5,6&7 IN ANY ORDER	10 on the Internet
B	

Section 2 Questions 11–20

11 30,000	16 A
12 200	17 A
13 bad weather	18,19&20 IN ANY ORDER
(conditions)	C
14 falling rocks	D
15 C	F

Section 3 Questions 21–30

21 Monday and Thursday	26 (nicely) organised
22 (a) (revision) timetable	27 key points
23 arranging (their)	28 author and publisher
materials	29 C
24 word for word	30 B
25 facts	

Section 4 Questions 31–40

31 C	37 B
32 A	38&39 IN EITHER ORDER
33 B	A
34 D	C
35 A	40 A
36 C	

TEST 3 Reading

Passage 1 Questions 1–12

1 contains	7 F
2 water fell	8 E
3 two metres	9 D
4 basement	10 A
5 B	11 G
6 H	12 C

Passage 2 Questions 13–27

13 FALSE	21 D
14 NOT GIVEN	22 C
15 TRUE	23 reduced
16 TRUE	24 endurance
17 NOT GIVEN	25 maintaining
18 B	26 burnt
19 D	27 production
20 D	

Passage 3 Questions 28–40

28 ix	33 C	38 A
29 iv	34 A	39 B
30 vi	35 B	40 B
31 v	36 A	
32 i	37 A	

TEST 4 Listening

Section 1 Questions 1–10

1 24 hours	6 anytime
2 snacks and taxis	7 1.30
3 debit card	8 A
4 2.30	9 A
5 5(.00)	10 B

Section 2 Questions 11–20

11 C	18 C
12 full time	19 B
13 ⅓ off / one third off	20 A
14 holiday offers	
15 £65	
16&17 IN EITHER ORDER	
B	
C	

Section 3 Questions 21–30

21 (the) second assignment	26 A
	27 B
22 24th November	28 A
23 17th November	29 C
24 (the) booking forms	30 C
25 19th November	

Section 4 Questions 31–40

31 formal eating	36 P
32 emotional state	37 E
33 positive and negative	38 P
34 overweight	39 P
35 E	40 C

TEST 4   Reading

Passage 1 Questions 1–16

1 FALSE	9 H
2 TRUE	10 D
3 TRUE	11 F
4 NOT GIVEN	12 A
5 FALSE	13 B
6 TRUE	14 E
7 FALSE	15 C
8 TRUE	16 G

Passage 2 Questions 17–27

17 C	21 F	25 E
18 D	22 B	26 B
19 A	23 F	27 C
20 E	24 G	

Passage 3 Questions 28–40

28 (tropical) storms	35 (massive) skyscrapers
29 flooding	36 C
30 coastal erosion	37 C
31 29 cm	38 B
32 lake bed	39 D
33 water (reserve)	40 B
34 mouth	

GENERAL TRAINING TEST A
Reading

Section 1 Questions 1–13

1 B	6 D
2 C	7 C
3 A	8 TRUE
4 B	9 FALSE
5 A	10 TRUE

11 FALSE	13 FALSE
12 NOT GIVEN	

Section 2 Questions 14–26

14 FALSE	21 i
15 FALSE	22 iii
16 TRUE	23 vii
17 FALSE	24 ix
18 NOT GIVEN	25 ii
19 TRUE	26 v
20 FALSE	

Section 3 Questions 27–40

27 i	32 v	37 A
28 viii	33 vi	38 B
29 iii	34 vii	39 C
30 iv	35 B	40 B
31 ix	36 D	

GENERAL TRAINING TEST B
Reading

Section 1 Questions 1–13

1 FALSE	£100
2 TRUE	£150
3 NOT GIVEN	10 favourite panto(mime) characters
4 FALSE	
5 TRUE	11 the (general) public
6 FALSE	12 direct debit
7 paying for / affording / financing	13 extra / more / additional
8&9 IN EITHER ORDER	

Section 2 Questions 14–26

14,15&16 IN ANY ORDER	20 D
A	21 i
C	22 vii
E	23 ix
17 C	24 v
18 C	25 viii
19 A	26 iii

Section 3 Questions 27–40

27 FALSE	35 cultural hero
28 FALSE	36 (historical) patterns
29 TRUE	37 B
30 NOT GIVEN	38 A
31 TRUE	39 C
32 TRUE	40 A
33 (wood) carvers	
34 (the) (village) craftsmen	

Writing: model answers

Test 1 Task 1

The table shows the changes in household types in Great Britain at 10-year intervals from 1971 to 2001 and again in 2007.

There has been a steady increase in households without children during this period. One-person households doubled from 6% in 1971 to 12% in 2007, whilst the percentage of couples with no children rose from 19% in 1971 to 23% in 1991 and to 25% in 2001. However, this figure levelled out in 2007. Even bigger changes have occurred when it comes to couples with dependent children. This category shrank from 52% in 1971 to 36% in 2007. In contrast, the percentage of lone parents trebled over the same period, rising from 4% in 1971 to 12% in 2007. The percentage of families with non-dependent children has remained more stable: 10% in 1971, rising only 1% over the next 20 years before falling to 9% in 2001.

In conclusion, the table shows definite patterns of change within the British family over the past 40 years, in particular the decline in the traditional model of one couple with dependent children.

Test 1 Task 2

It is certainly true that, taken as a whole, the tourist industry generates huge sums of money for the global economy. Moreover, the local economies of resorts around the world are often dependent on the influx of visitors every year, particularly with regards to local employment. My own country welcomes huge numbers of overseas visitors annually, and a significant number of people are employed in the hotel industry as a result.

However, it is sometimes argued that a significant share of the money generated goes not to the local economy but to the multinational companies that supply the transport to and from the destination and the hotel chains and shopping outlets that offer hospitality to these visitors. Critics also point to the negative effect of tourism on local culture. The way of life of indigenous people can often be undermined by developments that prioritize the needs of the visiting tourist. Finally there is the widespread effect of tourism on the environment. The arrival of huge numbers of tourists can be a drain on scarce local resources such as water, food and energy. Pollution, both through an increase in passenger flights and the local waste generated at the tourist destination, is another environmental concern. Then of course there is the physical impact on the landscape and ecosystem of large-scale construction.

Nonetheless, it is probably wrong to claim the problems are being ignored. The growth in sustainable tourism is evidence that people are aware of the impact they are having and are keen to contribute to a more positive experience, for themselves as well as for local people and the environment. As the market tends to determine how things develop, we can only hope that the demand for this form of responsible tourism continues to grow.

Test 2 Task 1

The bar charts compare the growth in holders of full car driving licences by age and sex between 1975 and 2006.

By 2006 the percentage of male licence holders peaked at just over 90% at ages 50–59 and over 85% for all ages from 30 to 69. Compared to 1975/76, there was a slight decrease in the percentage for males at ages 21–29, whilst the increases in certain other categories were slight: about 1% for the 17–20 and 30–39 categories, for example. Increases were more significant for older age groups, with the 70+ category doubling.

For females, in comparison, the increase over the 30-year period has been far greater amongst all age groups. For example, while just over 80% of males in the 40–49 category held a driving licence in 1975/76, rising to almost 90% in 2006, the percentage of women in the same category more than doubled, from just below 40% in 1975/76 to almost 80% in 2006. The percentage of women licence holders between 60 and 69 has more than trebled to over 60%, and the figure for the over-70s has increased by approximately six times to 30%.

These figures appear to show that the numbers of female and elderly licence holders have increased in line with their greater economic independence over this period.

Test 2 Task 2

The emergence of new technology over recent years has brought a wealth of learning opportunities into the home or workplace. Powerful computers aligned with the Internet mean that students can access websites and podcasts, and enter into even live communication with other students from around the world through video conferencing technologies. This, along with the explosion of freely available learning content should mean that students choosing to study English on a self-study basis have all the opportunities they need to progress. However, is this really the case?

One of the benefits of studying formally as part of a small group or class is that the school will have a system in place to manage the learning process. Each teacher will be required to follow a syllabus and will try to make sure that all the necessary content and skills are covered, and in the best order to facilitate learning. However, students working independently will often not have access to this expertise and will be left alone to organise their own learning. This might have serious consequences for students working to a tight deadline, for example, with an intention of passing an exam. Will they spend too long on practice tests and not enough time on learning exam strategies? Will they have an appreciation of how best to develop their English skills generally? Knowing what is required and when to learn it is probably something that the teacher has a better awareness of than the student.

To sum up, a great deal can be learnt independently and the main requirements for success are always motivation and hard work, qualities that the self-study student often possesses in abundance. However, I do feel that an experienced teacher can offer students a structure to their studies that will mean they spend their time more efficiently and effectively than when they study on their own.

Test 3 Task 1

This bar chart examines people's perceptions of being a victim of crime compared to the actual risks involved over two periods, 2009/10 and 2010/11.

For all three crime types, the fear of being a victim is far greater than the likelihood of becoming one. The highest figures relate to car crime and show that, during both periods, around 4% of the population were victims, with a very slight decline in 2010/11. In contrast, the fear of being a victim of this crime was recorded at about 21% in 2009/10, falling to approximately 17% in 2010/11. The perceived threat from the other two crimes, burglary and violent crime, were roughly the same over both periods: just over 15% in 2009/10, falling to about 13% in 2010/11. However, in both cases the real risk was far lower at between 2.5 and 3% for burglary and violent crime.

However, figures for the perception of the threat of crime have shown a marked fall in all three cases over the two-year period, falling by 2–4%. This may show that people are gaining a more realistic view.

Test 3 Task 2

Despite vast improvements in the position of women in society over the past half a century, we are still some way from achieving gender equality. Women who were around in the 1960s or 70s are surely struck by the significant improvements in the lives of women in the twenty-first century. However, they must also find familiar evidence of major inequalities.

Women in the West have made great headway in the fields of education and employment over the past 50 years. Women often out-achieve men educationally, and are entering occupations and professions that would once have been out of bounds. They often attain high positions within organisations and in some countries have even risen to the top of political power. Successful female entrepreneurs often appear in the media, perhaps leading some to conclude that women are now competing on a level playing field.

However, if we look more carefully we soon see that significant problems still exist. Women suffer inequalities in employment and have yet to achieve pay that is equal to that of men doing similar work. In addition, women are generally still responsible for child rearing and housework, creating a 'double burden' for those who work full time. Moreover, despite the success of some women in gaining positions of influence, these are the exception rather than the rule, and women are still outnumbered in positions of power. Finally, the dominant view of women in the media is not one of successful entrepreneur or public figure but of 'sex object', a situation that has barely changed over the past 50 years.

Consequently, despite some very real gains, I feel that women of the previous century must see much that they recognise when observing the position of women in society today.

Test 4 Task 1

The two tables together give a snapshot of the reasons people choose to stop smoking and when they intend to give up.

The main reason smokers give for stopping is for general health (71%), with financial considerations (31%) and the risk of smoking-related diseases (25%) being the next two most popular reasons. One fact to highlight from this table is that almost twice the percentage of heavy smokers cite present health problems as the reason compared to light smokers.

According to the second table, the majority of smokers questioned (71%) intended to give up, with light smokers more inclined to stop (79%) than heavy smokers (60%). 35% of smokers said they were planning to give up within the next six months and only 12% said they were prepared to try within the following month. Although only 29% of smokers on average were unwilling to give up, heavy smokers were almost twice as unwilling to try as light smokers, which perhaps reflects the level of addiction in the former group.

Test 4 Task 2

Taking a year off from education between finishing school or college and going to university is a popular choice for young people. Generally speaking, doing so does not negatively affect their educational progress and, depending on how the time out is spent, can lead to invaluable experiences before moving into higher education.

For example, one of the most popular reasons for taking an educational break is to travel. This offers the student an opportunity to come face to face with different cultures, to meet new people and in some cases will open up new opportunities abroad that may not have arisen at home. Alternatively, some choose to spend the period in work. This could be in the voluntary sector, on conservation projects or in paid work, for example as an au pair or even teaching English overseas. The skills and experiences gained can be extremely useful at university and when looking for employment afterwards.

However, taking a year out can have its drawbacks. To begin with, it means spending a year away from studying. Returning to it and regaining the discipline and focus required can be difficult for some. Additionally, the break can lead to carefully laid plans being blown off course if attractive offers of work or further travel become available.

Nevertheless, it is probably true to say that the benefits far outweigh the drawbacks. The time spent away from education gives the person the chance to reflect on life and any important decisions before signing up for a lengthy and expensive period of study. What is more, the experiences gained during the year out will build self confidence and maturity, qualities that will prove invaluable in the years to come.

General Training Test A Task 1

Dear Sir or Madam,

I am writing in reference to the advertisement you placed in the Stansfield Observer for waiters and waitresses.

I am 22 years old and I am a part-time student at college. I have held several positions in catering outlets during my studies and, as the restaurant where I am currently employed is due to close, I am keen to find another position as soon as possible.

I have completed and passed the advanced certificate in food hygiene and am therefore familiar with the requirements of working in the catering industry. In my current job, in addition to working as a waiter, I am also responsible for counting up takings at the end of the day.

I am very reliable and trustworthy, have a friendly, outgoing personality and enjoy dealing with the public. I would be very grateful if I could be considered for the position. My employer is happy to supply a reference and I am available for interview at any time except Tuesday and Thursday afternoons when I attend college.

Please do not hesitate to contact me should you have any questions.

I look forward to hearing from you.

Yours faithfully,

General Training Test A Task 2

The growth in supermarkets is a direct result of the convenience they offer consumers. Being able to park the car easily, and to put all your shopping in a trolley that can then be pushed to the car and home in an hour or two makes life a lot easier for people who are short of time. Furthermore, thanks to the competition between supermarket chains and the power they have in negotiating the lowest prices from their suppliers, the cost of goods is kept to a minimum.

Such convenience has a consequence, however, as small, independent shops find it very difficult to compete with these megastores. To begin with, parking in inner-city shopping centres can be very difficult, which makes if hard to attract customers to the area. And for those who are fortunate enough to find parking, the thought of carrying bags from one shop to the next in order to do the weekly shop is seen as rather cumbersome. In addition, these small shopkeepers are unable to compete on price with the supermarkets as they do not buy in such bulk. The result is that many high streets are littered with empty, boarded-up shops, increasing the likelihood of crime and vandalism.

Therefore, I would argue that supermarkets do have a negative impact on local communities. However, due to the convenience they offer it is unlikely that they are ever going to disappear. Consequently, in order to stay in business, small shops will have to use the advantage they have of being more personal, and offer a friendly, niche service.

General Training Test B Task 1

Dear Sir,

I am writing with regards to the complaint I made to you on 21st November concerning the stay I had at your hotel the previous night.

You may remember that on the day in question, you had a serious problem with your central heating system and that there was a great deal of noise, which started as early as 4 o'clock in the morning. Not surprisingly, this resulted in a very poor night's sleep for my wife and me. We complained about this to you when we checked out. You agreed that we had a cause to complain and assured me that you would be contacting us regarding compensation.

It has now been three weeks since that conversation and we have yet to hear from you. Could you please confirm that this issue is being dealt with? I would also be grateful if you could let me know when we can expect to be told the amount of compensation we will be receiving.

I look forward to hearing from you very soon.

Yours faithfully,

General Training Test B Task 2

Young people today are often reprimanded by their parents for living a passive lifestyle. In my country, for example, young children in particular are criticized for spending too long interacting with technology rather than being outside playing sports, climbing trees and doing all the other activities their parents claim they enjoyed as children. To what extent are these comments deserved?

On the surface, they would appear justified. There is a whole industry that encourages children to lead a sedentary lifestyle, for example sitting in front of a PC or games console. Dedicated satellite or cable TV channels for young people offer the chance to sit idly watching one programme after the next, often repeats of something that was on the day or week before.

However, it can also be argued that young people are adapting to the society they live in, a completely different place to the world their parents grew up in. Firstly, the roads today are far busier than they were in the past, which makes it very difficult for children to play outside. Secondly, children are often restricted from being outside by parents who have become overly concerned about dangers they imagine exist outside their four walls. Finally, it has to be said that many parents use the technology they complain about as a way of keeping young children occupied.

I think children today are less active and that it is something we should be concerned about. However, it is wrong to put the blame on technology. Children should be encouraged more to take up sports at school and parents should be more willing to support their children in exploring the outside world.

Speaking: model answers

Test 1 Part 1

In this first part of the exam I'd like to ask you some general questions about yourself. Where do you live?
I live in Portugal in a place called Figueira da Foz ... It's not far from Coimbra, ... which is a famous university city.

Is it a nice place to live?
Yes, very nice ... It's on the coast ... It's a tourist resort so there are lots of things to do there ... especially in the summer.

Do you have many tourists visit your area?
Yes ... it gets very busy in the summer ... with Portuguese and overseas visitors ... but I like seeing the place come to life when all these people arrive.

Let's talk about your interests. Do you have any hobbies or interests?
I really enjoy swimming and surfing ... We host surfing competitions in Figueira and I became interested in it when I was younger ... My father used to take me and I really enjoyed it.

Have you seen a good film recently?
I haven't been to the cinema for quite a long time actually ... I study most evenings and it's not something I often do ... go to the cinema that is ... I watch films on TV occasionally but I can't bring to mind any particular ones at the moment.

How often do you go out with friends?
Most weekends ... There are lots of bars and cafes near where I live and we also spend time hanging out on the beach after college when it's warm enough.

Test 1 Part 2

I'm going to give you a topic and I'd like you to talk about it for one to two minutes. Before you talk, you have one minute to think about what you are going to say. You can make some notes if you wish. Here is your topic.
...
A well-known person I admire ... That's a tricky question ... I can't say I've ever given it much thought ... I suppose an obvious person is someone like Nelson Mandela ... the ex-President of South Africa ... Most people who have admirable qualities also seem to have a darker side ... Maybe they're very ambitious or change their attitude or behaviour and you no longer find them quite so admirable ... That's often the case with politicians ... but someone like Mandela ... he spent all that time in prison because of his beliefs ... and he stayed true to what he believed in throughout all those years in prison .... He won over the hearts of the people of South Africa, whatever race they were ... I can remember the day he was released from prison and also the time South Africa hosted the World Cup ... Mandela made a speech and it seemed to capture the hopes of the whole nation. ... I think his reputation is based on values like courage, respect for others ... being a great statesman ... Whenever someone important – another politician for example – was pictured with him they always seemed to be insignificant in comparison ... I suppose I admire him for the same reason I admire anyone who stands up for their principles no matter what life throws at them ... and particularly with Mandela – he stood up for something that everyone should hold dear ... equality and freedom from oppression and prejudice ... Yes ... Nelson Mandela .... that's who I admire.

Test 1 Part 3

We've been talking about the subject of fame and celebrity. I'd like to discuss this subject with you with some more questions. Do you think being famous is a worthwhile ambition?
No ... not simply to be famous ... That's the problem with the people on reality TV shows – they sometimes say they want to be recognised ... to be famous ... I think the ambition should be for what you do ... not just to be well known.

Who are currently some of the biggest celebrities in your country?
Well ... I suppose our politicians are well known ... to Portuguese people anyway ... and then of course there's José Mourinho and Cristiano Ronaldo ... They're very well known ... if you like football that is ... I think I'm more proud of people like Fernando Pessoa ... our great poet – not a celebrity, I know, but very famous around the world.

Do celebrities deserve the attention they get from the media?
I think the media needs celebrities and celebrities need the media – they live off each other ... Most of them don't deserve all the attention but news about attractive celebrities sells newspapers and magazines so I suppose it's just natural.

Does fame generally bring happiness to the individual?
I don't know, really ... It's a little like the earlier question ... whether fame itself is worth aiming for ... If you are happy doing whatever it is that makes you famous, then perhaps yes ... but sometimes fame can interfere with your life.

Do well-known people suffer a loss of personal privacy?
Definitely ... yes ... As I just said ... fame can interfere with your day-to-day life ... Celebrities can be hounded by the paparazzi as soon as they leave their homes and stories can appear about them in the media that may or may not be true ... It's not something I'd like.

If you could be famous for doing something, what would it be?
I'd like to be well known for being a great surfer ... maybe like Gabriel Medina or Adriano De Souza – they're well-known surfers ... probably not famous to people who don't know about surfing but that wouldn't matter to me.

Track 30

Test 2 Part 1

In this first part of the exam I'd like to ask you some general questions about yourself. How long have you been studying English?
A long time ... I studied it at school for several years and then carried on when I went to college ... probably about six years now.

Do you enjoy learning another language?
I love it ... It's not learning the grammar and vocabulary that I enjoy – that's the hard part – but once you reach a level where you can listen to the radio or watch films in that language or read books in that language ... that's what I find satisfying.

What subjects did you find interesting at school?
Well ... as I said ... languages were fun ... once I reached a higher level ... but I suppose my favourite subject was art ... I still attend art classes and love drawing and painting ... It's something you can get totally engrossed in ... It's very relaxing.

Let's talk about travel. Have you been on holiday recently?
Not this year no ... but last year I went to France with my family, to Paris ... We spent a week there ... seeing all the sights and visiting some of the other important towns and cities ... Bordeaux ... Nice ... It was really good fun and the weather was excellent.

What is your favourite form of transport?
That's easy – the train ... I love travelling on my own on trains ... It's a great way to see the landscape you're moving through and you also get the chance to meet local people who share your carriage ... If I had the chance I'd spend a year travelling around the world by train.

Where would you like to spend a two-week holiday if you could go anywhere?
I suppose China ... although two weeks wouldn't be long enough to visit all the places I'd like to see ... It would be fantastic to travel on some of the main train routes between the major cities – second class of course – so I could share the journey with ordinary local people.

Test 2 Part 2

I'm going to give you a topic and I'd like you to talk about it for one to two minutes. Before you talk, you have one minute to think about what you are going to say. You can make some notes if you wish. Here is your topic.
...
I went on a caravan holiday with my parents once ... I was probably about nine or 10 at the time ... and the caravan park had a restaurant called 'The Matchbox Bar' ... The walls of the restaurant were absolutely covered with matchboxes from all over the world ... I can still picture it now ... it really was quite a sight ... Anyway it certainly grabbed my imagination ... I had friends who collected stamps ... but matchboxes ... I'd never heard of that ... so as soon as we got back home I started collecting them myself ... I used to ride around the streets where I lived looking for matchboxes people had thrown away ... You'd be surprised how many different ones you could find in one journey ... And relatives used to bring me some back from their holidays abroad ... That was always really exciting ... You used to be able to get packs or sets of them ... I remember the matches were waxy ... from Spain I think ... the boxes all with a different image on the front ... The collection just grew and grew ... I remember having over 3,000 different ones at one point ... That was a long time ago but now I think about it ... I remember really enjoying myself ... It was just good fun really ... seeing the collection get bigger and bigger ... As you get older it's difficult to re-create that sense of fun you have as a child ... It's a pity ... but anyway ... that's a hobby of mine I really enjoyed.

Test 2 Part 3

We've been talking about the subject of hobbies and interests. I'd like to discuss this subject with you with some more questions. What are the benefits of having a hobby or an interest?
I think there are several ... It allows you to switch off from work or your studies and focus on something else ... Depending on the hobby, it might help you keep fit or get out of the house ... You can meet other people with the same interest ... So there are lots of benefits.

Do hobbies change from generation to generation?
The young people I know don't have the hobbies my parents had – collecting stamps ... or, like me, collecting matchboxes ... I'm not sure that kind of thing interests people these days ... Perhaps children grow out of wanting to collect things at a younger age now ... Playing instruments is popular with my friends and that's timeless, isn't it?

In what ways can hobbies or interests bring people together?
Well ... taking my last point – playing music – this must be especially enjoyable when you play with a group of people rather than on your own ... I suppose it's the same with any interest – when you can share your love of it with others it brings you closer together.

Are there any hobbies that can lead to work in the same area?
Perhaps something like photography ... This could always lead to you being asked to take photos at weddings or birthdays ... Maybe eventually you could get a job as a photographer ... I suppose any creative hobbies could result in the person setting up their own business ... making jewellery ... art ... that kind of thing.

Has the use of technology in the home led to a decline in hobbies?
Possibly yes ... because we spend so much time on social networking sites and it's so easy to do ... You only need a smart phone handy and you can waste hours texting and browsing the web.

Are some people put off taking up some hobbies because of the cost involved?
Certainly ... yes ... If you take something like golf ... a lot of people I know play golf but it can cost a fortune ... There's the equipment ... the club membership fee ... I'm sure there must be lots of hobbies like that that deter a lot of people.

Track 31

Test 3 Part 1

In this first part of the exam I'd like to ask you some general questions about yourself. Are you currently studying at a school or college?
Yes ... I'm studying at a language school in town ... I came at the beginning of the year on a short course and liked it so much I booked myself onto another one.

Why are you taking the IELTS exam?
I need it to get into university ... It's a general entry requirement for all overseas students and I need to get 7 ... but I'm also doing an entrance test at the university as a back-up ... just in case IELTS doesn't go to plan.

What do you hope to do after you finish your studies?
I'm hoping to go into teaching ... After I've finished my degree I want to do a postgraduate course so I can teach in high school ... Ideally I'd like to teach history ... that's the subject I plan to study at university.

Let's talk about food. What kind of food do you like to eat?
I eat anything really ... but if I was going out somewhere for a special meal I'd probably choose a Thai restaurant ... I adore Thai food ... It's very expensive in my country ... but that's definitely my favourite cuisine.

Can you cook?
Yes ... I enjoy cooking a lot ... I only learnt recently ... after I left home to come here to study. I live in a shared flat so I've had to learn how to cook ... I'm not very good but I enjoy it.

Are there any regional specialities in your country you would recommend to visitors?
The most famous food from my country is pasta, of course, and there are lots of different kinds ... Most people know the famous dishes like cannelloni ... spaghetti bolognese ... I think I would recommend trying spaghetti alle vongole ... It's a seafood pasta from Rome ... It's delicious.

Test 3 Part 2

I'm going to give you a topic and I'd like you to talk about it for one to two minutes. Before you talk, you have one minute to think about what you are going to say. You can make some notes if you wish. Here is your topic.
...
I'm afraid it's not very imaginative but I think the most important possession I have is my phone ... At least that's the thing I use most often each day ... I'm not particularly attached to it ... It's only a phone, after all, and I'll probably change it for another one in time ... but it's so practical ... I think I'd be lost without it ... How long have I had it? Well ... I got it last year just before I came to England .... My parents bought it for me as a going-away present ... also, I think, because they wanted to make sure I kept in touch with them regularly ... It's a smart phone ... so I use it to text and speak with my mum and dad, but it's also a great way to keep up with the news ... I don't bother buying newspapers because I can read everything online ... In fact that's the first thing I do when I wake up – I check to see if I have any messages then read the main stories in the news ... What else? I listen to music on it ... I download podcasts from

some of my favourite radio shows ... watch videos .... take lots and lots of photos ... then there's the sat nav which is really useful as well ... The one in my car isn't very reliable ... The sat nav on the phone updates itself regularly so it's very accurate .... Yes ... I use it all the time ... I doubt if an hour passes without it being used for one thing or another ... so that's my most important possession.

Test 3 Part 3

We've been talking about personal possessions. I'd like to discuss this subject with you with some more questions. Do our important possessions these days tend to be technology based?
I think most young people want to have all the latest gadgets – phones ... PCs ... laptops ... games consoles ... I don't know which of these people regard as their most important though ... maybe none of them.

What kind of possessions often have sentimental value?
Probably things that have been bought as a present by loved ones ... and things like jewellery to celebrate a wedding or engagement ... Family photographs and videos as well – these aren't worth money as such but are really important memories of our past.

Does the advertising industry lead to us buying things we don't really need?
Definitely yes ... especially with things like technology ... We're always being told to upgrade our phone or computer when the one we have is perfectly okay ... When you walk around big stores there are shelves full of things that we don't really need but end up buying so ... yes I think it does.

How should parents deal with demands from their children for things they have seen advertised?
It must be very hard for parents ... In my country there are adverts all the time aimed at children and they probably always want to have things their friends have ... I think if I had children I would just explain that they can't have everything they see ... Otherwise they can easily become spoilt.

Are we happier the more things we own?
Not really, no ... We get excited about getting things we don't have – the trip to the shop to buy some new clothes is always enjoyable – but, once you have the things, I don't think it makes us any happier really ... we just end up wanting something else.

Is there anything you don't have that you would like to buy?
I don't think so ... I have everything I need ... maybe a new laptop but I don't really need one – it's just the idea of having a shiny new one that's appealing ... No, I don't need anything at the moment.

Track 32

Test 4 Part 1

In this first part of the exam I'd like to ask you some general questions about yourself. Do you come from a large family?
No ... just me, my mum and dad, and my younger brother ... My father comes from a large family ... I think he had 11 brothers and sisters when they were all alive ... but we're quite a normal sized family.

Have you got a favourite relative?
My Nan is probably my favourite ... She's very kind and a really good conversationalist ... always asking about my studies ... my friends ... She's the oldest of all my relatives ... 91, I think ... but still very active.

How often do you get to see your wider family?
Not very often actually ... We get together at big family celebrations but these don't happen very often ... so only once a year maybe ... We all live a long way from each other as well so it's difficult to meet up frequently.

Let's talk about work. Do you have any definite career ambitions?
Yes ... I hope to become an architect ... My father's an architect and I've always been fascinated by his work ... He's always building scaled-down models of buildings at home – there's always one on his table in his study – I think it's a really creative job ... That's what I want to do.

How easy is it to find work where you live?
Generally it's quite difficult ... I live in a small town and there aren't many opportunities to work locally ... You have to travel into the main cities ... and at the moment there's a lot of unemployment so it's not easy.

If you could do any job you liked, what would it be?
Well ... becoming an architect is my real ambition and I think I'll be very happy dong that ... I suppose a dream job would allow me to travel around the world and visit all the major cities ... Maybe if I can become an architect who travels the world ... that would be fantastic.

Test 4 Part 2

I'm going to give you a topic and I'd like you to talk about it for one to two minutes. Before you talk, you have one minute to think about what you are going to say. You can make some notes if you wish. Here is your topic.
...
I'm not sure I'd like to live there permanently but I'd love to have a flat in Amsterdam in the Netherlands ... I've been there two times – the last time was with my family and on both occasions I really enjoyed myself ... It's like a lot of big cities in some ways – a very busy centre with thousands of tourists ... We stayed in a suburb about 20 minutes from the centre ... It was very cosmopolitan ... lots of different restaurants with food from all around the world ... It was lovely ... There are a few things I really like about Amsterdam ... the architecture for one thing – we went into a library and it was so bright and spacious ... very modern looking – then there are the parks – we went to a couple and they were really peaceful ... even the one right in the middle of the city ... I can't remember the name now ... But the thing I liked most of all is how well cyclists are treated there – the roads seem to be divided up so that the trams and the cars can share one bit and the cyclists get a wide lane all to themselves ... There are cyclists everywhere and they all seem to be totally confident and safe ... In my country cycling on the busy roads is very dangerous – it's really not something I enjoy – but there in Amsterdam it seemed to be the best way to travel ... It gets quite cold there in the winter so I wouldn't want to be there all year ... but it would be lovely to have a place to stay in the spring and summer ... That would be good.

Test 4 Part 3

We've been talking about the subject of places we would like to live. I'd like to discuss this subject with you with some more questions. What is it about a place that makes it feel like home?
If you mean the area, I think people make the difference – having people you recognise and can say hello to ... that's a sign you feel at home ... As far as your own house is concerned, I think making it cosy and warm is the best way to make it homely.

Is it important to live close to your relatives?
When your parents get older and need taking care of ... yes it's important to live close to them ... Other people ... like brothers and sisters ... when you live a long way away from them it means you don't get to see each other very frequently so it would be nice to live quite close.

What are the main reasons people decide to move to another location?
Usually because of work I suppose – you might get transferred from one office or factory to one in a different city ... And when people retire they often decide to move away from the city into the country ... somewhere they can relax and enjoy the countryside.

What are the kind of things a family looks for when deciding where to live?
If you have young children it's important what the nearest schools are like ... Then the transport system – people usually like to live near a train station but not too close to busy roads ... Shopping as well – people like to have some shops nearby ... I think they also worry about crime and whether it's a safe place to live.

Why do some people choose to leave their own country and live abroad?
Possibly the weather ... they might live in a cold climate and want to live somewhere that gets a lot more sunshine throughout the year ... It might also be for the same reason I mentioned before – they move because of their job perhaps.

Do you think people who want to move to another country have a realistic idea of what it will be like?
I think often they probably don't ... not if they're moving because they spent a few weeks on holiday there once a year ... You probably don't get a true impression of a place when you're a tourist ... Maybe you see all the good things and don't get to discover things that might be a problem if you live there permanently.

Acknowledgements

The publisher and authors wish to thank the following rights holders for the use of copyright material:

Test 1: Writing
(Task 1)
Household Types: Social Trends 2008 Page 17
© Crown copyright 2008
Source: Office for National Statistics licensed under the Open Government Licence v.1.0.
http://www.ons.gov.uk/ons/rel/social-trends-rd/social-trends/no--38--2008-edition/index.html

Test 2: Writing
(Task 1)
Driving license holders: Social Trends 2008 Page 167
© Crown copyright 2008
Source: Office for National Statistics licensed under the Open Government Licence v.1.0.
http://www.ons.gov.uk/ons/rel/social-trends-rd/social-trends/no--38--2008-edition/index.html

Test 3: Writing
(Task 1)
Fear of Crime: ONS: (04/08/11) Correction Notice: Crime and Justice ST41
© Crown copyright 2008
Source: Office for National Statistics licensed under the Open Government Licence v.1.0.
http://www.ons.gov.uk/ons/publications/index.html?pageSize=50&sortBy=none&sortDirection=none&newquery=social+trends+41+-+crime

Test 3: Reading
(Passage 1)
Article name: Seas Beneath the Sands
Authors: Louis Werner and Kevin Bubriski
This article appeared on pages 34-39 of the January/February 2007 print edition of Saudi Aramco World.
http://www.saudiaramcoworld.com/issue/200701/seas.beneath.the.sands.htm

(Passage 3)
Article name: Ksar Aqil: At the Crossroads Out of Africa

Authors: Christopher Bergman with Ingrid Azoury and Helga Seeden.
This article appeared on page 34 of the September/October 2012 print edition of Saudi Aramco World.
http://www.saudiaramcoworld.com/issue/201205/ksar.aqil.at.the.crossroads.out.of.africa.htm

Test 4: Writing
(Task 1)
Smoking: ONS Opinions Survey Report No. 40, Smoking Related Behaviour and Attitudes, 2008/09 Pages 21 and 23
© Crown copyright 2008
Source: Office for National Statistics licensed under the Open Government Licence v.1.0.
http://www.ons.gov.uk/ons/publications/index.html?pageSize=50&sortBy=none&sortDirection=none&newquery=Smoking%3A+ONS+Opinions+Survey+Report+No.+40%2C+Smoking+Related+Behaviour+and&content-type=publicationContentTypes

General Reading Test A
(Section 3)
Source: Article reproduced under the creative commons licence:
http://www.plosbiology.org/article/info%3Adoi%2F10.1371%2Fjournal.pbio.1001391

General Reading Test B
(Section 3)
Article name: The Carvers of Bukittinggi
Author: Sigrid Laing.
This article appeared on pages 29-31 of the July/August 1991 print edition of Saudi Aramco World.
http://www.saudiaramcoworld.com/issue/199104/the.carvers.of.bukittinggi.htm

Sample answer sheets
Reproduced by permission of Cambridge ESOL.

The publisher also wishes to acknowledge the following sources used for information when writing articles:

Test 1: Reading
(Passage 1)
http://www.invasivespeciesinfo.gov/aquatics/mittencrab.shtml - .UHGAOo6h7fA
http://www.dpi.vic.gov.au/agriculture/pests-diseases-and-weeds/pest-animals/lc0298-rabbits-and-their-impact
http://www.dpi.vic.gov.au/agriculture/pests-diseases-and-weeds/pest-animals/lc0298-rabbits-and-their-impact
http://www.australian-information-stories.com/camels-in-australia.html
http://news.discovery.com/animals/swine-flu-animal-trading.html

http://www.dfg.ca.gov/delta/mittencrab/life_hist.asp
http://mittencrab.nisbase.org/page/impact
http://www.iisgcp.org/exoticsp/chinese_mitten_crab.htm
http://www.environment.gov.au/biodiversity/invasive/publications/camel-factsheet.html

(Passage 2)
http://knowledge.wharton.upenn.edu/article.cfm?articleid=3018
http://www.economist.com/blogs/babbage/2012/10/spacex-goes-iss
http://www.independent.co.uk/news/science/private-

Acknowledgements

rocket-blasts-off-for-iss-8202905.html
http://www.businessinsider.com/how-the-private-sector-revolutionized-the-space-race-in-a-few-short-years-2012-8

(Passage 3)
http://www.guardian.co.uk/environment/2012/sep/17/arctic-collapse-sea-ice
http://www.newscientist.com/article/mg21528831.700-can-geoengineering-avert-climate-chaos.html?full=true
http://www.sciencedaily.com/releases/2008/02/080217094602.htm
http://www.sciencedaily.com/releases/2012/08/120830191017.htm
http://www.guardian.co.uk/environment/2010/may/14/bill-gates-cloud-whitening-dangerous
http://en.wikipedia.org/wiki/Geoengineering
http://lajicarita.wordpress.com/2012/08/03/geoengineering-new-mexicos-climate-future-or-screaming-for-sulfur-seeded-sunsets/
http://www.guardian.co.uk/environment/2009/oct/21/geo-engineering

Test 2: Reading
(Passage 1)
http://www.foods-healing-power.com/health-benefits-of-beans.html
http://www.newscientist.com/article/dn16573-eating-less-meat-could-cut-climate-costs.html
http://www.bupa.co.uk/individuals/health-information/directory/f/fibre
http://www.foods-healing-power.com/health-benefits-of-beans.html
http://books.google.co.uk/books?id=-4OHxYNRdhAC&pg=PA73&lpg=PA73&dq=beans+hittite&source=bl&ots=EKOBXEvSB4&sig=KckLC-Vnh5bgD1kRojh6Z1GAm9Q&hl=en&sa=X&ei=XpWCUKaOKcPQ0QWYgoHYBA&ved=0CFUQ6AEwCQ#v=onepage&q=beans%20hittite&f=false
http://www.hurriyetdailynews.com/default.aspx?pageid=438&n=ancient-seed-came-into-leaf-2009-12-16]

(Passage 2)
http://www.dyscalculia.me.uk/background.html
http://www.bdadyslexia.org.uk/about-dyslexia/schools-colleges-and-universities/dyscalculia.html
http://en.wikipedia.org/wiki/Dyscalculia
http://www.mathematicalbrain.com/preface.html
http://www.aboutdyscalculia.org/author.html

(Passage 3)
http://www.mision4636.org

Test 3: Reading
(Passage 2)
http://www.glucalite.com/insulin-sensitivity/
http://www.sciencedaily.com/releases/2009/01/090127190344.htm

http://www.sciencedaily.com/releases/2010/03/100311123639.htm
http://www.bbc.co.uk/news/health-17177251
http://www.topendsports.com/weight-loss/weightloss-intensity.htm
http://www.medicalnewstoday.com/articles/251413.php
http://www.sportsci.org/jour/0101/cf.htm
http://www.health.gov/paguidelines/
http://www.cdc.gov/physicalactivity/everyone/guidelines/adults.html]

Test 4: Reading
(Passage 1)
http://www.telegraph.co.uk/news/worldnews/asia/china/9263425/40-killed-during-hour-long-hailstorm-in-China.html
http://www.azcentral.com/news/articles/2011/10/02/20111002weather-phoenix-hail-damage-year-later.html
http://www.chaseday.com/hailfall.htm
http://www.nssl.noaa.gov/education/svrwx101/hail/
http://www.islandnet.com/~see/weather/elements/hailform.htm
http://www.torro.org.uk/site/hscale.php

(Passage 2)
http://news.cnet.com/8301-30686_3-20112534-266/wireless-spectrum-shortage-what-spectrum-shortage/
http://dvice.com/archives/2012/06/how-twisted-lig.php
http://www.extremetech.com/extreme/120803-vortex-radio-waves-could-boost-wireless-capacity-infinitely
http://io9.com/5921078/scientists-twist-light-to-carry-an-astounding-25-terabits-of-information-per-second
http://arstechnica.com/science/2012/06/twist-light-carry-terabits-of-data/]

(Passage 3)
http://www.china.org.cn/video/2012-02/21/content_24692583.htm
http://www.freemalaysiatoday.com/category/leisure/2012/07/19/shanghai-%E2%80%93-sinking-by-the-second/
http://www.science20.com/news_articles/northwest_houston_sinking_fast
http://www.upi.com/Science_News/2010/09/28/Geologist-Parts-of-Houston-are-sinking/UPI-50181285721438/
http://news.asiaone.com/News/Latest%2BNews/Asia/Story/A1Story20111109-309598.html
http://www.guardian.co.uk/environment/2011/sep/06/bangkok-thailand-risks-steadily-sinking
http://seattletimes.com/html/nationworld/2016310507_mexicosinking25.html]

If any copyright holders have been omitted, please contact the publishers who will make necessary arrangements at the first opportunity.

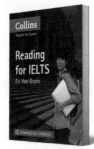
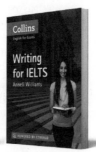

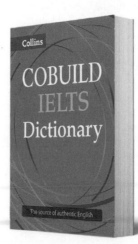